VOICE - OVER
VOICE ACTOR

THE EXTENDED EDITION

YURI LOWENTHAL
AND TARA PLATT

VOICE-OVER VOICE ACTOR: The Extended Edition
by Yuri Lowenthal and Tara Platt

Bug Bot Press
1335 N. La Brea #2233
Hollywood, CA 90028
orders@bugbotpress.com
www.BugBotPress.com

Edition ISBNs
978-0-9840740-5-1   0-9840740-5-8 (print)
978-0-9840740-6-8   0-9840740-6-6 (ebook)

Cover design, layout and typesetting by Michelle Landry.
Illustrations by Jerzy Drozd. Photographs by Mikel Healey.

Printed in the United States of America

Library of Congress Cataloging-in-Publication Data
Names: Lowenthal, Yuri, author. | Platt, Tara, author.
Title: Voice-over voice actor : the extended edition / Yuri Lowenthal and Tara Platt.
Description: Includes bibliographical references and index. | Hollywood, CA: Bug Bot Press, 2018.
Identifiers: ISBN 978-0-9840740-5-1 (pbk.) | 978-0-9840740-6-8 (ebook) | LCCN 2017954792
Subjects: LCSH Acting. | Television announcing--Vocational guidance. | Voice-overs. | Voice culture. | Television advertising--Vocational guidance. | Voice in motion pictures. | Animation (Cinematography). | BISAC PERFORMING ARTS / Acting & Auditioning
Classification: LCC PN1995.9.V63 .L69 2018 | DDC 778.5/347--dc23

WHAT OTHERS ARE SAYING ABOUT
VOICE-OVER VOICE ACTOR: THE EXTENDED EDITION

"This was one of the first books I bought when I started my journey into voice-over, and has been by far the most helpful. To have this kind of information from two of the most successful people in the business in a single book is absolutely invaluable."

~ CISSY JONES LIN, ACTRESS,
BAFTA WINNER FOR *FIREWATCH, DESTINY 2*

"Have you ever met beautiful, intelligent, thoughtful humans who are successful in every aspect of their lives, not just their chosen professions? Wouldn't you like to know what it is they do so you might be able to incorporate some of their successful habits into your life, and who knows, maybe achieve your dreams, as well? Wouldn't it be great if they wrote a book in which they shared their experiences and advice, helping you to achieve your own success? Well, lucky you. I'm talking about Tara and Yuri and VOVA, if it isn't clear. And if it isn't clear, boy, oh, boy, do you ever need this book."

~ ROGER CRAIG SMITH, ACTOR,
SONIC THE HEDGEHOG, PLANES, ASSASSIN'S CREED

"A delightful and insightful book filled with firsthand knowledge of this crazy business called voice-over from two of the finest vocal performers I know. But don't be fooled. I wholeheartedly agree with Tara and Yuri in that VO is not just using your vocal skills and talents: this is an ACTING JOB!"

~ KRIS ZIMMERMAN SALTER, DIRECTOR,
METAL GEAR SOLID SERIES

WHAT OTHERS ARE SAYING ABOUT
VOICE-OVER VOICE ACTOR: WHAT IT'S LIKE BEHIND THE MIC

"As professionals, we attempt to recognize talent and integrity. Yuri and Tara are heads and shoulders ahead of their contemporaries. Their combined integrity and work ethic, along with a strong acting aptitude, keep them on their own personal and joyous track for success."

~ HARVEY & CATHY KALMENSON, KALMENSON & KALMENSON, INC., VOICE CASTING & INSTRUCTION

"In my eight years of coaching actors of all levels, I have never seen such a comprehensive and clear explanation of the ins and outs of the voice industry. Yuri and Tara offer up a book that is not only easy to follow, it's also in-depth, inspiring, and funny at the same time!"

~ DALLAS TRAVERS, FOUNDER OF THE THRIVING ARTIST CIRCLE, AUTHOR OF *THE TAO OF SHOW BUSINESS*

"Lowenthal and Platt delve deep into the world of voice acting, with stories from behind the mic and trenchant observations from fellow performers. They bust the jargon-packed world of loop groups and walla work, voice matching and phone patching. They have produced an excellent road map of the surprisingly wide world of vocal performance, including unexpected areas like studio socializing, the ethics of networking, audition tips, and even health and hydration. The result is an invaluable guide to professional voice acting from two of its leading stars."

~ JONATHAN CLEMENTS, AUTHOR, *SCHOOLGIRL MILKY CRISIS: ADVENTURES IN THE ANIME AND MANGA TRADE*

"Whatever Yuri and Tara say, I wholeheartedly disagree with. They're a couple of shysters. And if you believe that, then I am Elmer J. Fudd, millionaire. I own a mansion and a yacht. Buy this book, you maroons!"

~ JOHN DiMAGGIO, ACTOR, *FUTURAMA, GEARS OF WAR, HALO 3*

"If you want to know the nuts and bolts of becoming a working voice actor, this is the book for you."

~ DEE BRADLEY BAKER, ACTOR, *AMERICAN DAD, AVATAR: THE LAST AIRBENDER, STAR WARS: THE CLONE WARS*

TABLE OF CONTENTS

ACKNOWLEDGMENTS

We must first take the time to acknowledge every reader of the first edition of *VOVA*. You helped inform the changes and additions to be found within these pages, and inspired us to even consider putting out a second edition! Particular thanks for this edition go to Walt Gray IV (and all his previous clones) for his friendship and help getting the new PCap additions right, to Michelle Landry for the fresh look, to Mikel Healey for new photos, to Rob Paulsen for the fantabulous foreword, and to the talented people who contributed new anecdotes and success stories, as well as to all of the original contributors (below) that are just as appreciated today as when we first wrote the book.

The original book would never have been possible without the generous help of our fellow VAs, our friends, our families, and most of all our fans. And here's to those who really got their hands dirty: Jennifer, Juan, Stephanie, Candace, and Jonathan, who read what we had written and gave their honest opinions so that we might bring you, the reader, the best possible book. Tod and the gang at Thomson-Shore, you helped demystify and yet romanticize the process of actually printing a physical book. To our fantastic design team Scott and Sarah at Cyanotype, for making things, well, *look* so darned good. To Casey and Rudy for making us look cool on the intarwebs. To Boris for so much more than the pretty photos you took of us. To Jerzy for finally turning us into what we've always wanted to be: cartoons. To Paul for writing a kick-ass foreword. To SomeAudioGuy for taking us to technology school. To Dallas for lending guidance and support. To Wil for being a trailblazer whose path we could trust. To Dr. Bear for making a last-minute house call on the book. To our amazing and immaculate editor, Candace, for catching all our little oopsies but not messin' with our style. So thank you. Thank you to the wonderful team of people who actually made this book possible.

DEDICATION

This book is dedicated to our parents Barry, Candace, Heidi, and Jim, who have always supported our crazy ideas and relentless pursuit of our dreams.

This book is dedicated to the ridiculously talented voice-over community, whose members rarely get the acknowledgment they deserve.

This book is dedicated to the fans, who make it possible for us to do what we do.

This book is dedicated to anyone who has passion, a dream, and the drive to succeed.

This book is dedicated to you, the next generation of performers to whom we will be listening as you make your mark on the world.

DISCLAIMER, AKA "WHAT EXACTLY ARE YOU PROMISING HERE?"

First, what our lawyer told us to say:
This book is designed to provide information on voice-over, voice acting, self-promotion, vocal health, and warm-ups. It is sold with the understanding that the publisher and authors (and guest experts) are not engaged in rendering legal, medical, or other professional services. If legal, medical, or other expert assistance is required, the services of a competent professional should be sought. There are physical exercises described in this book; we do not recommend engaging in any type of new physical activity without first consulting a physician.

It is also not the aim of this book to imply that there is only one way to build a voice-over career; nor is there a guarantee that by reading this book, you will have a successful career in the world of voice-over.

Voice-over is not a get-rich-quick endeavor. Anyone who decides to pursue a career in the entertainment business must expect to invest a lot of time, energy, and very likely, money, into it. For many people we know, voice-over is an exciting, rewarding career, and a lot of them have built solid names for themselves in this business.

Every effort has been made to make this book as complete and accurate as possible. However, there may be mistakes, both typographical and in content. Therefore, this book should be used as a guide and not the ultimate source in voice-over, voice acting, the care of your voice, and related subjects that we touch on.

The purpose of this book is to educate and entertain. The authors and Bug Bot Press shall have neither liability nor responsibility to any person or entity with respect to loss or damage caused, or alleged to have been caused, directly or indirectly, by the information contained in this book.

If you do not wish to be bound by the above, you may return this book to the publisher for a full refund.

And in our own words:
We're going to try to answer a couple of questions you may have while flipping through this book, contemplating its purchase:

"If I read this book, will I become a famous voice actor?"
Maybe. Certainly not just because you read this book. It's going to take a lot more than reading this book (or any other, for that matter) for you to become famous. The *only* thing we can guarantee is that by reading this book you'll be more well-read and slightly older. But here's the deal: we've geared this book towards your having fun, learning stuff, and getting excited about voice acting, not towards your getting famous. This type of work has no guarantee, no *A+B=C* plan. But it *sure* can be a lot of fun, and the people we've seen succeed have never forgotten that. If you try this stuff, and after a while you're not having fun anymore, find something that you *do* have fun doing. You'll be happier for it. Trust us: fun is way cooler than fame.

"Will everything you say in this book work for me?"
Probably not. Everybody's different. If everything worked the same for everyone, there'd be no surprises. Did the stuff we talk about in this book work for *us*? Yep. And that's what you wanted to find out, right? How we do what we do? What have we seen? Well, that's what we intend to give you … and then some. And, hey, while we don't guarantee everything, check out Chapter 15 in this brand-spanking new edition to hear from some people who *have* found some success after reading this book!

FOREWORD
TO SECOND EDITION

The first thing you'll notice upon meeting Tara Platt and Yuri Lowenthal is how utterly out of Yuri's league Tara is. Yuri's a nice enough boy; but Tara? Well, let's just say Yuri should be grateful every day that Tara lowered her standards enough to consider him to be the stuff of husbandhood.

The second thing you'll notice is the fantastic sense of humor with which these crazy-talented kids are gifted. (I say "kids" because although I behave like a kid, I am, in fact, VERY old.)

One of the few kindnesses age has bestowed upon me is the ability to know the difference between truly skilled, kind, honest, helpful show-folk and assholes. Now you might think it'd be obvious, but trust me, it is not. Having made my living as a singer/actor in Hollywood for 35 years, I've lost count of the number of acting "teachers" and VO "experts" I'm aware of who've taken hard-earned American dollars from deeply passionate, wide-eyed and sweet, but naive young actors (and some veterans who should know better) who are in L.A. for the same reasons Tara, Yuri, I, and countless others are: to follow our creative jones and find a way to make a living doing pretty much what we'd do for free. Look, no one I know has ever been forced at gunpoint to be an actor. It's a choice. A brave one. And unfortunately, there are, in fact, many people who were never able to make it as performers and turned to "teaching." There is no standard, no regulation, no necessary degree, and no law which prohibits anyone from charging whatever they wish to "teach" acting, voice or otherwise. Caveat emptor, baby. There will ALWAYS be more actors than gigs. But there will NEVER be too many actors who're willing and able to give affordable, practical, experienced-based, and real-time information which, at the very least, is going to give budding actors (and experienced ones for that matter) excellent tips and help them navigate many of the issues voice acting pros deal with in their careers.

Is *Voice-Over Voice Actor* a step-by-step guide to VO stardom? No. NO ONE has that kind of info to sell, whether in a workshop, showcase, on line, or in a book, and anyone who implies such is lying. And an asshole. In *Voice-Over Voice Actor*, you'll receive good, honest, smart information from people who make their living as actors in Hollywood. NOW. TODAY. TOMORROW. Tara and Yuri will never become wealthy from the book. That'll happen as a result of the day-to-day hard work they put into their careers in which they are, by any measure, already successful. They wrote *Voice-Over Voice Actor* because they, like us, are passionate about the art form. And unlike the assholes, they're not, um...assholes. And they're pretty. Both of them.

Rob Paulsen

Los Angeles, September 2017

Rob Paulsen is a strikingly handsome award-winning voice actor and singer. His awards include an Emmy and three Annies for the role of Pinky in Pinky and the Brain. *He has voiced multiple teenage mutant ninja turtles, and fans love his rendition of the song "Yakko's World" from* Animaniacs. *As if that weren't enough (and there's more, believe us), Rob recently added voice directing to his credits. You can catch him on his podcast "Talkin' Toons" on the Nerdist network at projectalpha.com.*

FOREWORD
TO ORIGINAL EDITION

S o you want to be a voice actor? Close your eyes for a moment and listen.

All of those noises you hear – the murmurs and whispers, dripping taps and distant engine rumbles – are waves on the ocean of sound we swim through each day. Our emotions respond most viscerally to what we hear. Our lives are constantly awash with sound, though we rarely acknowledge it.

Sound is everything. If you don't believe me watch a movie minus the post-production sound design. You'll get a new appreciation for sound engineers, sound designers, and musicians. The visuals may draw us in but it's the sound that keeps us in. I believe this is why we hang on every word uttered by that chap who voices over movie trailers, and why we are equally compelled to go and beat up a mime.

Professional voice actors understand the importance of conveying information using sound. They're among the most underappreciated and they're among the most talented. Consider that a film or television actor can convey emotion or meaning with a raised eyebrow or a nuanced expression. Voice actors enjoy no such advantage. If it can't be done with just the voice, then it can't be done.

If you haven't run screaming thus far – and assuming you've

opened your eyes and read down to here – don't fret; because you've come to the right place. Tara Platt and Yuri Lowenthal are among the best at what they do, and they're here to guide you gently and whimsically through the pieces you'll need to know. *Voice-Over Voice Actor* is the essential handbook, specifically geared towards what really happens when you do this for a living. You'll read this book over and over again.

In addition to being accomplished and talented voice actors, Tara and Yuri are two of the sweetest and funniest people I know. That sense of fun jumps from these pages and will put you at ease now that I've frightened the life out of you. If we are all afloat on this ocean of sound, they're piloting the lifeboat.

Let's go test the water.

PAUL JENKINS
Atlanta, June 2009

Paul Jenkins is an Eisner Award-winning author and comic book creator. Some of his many stand-outs include The Sentry, The Spectacular Spider-Man, Wolverine: Origin, *and* Captain America. *In addition to his prolific comic works, he has written and directed numerous voice-overs for video games, including his own award-winning hit game* The Darkness.

INTRODUCTION

"The supreme accomplishment is to blur the line between work and play."

ARNOLD TOYNBEE,
ENGLISH ECONOMIC HISTORIAN

WHY THE NEW IMPROVED EDITION?

It's been almost 10 years since we first began writing *Voice-Over Voice Actor* and we've got a lot more to talk about. More importantly, we have observed first-hand the rapidly changing industry. Technology is shifting, as is the way people consume entertainment, and that means VO has had to change along with it. And while we could dig in our heels and fight the coming tide, we've found it much more useful (and fun!) to become a part of the changing landscape and play in this wild west of wonder.

Over the years, people have requested more information on various growing areas such as performance capture and its relationship to the voice actor, and we were listening. So as we revised this edition, we felt we had to make additions to the book to address some of these changes to better help you stay on top of the business of voice-over. We may not be the only source of information in this industry, but we appreciate the trust that many of you have put in us. Our thanks go out to the countless friends and fans for continuing to read this book over the years, recommend it, and share their post-*VOVA* success stories. We are so happy for you, and couldn't be prouder of this amazing and talented community.

WHAT'S NEW IN THIS EDITION?

If you've read the previous edition, you will find pretty much everything just where you left it; but if you keep your eyes peeled, you'll notice several additional chapters and some slight alterations. We have improved the content and expanded certain topics based on questions we have been asked as well as on our experiences in the voice industry in the years since writing the original book. There are three additional chapters (with new cartoons!), plus an added workbook section with practical steps on which you can take action. Hopefully, it won't matter whether you're picking up this book for the first time or if you're re-reading it for the umpteenth time. We hope you'll dig in and enjoy the ride just the same. We've had a blast coming back to it.

WHY WE WROTE THIS BOOK (THE ORIGINAL ONE)

It certainly wasn't our intention to write a book when we started out in this crazy business. All we wanted to do was make a buck doing something we love, and that thing was acting. So we acted.

First, we acted before we even knew we could make any money at it. We were the self-styled hams at family gatherings, the class clown in elementary school, Juliet on a high school stage, comedians in cafes and clubs, a thousand-and-one characters (and most of the crew) in summer stock theatre. We made our own Super 8 films (what the kids today are calling "YouTube") and bared our souls (and on occasion, more than that) in dark basement theatres off-off-*off* Broadway, where often there were more of us on stage than in the seats. It wasn't always easy, but something kept us going.

Then miraculously, a time came when somebody paid us for our acting. Now it may not have covered even our bus fare to the theatre, but it didn't matter. We weren't doing it for money. But the thought arose: *I've already made this my life. Could I actually make a living at it?* We started reading the papers, looking at billboards, watching TV. We could see the people who were making a living doing what we love. The *stars*. If they could do it, why couldn't we? So we set out to be the next overnight success (forgetting, for a moment, that we'd already been doing this for years).

And it was hard again. Most people didn't want to pay us, and those who did, couldn't pay us what we needed to survive. But survive we did. We took other jobs that had nothing to do with acting (unless acting like you really wanted to be there counts), and that allowed us to do more acting. And more ... and more. We took classes, auditioned for anyone who'd let us in the door, worked on student films, assisted famous directors, wrangled pigs for eccentric Japanese performers. (These are, of course, stories for a*nother*-nother book). We lived our lives, and every odd little experience helped prepare us for the next acting job, whether we knew it, or not.

Then it started to happen. We found that what we practiced for every day, what we trained for, sweated and bled for, is what we were starting to become. We were actors. People started paying us a little more regularly ... for things that had started out as fun and games, mind you.

Even then, it was still a surprise when we stumbled into voice acting. I mean, we'd watched cartoons for years (one of us a little more than the other), and we still had memories of their callouts:

GO, SPEED RACER!

AUTOBOTS, ROLL OUT!

AND KNOWING IS HALF THE BATTLE!

S.I.G. SPECTRUM IS GREEN!

WHEN CAPTAIN AMERICA THROWS HIS MIGHTY SHIELD ...

SWORD OF OMENS, GIVE ME SIGHT BEYOND SIGHT!

MEANWHILE, BACK AT THE HALL OF JUSTICE ...

But that's not a *real* job, is it? Is it? *Hmm. I don't know. Let's take a voice acting class and find out.*

So we did. We went to class. We recorded voice-over demos. We sent them to agents. And it finally started to click. We started to work. We learned more. And, astoundingly enough, we even started to get paid for our voice acting. On a somewhat regular basis, no less! Soon, we were making enough money so that we didn't have to work as secretaries and bartenders anymore. We were working on projects we could write home to our families about, and that they could watch on their TVs at home in Michigan and Tennessee.

It was an interesting time. And an interesting thing happened: we started to get letters. (Okay, well, *emails*, mostly. But in the olden days before computers were so widely used, actual papers were delivered to your house; we called those *letters*.) They were from people we didn't know. People from the U.S., people from the U.K., people from Canada and France and the Philippines and Dubai and New Zealand. And they wanted to know how they, too, could do what we were doing. *How did you get to where you are?*

Hold on; wait! We *did* know those people. They were us. We remembered that not so long ago, we, too, wrote letters to people we looked up to, asking for encouragement and advice. We stood in line for hours at sci-fi and comic book conventions (okay, once again, one of us more than the other) for a chance to ask those people, our heroes, how we could do what they were doing. The more emails we got asking us those same questions, the more it became important to write a book. Through love, relentlessness, and a little luck, we had gotten to a place other people wanted to get to as well. How could we not share the fantastical world we live in? And now we can expand on that information with a combined two decades more of experience!

Actors have a pretty cool job. We get to try on different ... people. We get to create characters that have unique mannerisms or personality quirks that we ourselves might not actually share. For on-camera actors, these characters are limited only by the actor's imagination and appearance. Imagine how often you see on-camera actors in an interview and realize that they aren't what you had imagined based on the characters they play.

Now take that one step further: as voice actors, we aren't constrained by age, gender, race, or even *species*. If we can create a voice for a character, we can play that character!

Voice-over is an amazingly empowering medium for any actor with an imagination and an inclination to play. There's no age, sex, or race discrimination (okay, there's never *none* of that stuff, but you will find less of it around here). Why keep it a secret?

We wish someone had told us some of this stuff sooner, so now we're taking it on ourselves to share the information with others.

So here you go. We're throwing you a rope. It may not get you all the way here, and you're gonna have to grab it yourself, but it'll be an exciting climb if you decide to make it. That we can promise.

AND WHO ARE WE ANYWAY?

Well, for now we'll tell you that Yuri's been a prince of Persia, a man of steel, and a boy who smacks his watch and turns into ten different aliens; while Tara has repelled inter-dimensional invaders with her Lasso of Truth, fought ninjas, and saved the universe by dreaming the future. And that's just a *taste* of who we are. If you want more details, you can check out our websites (*www. TaraPlatt.com* and *www.YuriLowenthal.com*) or go to the back of the book to see the *Author Bios* for a partial list of our work.

In short, we're actors who have been working professionally for the last 25+ years, with the last 15 years or so heavily steeped in voice acting. Our work in voice-over has run the full spectrum, ranging from TV and radio commercials to podcasting to promos to narration to animation to voice matching to looping to video games (from VO to full performance capture), and this exciting work continues to keep us busy.

We're storytellers no matter the medium. When we're not behind the mic, we're likely to be found on stage, in front of a camera, or at a convention with our fans. We love what we do and we hope that it shows.

TAKE ACTION!

We invite you – nay, implore you – to go above and beyond this book (or as a certain caped hero would say, "Up, up and away!"). To take the things you've learned here and put them into action. In fact, for this edition, we've added an appendix containing exercises to help you hone your skills!

We wish you much success and joy as you begin your exploration of the world of voice acting. Good luck and enjoy your adventure!

Raise your voice!
Yuri & Tara

CHAPTER 1
SO, WHAT IS VO ANYWAY?

"Imagination is more important than knowledge."

ALBERT EINSTEIN, GERMAN NOBEL
PRIZE-WINNING PHYSICIST

AND ... *WE'RE ROLLING* ON TAKE TWO...

In the world of voice-over (VO), *rolling* means that the engineer has begun recording, and you're clear to begin doing what you do: speak ... or in our world, yell, scream, growl, moan, bark, trill, warble, coo, guffaw, gurgle, pant, gasp – the list goes on, as you'll see. *And ... we're rolling* is sort of the VO equivalent to the film/TV world's *A-a-a-a-nd ... ACTION!*

The *rolling* part refers to when sound used to be recorded on big rolls of magnetic tape. Some of us (ahem!) remember those days. Of course, nowadays, most everything is done digitally, and there's no real need to physically roll anything. But the saying is industry standard and it still applies. You see, here's where it begins – where we take things from a stop into motion. That's when the fun stuff really starts to happen.

So let's get things rolling, shall we?

WHAT IT IS

Well, here's what the dictionary (*Merriam-Webster's*) will tell you: "a *voice-over* is the voice of an unseen narrator speaking (as in a motion picture or television commercial); the voice of a visible character (as in a motion picture) expressing unspoken thoughts."

Wikipedia, the online (or *people's*) encyclopedia, says: "the term *voice-over* refers to a production technique where a disembodied voice is broadcast live or prerecorded in radio, television, film, theatre and/or presentation; the voice-over may be spoken by someone who also appears on-screen in other segments or it may be performed by a specialist voice actor; voice-over is also commonly referred to as 'off camera' commentary."

While we love the idea of a "disembodied voice" because it appeals to our love of horror movies and ghost stories, basically voice-over boils down to this: any time you hear a recorded voice (or, for that matter, a *live* voice) and you can't see the person who's actually speaking, that's voice-over.

THE WONDERFUL WORLD OF VO

The world of VO is an incredibly creative one where I've worked with the most talented actors I've ever been around. All of them have their own unique abilities and sounds. The best ones have never left their "child-like" honesty, and are able to go into the most amazing vocal areas. I think that as long as you never grow up, have some acting ability and a healthy, passionate interest in your fantasy life, VO can be one of the most satisfying experiences you can have in this crazy business, and I have made life-long friends as a result.

~ PHIL MORRIS, ACTOR

WHERE CAN YOU FIND VOICE-OVER?

Disembodied voices come from everywhere. Put that way it sounds almost creepy, doesn't it? Well, not really. Think about it. Whether it's TV, film, or radio; whether it's in commercials and advertising, or cars and computers; it seems that some voice is always telling you something.

Consider all the places in your life where you hear voices. How many things talk to you every day? Your alarm clock, the radio, your voice mail, the TV, the GPS in your car, that audiobook or podcast you listen to during your commute, your computer, your Xbox, your tablet.

This is good news for voice actors because we're going to bet that, in most of those cases, someone got paid to do the talking. In other words, all of these venues equal jobs that a crafty and talented voice actor could go out and get! Next time you wake up, start counting every time you hear a voice-over of some kind. It shouldn't take you long to become aware of how many opportunities there are to make a buck and have a good time doing it.

So how do I start doing some of those jobs? you might be asking; and we're getting to that, we promise. But before we get you into the studio to really start playing around, let's take a look at some of what's out there and where it came from. Because, as many of you are already aware, *Knowing is half the battle.*

HISTORY AND THE DIFFERENT KINDS OF VOICE-OVER

Radio and TV broadcasting have used voice-over for both advertising and entertainment since the beginning of time – or since the beginning of radio and TV anyway. Starting with the advent of radio in the late 1800s and then continuing with the launch of television in 1928, voice-over has been a popular way to convey news, entertainment, and advertising. DJs and commentators are voice-over artists as long as they are not seen. However, with the rapidly changing Internet and alternate medium programming, the distinctions between who qualifies as a voice actor versus who is considered a DJ or commentator are becoming more and more blurred. Especially now, with the growing abundance of podcasts, where the personalities who host may or may not consider themselves actors. And as the thirst for new content increases dramatically each day, the need for voice-over actors grows dramatically as well.

MIC SAYS: The October 30th, 1938 radio broadcast of the Mercury Theatre's *The War of the Worlds* made international headlines – "Radio Listeners in Panic, Taking War Drama as Fact" – all without a single photo or moving image.

Radio plays, while most popular before the proliferation of television, still enjoy a wide audience in countries such as England. They are finding a new and growing audience thanks to the Internet where they are available in the form of podcasts. Not unlike listening to an audiobook, listening to these audio dramas can take the audience on vivid and detailed adventures using only sound effects, music, and dialogue. The art form remains a wonderful example of how profound and affecting a voice-over artist's skills can be.

Podcasts are audio programs you can stream or download from the Internet that serve much the same purpose as the old radio shows. Once upon a time, you had to work at a radio station to host your own show; but now (again thanks to our friend technology), anyone with a computer, an Internet connection, and a mic has the tools to create their own hit show and make it available for download to a computer or mobile device. The Internet has done wonders to help a huge variety of shows connect with their audiences. In days gone by, two friends waxing poetic about *MAD MAX: FURY ROAD* for a year wouldn't have been a show; it would've been two friends sitting in a basement, talking about a movie. And a journalist's deep dive into a little-publicized murder case to try and ascertain whether or not an innocent man had been imprisoned wouldn't have set the Internet on fire like some sort of true crime *Game of Thrones*. But now, podcasting has become just as legitimate a medium as television or radio, with some popular shows garnering millions of listeners and lucrative advertising contracts. Podcasting has become a storyteller's playground, and an excellent place for aspiring voice actors to cut their teeth. But more on podcasting in the next chapter.

Animation has long been the home of character voices – whether film, television, Internet, or video games. The voices created by the voice actor (VA) help bring life to animated characters who were, in turn, created by writers and designers. More often than not, these characters (e.g. Bugs Bunny, Betty Boop, SpongeBob SquarePants, Naruto) spring to mind when people think of voice-over or voice acting. More and more animated video games and toys are using voice-over to tell a story, entertain, or otherwise engage the player as fully as possible. And in addition to actors' vocal performances, their movements and facial expressions are more and more likely to be filmed or recorded to help animate characters for film, TV, and games these days.

Live-action with voice-over is found where recorded tracks of a character's thoughts or internal dialogue are played over the images or action, and are often used for dramatic effect (such as memories, after death, etc.). This type of voice-over is used in television, film, and theatre. For example, in the film *The Shawshank Redemption*, Morgan Freeman's character "Red" narrates, as does the (deceased) character of Mary on the television show *Desperate*

Housewives. One of the great things about film, TV, and animation is the opportunity to actually communicate what the character is thinking – directly to the audience. Think of how much more effective it is on the TV show *Heroes* that not only can the character of Matt Parkman hear people's thoughts, but so can we, the audience. Some shows or movies may also mix animation into an otherwise live-action show, like *Who Framed Roger Rabbit* or *Son of Zorn,* and the animation requires voice-over.

Commercial/Promo is a use of voice-over that's at least as old as radio broadcasting. If you can hear but not see an announcer trying to sell you something, consumers telling you about their experiences, people talking about a product, that's commercial or promo VO. Heck, it was the job of the original carnival barker. It might be presented as a dialogue between two or more people, or it might simply be information about a product or service, addressed directly to the consumer. Think about the differences between commercials for McDonald's, Dell, or Micro Mini Machines, for example. A promo (short for *promotion*) tends to be like a commercial, but is most commonly used to promote a network or show. The announcer of the Academy Awards, or the person you might hear say, "Up next on The Travel Channel," is basically doing a commercial, or *promo,* for the network.

Narration could be considered a sub-category of the aforementioned live-action with VO. It is commentary that describes a scene, or tells a story, or explains whatever's happening on screen or as part of an audio program. Narration might be in the form of a nature expert commenting while you watch polar bears bound about, or it might be Shakespeare's *Twelfth Night* as read by Sir Ian McKellen. Documentaries often have someone narrating the events you're watching. If you want words and don't need visuals, you can listen to narration as an audiobook.

Instructional voice-over is similar to narration but can pop up almost anywhere. Phone systems, computer programs, and corporate educational courses are all examples of this type of voice acting. When the elevator tells you what floor you're on, or when your GPS tells you to turn left in fifty feet, you can be sure that someone recorded those instructions. Unless, of course, they're using a computer-generated voice; but we all know that, despite recent and impressive technological advancements, those never sound *quite* as natural as a human-generated voice: *Wo-ould yo-ou li-i-ike to-o pla-ay a ga-ame?*

CHAPTER 2

YOU REALLY WANT THE JOB, BUT WHICH ONE?

"Variety is the very spice of life that gives it all its flavour."

WILLIAM COWPER, ENGLISH POET

SO MANY DELICIOUS FLAVORS ...

VO is a many-splendored thing. You can work in promos, commercials, animation, video games, narration, toys, and foreign language dubbing. The list goes on and on. Each of these areas, although similar in many ways, will have its own unique flavor. One variable is the time required for a recording session. While a commercial session may last only fifteen minutes, a video game session may last four hours, and a loop group session may take *all day*. And each one will have its own rate (and sometimes *rates*) of payment.

You may find that you're very well suited to one of these areas, or you may take to all of them. We have friends who specialize in one specific area and typically don't seek work in any of the others, and friends who will do any job that comes their way. Still others will go to great lengths to create their own projects when they aren't working for someone else. There's no right or wrong here. Whatever works for you is whatever work you'll do.

We've given you a brief look at the most common types of VO

work. Now we'll break those down a little more to see if we can give you a more detailed idea of what's out there waiting for you.

ANIMATION

You may have picked up this book because you're a fan of animation. Well, you're in luck: we're big fans, too. Voice work for animation pretty much falls into two categories: *original* (where you originate and record the role from scratch) and *dubbed* (where you rerecord the dialogue into a language different from the original: in our case, English). We've done a fair amount of work in both kinds of animation. While they're both fun, they each have their joys and challenges as well as their own specific techniques.

MIC SAYS: The longest-running American prime time entertainment series is a little animated show you may have heard of called *The Simpsons.*

Original

Original animation is sometimes called *pre-lay* because the voices are recorded before the animation is commenced. (*Pre* means before, and to *lay* down a sound track is to record it.) More often than not, you will record original animation with other actors – at the same time, in the same room. This is generally more fun, and can actually help create better performances because you get to act and react based on living, breathing people. But it also means that you'll have to pay attention to things that you might not be worried about if you were recording in a booth by yourself.

For example, each actor will have an individual mic, but you must be careful not to talk over someone else's line (or shuffle your script, or sneeze, or play with Velcro, etc.) or it may become unusable. Also, while your instinct will be to turn toward the actor you are speaking to, you have to be careful to maintain a consistent position behind your mic so that your voice is recorded evenly.

Having everyone in the same room can also help the director, writers, and producers see immediately if something works or doesn't work. Think of how many shows are successful largely because of the chemistry between the cast members. While it can be great fun and an important learning experience to work with other talented and skilled actors, just remember: You're there to do a job, so avoid the temptation of having *too* much fun. (Sometimes having a bunch of talented, funny people in a room together can actually slow things down, if you get what we're saying.) So, have fun, but make sure that the fun isn't getting in the way of the work.

Because the voice recording comes first and the animation is created second, the recorded dialogue is used as a guide for the animation. This means that when you first go in to record, you won't have anything visual to refer to while you're acting.

Sometimes when the completed animation comes back, it doesn't exactly match the audio that was recorded. Or perhaps there have been rewrites to the script. In either case, the actors may be asked to come back for a *pickup session* to rerecord some of their dialogue, or perhaps to record entirely new dialogue. This process is called *ADR* – additional dialogue recording, or sometimes either "automated" or "automatic" dialogue replacement.

In the pickup session, actors will have a chance to watch the animation as they record. Oftentimes, this additional session is when you'll be asked to record fight sounds or *efforts* (non-dialogue vocalizations such as grunts, groans, moans). Recording dialogue and efforts to animation that has already been created leads us right into our other category: dubbed animation.

THE DUB: A BRIDGE TO THE WORLD

Film dubbing can be described as a bridge between cultures. Its role in communicating in the twentieth century has been crucial and extends to present day. The art of dubbing has been around more than 70 years. However, most of those who have given their voices and their work to recreate the performances done by foreign artists or animated characters are basically unknown.

Cary Grant said that 80% of the work of an actor was the voice. In the twenty-first century, in addition to movies and TV series, actors' voices are heard in commercials, video games, telephone messages, and a wide range of applications in the media.

Dubbing is an international industry which is expanding due to the needs of a globalized world. In Asia and Africa, where professional dubbing has been developed only recently, new studios are proliferating, and the technology is being adopted by a new generation hungry to participate in the magic of working behind the microphone.

Times certainly have changed. Hollywood must now face competition from products filmed in places like Japan – with its popular *anime* cartoons, as well as films from Thailand, Korea, and China. Mexican, Brazilian, and Venezuelan soap operas have attained international status through dubbing.

Dubbing is also opening the doors of global markets to French, Italian, German, Spanish, and Russian animation companies. The biblical confusion of languages finds a practical solution in the replacement of voices. Since its development, dubbing has provided the greater public a way to understand the original message from the filmmakers.

~ EXCERPTS FROM HIS BOOK ¿DE QUIÉN ES LA VOZ QUE
ESCUCHAS? "WHOSE VOICE ARE YOU LISTENING TO?"
© BY RUBEN ARVIZU, ACTOR, DIRECTOR

Dubbed

In *dubbed animation* (in most cases coming from Japan, and often referred to by fans as *anime*), your job becomes more difficult as you find yourself with a lot more balls to juggle. Here, you are attempting to say the dialogue in a different language than originally recorded while matching the mouth movements in the animation that has already been created; and at the same time, you are also trying to match the *emotional integrity* of the original performance.

Add to all this the fact that you'll more than likely have to imagine the other actors because you'll be recording by yourself in the booth. (Because dubbing carries its own technical challenges, it has been established that recording each actor separately is the more efficient way to do it.)

Luckily, the scripts will already have been translated and adapted into English, but you'll still find yourself with plenty of things to think about. It takes practice, focus, relaxation, and timing, to say the least.

Here's generally how it works: you're in the booth (sitting or standing), and in front of you is a monitor on which the engineer will play the animation for you. Your script is on a music stand in front of you. Usually your dialogue is broken down into bite-sized pieces called *loops*. You may watch a loop a couple of times to get a feel for both the timing and what the mouth movements (or *flaps*) look like before trying to lay down the dub track.

Oftentimes the director has the engineer play the track in the original language so that you get some context from the original performance. How close you try to get to the original performance is up to the director. This process definitely takes some getting used to, and can, at times, be like juggling a ball, a bowling pin, and a chainsaw. But you will usually have your guide: the *beeps*.

Immediately preceding the moment when you need to begin speaking, you hear (in your headphones) *The Three Beeps*. These beeps are timed so that you begin speaking on the beat where the imaginary fourth beep would fall. So: *beep … beep … beep …* SPEAK! (For a more detailed explanation of The Three Beeps, you can check out "What's That Sound?" in Chapter 6, *The Booth*).

As we mentioned when discussing ADR, the skills developed in dubbing will sometimes serve you well even when you're working on original animation. And while dubbers are almost always paid less for their work, and are oftentimes looked down on by actors accustomed to working in the pre-lay animation world, the dubber's job is more often the harder one. If you can master the skills required for dubbing, you'll look really good in a pickup or ADR session for a pre-lay animation project. The engineer will love you, and you'll save everyone time and money.

Is It Crazy in Here or Is It Just Me?

My very first voice-over job ever was working on an anime dub. I landed a fairly decent part for it being my first time out, and I later found out that the producer was slightly nervous to use someone so new in the role. Luckily I had a knack for dubbing, though, and his worries quickly abated.

That same producer, however, did manage to scare the crap out of me during that first session. We got to a part in the show where I had one super-long chain of sentences that had to match up to a never-ending series of mouth flaps. Lines like that in anime can be tricky because the animation doesn't really allow for you to inhale when you start to run out of air. You just have to take one giant gulp of air at the top and hope it skids in across the finish line at the end.

Well, somehow, the stars aligned and I made it all the way through the line in one take, and managed to make the moment work, although I had no idea at first. I was still getting my sea legs.

Just as I began to reread the line to myself to see how I might improve for the 2nd take, the producer leaped forward without warning, yowling loudly like a Viking, and slapped a Post-it note on the glass separating me from the control room. *Hard.* I practically leapt through the ceiling, it startled me so badly. A second later, I looked at the Post-it, and read the letters *FB* on it. I was a much greener actor then, with zero reps in the recording studio, and I had no clue what was going on. I wasn't sure if I had messed up the show, or was being fired, or what. It certainly SEEMED bad. After I stared at the guy blankly for a few seconds, he jabbed his finger at the Post-it and yelled **&@#ing Brilliant,* baby!" Hence the *FB.*

The lesson learned being: just because you've made it to the big time, don't necessarily expect the people you find there to be 100% sane.

~ LIAM O'BRIEN, ACTOR, DIRECTOR

VIDEO GAMES

Similar to dubbing animation, voice-over for *video games* is most often recorded one actor at a time, alone in a booth, because it's easier from a technical perspective. Characters may have scenes with other characters, but the bulk of their dialogue will usually be stand-alone callouts, and those are recorded more efficiently one actor at a time. Are actors ever recorded together in studio? Yes. But it's uncommon, and has its challenges (overlapping dialogue becomes unusable, etc.). Performance capture, however, is a different story. If you're recording a scene with other actors on a PCap stage, you'll definitely be recording together if all actors are available. But even then, you may need to pick up dialogue at a later date in a studio. When you do begin recording, you may have a character sketch or some sample *gameplay* (a demonstration of what the game will look like when the player is playing it), but there's rarely more than that to hang your hat on.

There are, of course, a few exceptions to this – the first being when you're recording a version of a game that was originally produced in another language. In that case, you may have reference tracks in the original language, cut scenes (the short movies that play in between gameplay) that you'll have to match, and strict timing concerns to be aware of.

In another scenario, you may have done some work near the beginning of a game's development while no animation was yet available; and then eight months later the producers ask you to come back and do more work on it. Only now they've got animation and gameplay to show you as a reference.

But most often you'll have very little (if any) preparation, and not a lot of time to learn about the game before you're thrown into the fire. And this is where the director will be your best friend, giving you context for your dialogue – which you will sometimes record very quickly, one line after the other, two or three *takes* per line (i.e. two or three different recordings of the same line), with not even the other characters' dialogue for reference. Other times you might get the entire script, but it's unlikely you will have the time to do much more than scan it as you jump from line to line.

We've said that a strong imagination will help you in this business. To make this stuff work, you're gonna have to imagine quite a bit. So, listening to the director, using your imagination, and making bold choices – all at high speed – are important, and together can often be the key to finding yourself on the top of the call list when a studio is auditioning and booking future jobs.

Very often these days, video games are developed in tandem with major motion pictures so that when the movie comes out, the game based on that movie is also available. Now before you get too excited about doing the VO for these video games, we have to let you know that voice actors in video games get paid a lot less than their on-screen counterparts. Why? Well, we used to say, "Because the budgets for video games are nowhere near the budgets of the movies they accompany." But that's not always true. The budgets for some AAA titles can be greater than many Hollywood blockbusters. So, a better answer may be, "Because the commonly held opinion is that voice actors, no matter how good or well known they are, don't sell a game like Channing Tatum's face sells a movie." Is that unfair? Maybe. I dunno: that Channing Tatum is damn handsome. But you won't read anywhere in this book (or in the world) that life is guaranteed to be fair.

But now's your chance to get excited again because, in most cases, major motion picture actors will not want to lend their voices to the video game; the salary paid is simply not worth the time involved. This is where you come in: the game will likely require a voice actor to *voice match* the actor from the film. See, you always knew those impressions would come in handy one day.

Let's talk about voice matching for a second. It's not limited to video games, but can be found in any VO medium where the person hiring you is trying to match a voice that's already out there: usually, but not always, a celebrity voice. Maybe certain actors are unavailable or difficult to work with; maybe the budget can't afford them; maybe they're not good at ADR; or maybe an actor is dead and the producers still need to finish the project. Tara has matched celebrity voices for "plane/TV-safe" versions of films where profanity had to be dubbed out, and Yuri has matched celebrities who weren't available to do the video game based on the movie. If you have a talent for this sort of thing, make sure people know about it.

Whether you are voice matching or creating your own character voice for a video game, the recording session can be very stressful on your voice if you're not careful. Because of the nature of video games themselves, vocal control is extremely important. If you play a lot of video games, you know that they're chock-full of shouting, screaming, yelling, getting blown up, being set on fire, and falling from great heights. And that's just in the opening cut scene.

These recording sessions can last up to four hours at a time. There have been times when we've emerged from them sweaty, hoarse, and shell-shocked – as if we've actually been through the war we were just playing at. Many voice actors refuse to do video games for this reason, and some will intentionally schedule VG sessions in the afternoon on a Friday so that they have the whole weekend to recuperate. But don't let that scare you. Just keep reading: we have ways to help keep you safe.

MOTION CAPTURE AND PERFORMANCE CAPTURE

With the abundance of video games and even animation and film utilizing the exciting technologies that allow for motion capture, more and more jobs are looking for talents who can provide both the vocal and physical performance for the character. *Motion capture* (MoCap) refers to recording, on a soundstage, an actor's physical movements for a character, and then using that data to create digital animation. The actor's performance, which often includes stunts, is filmed (or "captured") by a battery of specialized cameras that feed their data right into a computer. Later the actor's recorded motion is used to assist animators in giving movement to characters in video games or animated TV shows, or to create computer-generated effects in films.

Performance capture (PCap) is similar to the work of motion capture but instead of just the overall physicality, the actors are also lending their individual performances (voice and face) to the character. As technology has gotten better, capturing an actor's full performance, even minute facial expressions, has become possible. Until only recently, it was all called motion capture, but the term "performance capture" makes it clear that it is truly the actors' performances, not just their movement, that is seen in the resulting animated or CG character. Performance capture has become de rigueur with most AAA games' creators who want their lead actors playing the role from start to finish, with the exception, sometimes, of specific specialized movements (stunts, acrobatics, martial arts, creature work) that may be awkward, unfamiliar, or even dangerous to an actor.

While MoCap and PCap work is not entirely new, it finally started to receive the attention it deserves when the world was treated to behind-the-scenes videos of Ahmed Best performing as Jar Jar Binks in the *Star Wars* prequels; and then Andy Serkis performing as Gollum in *The Lord of the Rings* films, and subsequently as Kong in *King Kong*, and then as Caesar in the *Planet of the Apes* films. But the business is slow to change, and major awards entities still struggle with honoring the work by an actor doing motion capture – or performance capture – with the same respect accorded to any other performance. More and more we see video games incorporating PCap, with characters ultimately bearing a striking resemblance to the actors who portray them. The technology has gotten so good that games like *L.A. Noire* were filmed with extensive facial performance capture and then used a gameplay mechanic that required the player to pay close attention to other characters' facial expressions to determine if they were lying.

So the good news is that all your years of doing plays in college or summer stock will come in handy when doing MoCap and PCap – with a few adjustments. While you'll be working on a soundstage similar to a film or television stage, and the acting will require the same skills, you'll be dressed in a tight-fitting body suit covered in reflective sensors (markers) that help the cameras read and record your every move. Add dots to your face, a camera and microphones strapped to your head, and a hard drive and batteries to round it out, and you'll find there's an adjustment period, acting-wise. Unlike for a theatre or film performance, the props and sets are merely "suggestions" of actual objects; and instead of wearing a unique costume, you'll be dressed pretty much like every other actor onstage. Clearly, interacting with the PCap "world" can be unnatural at first. But don't get your markers in a twist. We'll give you a few tips in Chapter 8, *The Soundstage*, that'll help put you at ease the first time you step into the void.

FILM/TV

Even though they call it tele*vision* and moving *pictures* (okay, so they don't really call it moving pictures anymore, and most of you probably watch all that stuff on the Internet anyway; but just nod and smile, or we'll start to feel old), *sound* plays a huge part in both of these media. And a lot of the sound work happens *after* the film/show's been shot and the on-camera actors have gone home. That's often when *we* get hired.

As we've mentioned in regard to foreign animation, you might be hired to dub an actor's dialogue into English (or possibly another language if you're multi-lingual). Some people just don't like to read subtitles, and that ends up being good for voice actors. A film or TV show might also need narration, another job for which the producers could potentially hire you (you know, if Morgan Freeman isn't available …).

Another good opportunity within the TV/film industry comes in the form of the *loop group* or *walla group* (usually a team of five to eight actors hired to record all the extra or *background* dialogue necessary in film, TV, or games). These groups join the project after a film/TV show has been shot, to *fill in* the audio *soundscape* (sounds that make up the environment). That generally means creating crowd or ambient noises that weren't recorded during filming.

Typically there is little to no scripted dialogue: the walla group actors simply make up lines based on research they've done about the location of the scene. But occasionally, a member of the loop group will be asked to match or replace a small character with scripted lines.

You see, in order to get the best quality sound on set when a movie or show is originally shot, the only people who are allowed to actually speak and make noise are the principal actors. This means that everyone you see in the background of any scene (in the coffee shop, hospital, or sports arena) is simply miming speaking and is not actually saying anything. So it is often necessary to have a loop group come in to the recording studio and fill in the voices that are missing.

Sometimes doing loop group or walla group work means adding in efforts (those non-dialogue vocal sounds) and possibly dialogue (ADR) that was somehow missed or perhaps left until later. Or it could involve replacing dialogue that didn't work out. Say, for example, that the film was shot in Romania, but the story is supposed to be set in New Jersey. Some of the actors who were hired locally may not have sounded *Jersey* enough, so the loop group may be asked to replace the dialogue with a more authentic accent.

These looping sessions can be some of the most sought-after work in the VO business. The prestige is low, but the pay is high, and the work can be profitable if you become associated with a group that works frequently.

Also, contrary to how we've described the workspace for most VO work, if you are working as part of a loop group, you'll have plenty of room to move around. The microphone is often set up fairly high in a larger-than-average room so that the actors can walk and move around and create different depths of background sound.

These different depths of sound are achieved through a number of techniques that have their own specialized vocabulary. One example is the *pass-by*, where people in conversation stroll across the pickup area of the mic to give the illusion of movement.

Another technique is the similar *donut*, where the group circles like a wagon train in front of the mic, and actors converse while continuing to circle. Sometimes it's just a stationary lineup of the group in front of the mic, with every member taking a turn shouting *callouts* (shouts) that may be used to break up the walla *bed* (a continuous layer of background dialogue). The first time we worked with a loop group, it was as if we had traveled to a foreign country and had to learn a whole new language.

As a member of the loop group, you are responsible for doing your own research so that you can bring in terms and vocabulary specific to certain settings or locales that are featured in the film/show. For example, if the movie you're looping is about the crew of a submarine, you'd better ask the Internet (or your favorite uncle) a lot about submarines before you come in to work. You must be prepared to improvise dialogue realistically and within the specific context of the project. But don't worry; a good loop group director will go over what you'll need to know for a specific project enough in advance that there will be time for you to do some research.

Since the first edition of *VOVA*, a lot of people have asked us to talk more about loop groups, mostly in terms of, "How can I get this kind of work?" Fortunately or not, our answer is simple: *It's really about who you know.* And the best way to know people is to get out there and work. So, work, get good, and let them find you. Or be a friend of a producer on a TV show. Often, the producer can call the director of that show's loop group and ask for you to be a part of the group. But remember, to the other actors, you'll be "the producer's friend who took up a valuable slot in our group." So if that's your path, then be nice, be extra prepared, show up on time, and don't hide in the back.

COMMERCIAL OR PROMO

Here, we're grouping together all advertising and promotional VO. We could break down this section into individual commercial/promotional types, but let's keep it simple.

Recording VO for commercials/promo can be a fun and extremely speedy process. You may have only one line – or sometimes even one word! – to say; and then your session will consist of your going into a studio and saying that one line or word several different ways, and having the client or ad exec say, "Fantastic! You're brilliant! Thanks so much. Have a great day!" and then send you on your way. Not a bad way to earn a living.

But it doesn't always work out quite like that. Sometimes, as a promo announcer for a TV series or show, you might have pages and pages of copy per session, and you could be in the booth for several hours. Or, you may have only one line, but they'll want it a hundred different ways (and probably still use your first take) and have to go through several lengthy layers of client approval before letting you go on your merry way.

And we certainly don't want to make you think that these kinds of jobs don't require as much skill or technique as the other types of jobs we've been talking about. They most certainly do.

Usually, for commercial/promotional copy you'll be recording alone unless it's a commercial with two or more people talking to each other (often called a *partner read*). But unlike in original animation, there won't be a need for you to worry about stepping on another actor's lines. As a matter of fact, the producers will usually be looking for funny, natural mistakes that bring realism to the spot. Also, we've noticed an increasing amount of improvised comedy, so make sure you're taking those improv classes.

Sometimes the clients will be in the control room, but more often they'll be absent, trusting the advertising team to get the job done with you. Sometimes, even the ad team won't be in the control room: they'll be on the phone, and you and the engineer will be the only ones physically in the studio!

Often, timing will be a major concern because the commercial has to stick to a fifteen, thirty, forty-five, or sixty second limit, and the ad copywriters will have spent many hours crafting words to fit that time exactly. Sometimes, though, it doesn't work, and they rewrite on the fly; so always be flexible.

You may have in your head an idea of what kind of voice sells products: the *Announcer Guy* voice. Well, allow us to tell you about a little trend that's been going for years: *Less announcery. More natural. Girl-next-door feel. Like you're talking to your best friend.* Gone are the days of the "voice of god" commanding you to buy something. Today's methods are a little more tricky, so it'll behoove you to practice and become very aware of what sounds *put on* and what sounds *natural*.

NARRATION

When performing a narration, or an audiobook, a PSA (public service announcement), or other long-form narration, you will find that the setup is usually similar to commercial copy. Sometimes you'll be in a studio, and sometimes (especially with audiobooks) you'll be at home recording by yourself.

Most often with narration, you will either record a paragraph at a time or just keep recording until you flub (that's fancy voice-over talk for *make a mistake*), and then stop. Other times, the engineer will continue recording and will simply ask you to say "pickup" after making a mistake, then say the corrected version and keep going.

Your saying *pickup* is just an indication to whoever will be editing that you've flubbed that last bit, and you're taking it back to the last easy break in your script (usually the beginning of a sentence, or maybe even at a comma break) and starting again.

You can always check with the engineering team to see how they prefer you do pickups. It's just important for you to be aware that when the whole piece is cut together, it will need to flow smoothly. So be sure that you're working to maintain a consistency to your read throughout the entire piece.

PODCASTING AND RADIO SHOWS

When we first wrote this book, podcasts (the modern version of the radio show) weren't really a thing. Now, podcasts are ALL THE THINGS. So we figured it'd be good to talk about them this time around, even though one could argue that they don't fit solidly in the world of VO. And while it certainly is hard to monetize a podcast, there are many other benefits to be had by creating your own show.

Now more than ever, it is increasingly easy to create your own content and get it out there. Hosting a podcast is as simple as deciding on a topic that interests you, recording yourself, and then making your program available on the Internet for others to listen to. Yuri has a list of podcasts he listens to regularly, and it seems like the list is as long as or longer than our Netflix queue!

There are a number of available hosting platforms that allow you to publish your podcast online once it is recorded; and once it's up, you can make it available in the iTunes and Google Play stores for the world to download and listen to while commuting.

One of the major benefits of creating your own show is *control*. You are your own producer, client, and talent rolled into one. You don't have to wait on anyone to say yes, and maybe most importantly, there's nobody to say, "No. That's a stupid idea. Nobody would listen to that show." Of course the downside is you have to do all the work yourself – recording, editing, promotion, scheduling guests (if it's that kind of show) – and you don't have anyone else to keep you motivated and on schedule. Obviously you could hire someone to do that stuff, or team up with someone who *likes* to do that kind of stuff.

We once attended a Kevin Smith talk (you should certainly do this if you have the chance) in which he spoke about creating his own very successful podcasting empire, and he basically said that if you make a hundred episodes of a show, no matter the topic, you will eventually find an audience that loves and adores it as much as you. He's not wrong. If the Internet has shown us anything, it's that there's an audience out there for everything, no matter how "niche" you think it may be. The key to podcasting is making something you're passionate about and being dedicated to getting it out into the world *on a regular basis*. Audiences love regular content, consistency, and engagement (interacting with them on social media, taking their questions/comments on the show). You can have the best show in the world, but if people don't know when it comes out, or have to wait too long for the next episode, they'll go somewhere else for their free entertainment. So plan ahead, and don't just wait for inspiration to strike whenever it feels like it.

So how is this voice acting? Well, you're telling stories using only what your audience can hear, so...

Build up a big enough audience over time and maybe you can attract sponsors. Even if you don't, now you've got an audience that may follow you beyond your show. And at the very least, it's good practice. We can't say it enough: *make your own stuff*. Heck, get meta on it, and host a podcast about your favorite podcast! Mind ***blown***.

CHAPTER 3
FINDING YOUR VOICE

---

*"When you are content to be simply yourself and
don't compare or compete, everybody will respect you."*

LAO-TZU, CHINESE PHILOSOPHER

It seems a little obvious, but your voice is going to be your most important tool in this kind of work. So let's talk a bit about your voice and what you might be expected to do with it.

KNOW YOUR VOICE

This is something that can't be said enough: you must know your own voice. No matter how long you've been living with your voice and how well you think you know it, you're about to start doing things with it that you've probably never done before. So take the time to get friendly with your beautiful and unique pipes. You'll learn to recognize your limits and your strengths.

Believe it or not, if you don't know your voice, sometimes booking the job is the worst thing you could do! For example, let's say you really push your voice way out of your comfort zone in the audition, and you book the job. Well, that's great, you got the job! But now you have to *do* that voice (maybe for 52 episodes!), and if you've made a choice that your vocal apparatus can't keep up with (say, a deep gravelly voice that you can only maintain for a few minutes before you get hoarse or keel over in pain), then you'll end up embarrassed because you'll have to back out of the project, and the producers will have to find someone else.

In that case, everyone loses, and no matter how many times you apologize, everyone will remember what a snafu you caused. We're gonna bet most voice actors have a story like this; and you only need one such experience – where you risk losing your voice (and your pride) – to drive home the importance of knowing your own limits.

This isn't to say you shouldn't push yourself or that it isn't possible to expand your range. That's the fun part! But the key here is staying healthy. Start by becoming conscious of when you are speaking *on* your voice or *off* your voice. Just as our fingerprints are unique to each of us, our vocal folds vibrate to create specific vocal patterns that make up our personal and unique vocal signature. Practice creating interesting and specific characters with the voice you *do* have, and not the voice you *wish* you had.

Sure, it's possible to imitate someone who has a similar sound or register, but ultimately we are each built differently, and our vocal quality is one more example of this. (You really are unique, just like your mom told you.)

You can expand your healthy vocal range just as you would build muscles at the gym – by working out. Taking a singing class or voice class can often provide you with the exercises you need to broaden your range.

"SO HOW DO I FIND MY OWN VOICE?"

You can start identifying your *own* voice by making a list of adjectives that you feel describe your voice and your way of speaking. Then (because we often have trouble being objective), pick five people who know you well and five people who know you less well, and ask each of them to come up with five adjectives to describe your voice. Remind them that they're not trying to describe *you* or the way you *look*, but specifically *your voice*. If they have trouble coming up with descriptive words, maybe you could compile a long list of adjectives to make it easier on them. Here are a few adjectives you might choose (also see our suggestions in "Play to Your Strengths" in Chapter 12, *The Demo*):

abrupt	**energetic**	**sincere**
curt	**fun-loving**	**smooth**
confident	**guarded**	**upbeat**

See which of the words suggested by your friends resonate with you, especially if a certain adjective comes up more than once. That means there's usually something to that suggestion.

As you become more familiar and comfortable with your voice, you may find that you can start to identify the attributes that are specific to you. Your voice might be raspy or it might be crisp and clear. Maybe you have a slight drawl from living in the South, or a particular vocal pattern that people identify with you. Identifying your vocal characteristics is a good way to start homing in on what types of characters and qualities you might be able to bring to the table.

Some people call this description of your voice and delivery a *vocal signature* or *style*; others simply call it *your sound*. As soon as you zero in on your sound, you've got a strong place to start and to build outward from. It'll be your safe place that you can always fall back on, and probably the place from which you'll do most of your work.

Vocal signature comes up a lot in commercial VO. You might get hired because of your specific sound and attitude – which the client feels perfectly represent the product, and suddenly you're the *spokesvoice* for that brand.

Remember, the most important thing here is that you are discovering for yourself your own personal and particular vocal quality and sound. There are so many opportunities in the field of voice-over that there's no reason for you to feel the need to alter your own sound. Simply learn to market what you have and who you are, and that's when things will really start popping!

ADJECTIVE/ADVERB QUALITY LIST

Here's the next step in discovering your sound: create a *quality list* that is unique to you. This list is a refined version of the adjective list you've already started.

Put together for yourself a portfolio of the sounds and qualities that you feel accurately describe your natural vocal delivery. Start with the list of descriptive words that you and other people came up with to describe your voice. Add your favorite characters and even pictures of things that remind you of these qualities.

Then start listening to commercials on the radio or the VO in TV commercials. What audience is the commercial/show geared to? What voices do you connect to? Where do you see yourself fitting in? Do you think you might be better suited to voice the father in an oatmeal ad or the high school football star in the soft drink ad? Would you be more believable as the voice of the young mom in a detergent ad or of the pre-teen girl in the back-to-school fashions ad? Where are you comfortable?

Think about gender, age, race/ethnicity, personality, profession, attitude, and all the elements that are central to the spot, the character, or the story. Now use all of this information to build your own quality list, one that expresses your signature style. Here are some more examples of qualities you might include on your list:

manly	professional	bubbly	trustworthy
feminine	down-to-business	calm	sly
boyish	carefree	eager	slick
girlish	laid back	slow	honest
motherly	straightforward	warm	nurturing
fatherly	happy-go-lucky	aloof	wry

Pick one or two qualities from each column above to create a quality list. For example, are you *manly, fatherly, laid back, calm, trustworthy,* and *wry*? How can you channel *your* warmest or slickest quality?

If the suggestions above don't work for you, come up with your own. Decide which mix of words describes your voice when you speak. The qualities you identify make up your quality list.

Voice-over, like so many industries, has to adjust to changing fads and trends: voices come and go in popularity. When you listen to the radio or to commercials or shows, what attributes are prevalent in the actors' voices? Sometimes bubbly and perky will be in, other times sexy and sultry, still other times dry and sarcastic. The better you know your own voice, the more prepared you'll be when "your voice" is selling.

In the meantime, don't despair. Even if your sound is not *hot,* there's still room for every kind of voice in this biz. And, as we've said, *hot* changes from day-to-day...

MIC SAYS: To help define your own voice, write yourself a sentence listing your vocal qualities. "I have a _____, _____, _____ voice."

"BUT I LIKE HOW THAT GUY SOUNDS!"

Good! Part of developing your voice involves listening to how other people's voices sound. Become a keen observer not only of the way *you* speak, but also of the ways people around you are speaking. Being observant will help you to become more aware of vocal variations, a skill that'll come in handy when you're playing around with your own voice.

You know how people with pets have a tendency to resemble them? Well, you might start to notice that, for the most part, people's voices have a tendency to suit them. Therefore, we often find comedy when someone's voice doesn't seem to fit the character's appearance.

For example, imagine a large male bodybuilder who opens his mouth only to speak with a very high-pitched, delicate, feminine voice. You might find it funny because the voice seems the opposite of what you'd expect. On the other hand, if a distinguished-looking male doctor opened his mouth and spoke with a grave and authoritative voice, you would probably take his word for fact because his appearance and his voice seem to match perfectly.

It's the nature of our minds to make judgments and presuppositions about things. Knowing this, we can learn to play around with these assumptions to create interesting characters. Perhaps you have a meek sound. Would that lend itself to playing a librarian or a mousy creature? What if you have a very deep, resonant sound? Might you be a dragon or a politician? Now what if you switched it up and created a mild dragon or a meek politician?

Playing with opposites is fun. Next time you're watching a cartoon, note how many characters have voices that suit them physically, and how many "play against type." You might say that Homer Simpson has a voice that suits him; but Bender sounds about as far from what you'd think a robot sounds like as humanly (robotly?) possible, and that's one of the things that makes him interesting.

YOUR STRENGTH IS *YOU*

When I was 10 years old, I did a voice for the film *The Secret of NIMH*. I then spent twenty years acting on-camera, and my voice acting career didn't actually *begin* until I was well into my 30s and I became a recurring character on *Teen Titans*.

Working on *Titans* led to *Legion of Superheroes*, *Ben 10: Alien Force*, and *Batman: The Brave and the Bold*. Along the way, I've been fortunate to work with some of the greatest talents in the industry, and I've learned a great deal about the craft of voice acting simply by being in the same room with them and paying attention to how they work.

One afternoon, while listening to Phil Morris blow us all away as Imperiex, I thought, *"I'm never going to be able to do voices like that. I'm never going to make it as a voice actor if I can only sound like myself."*

Then, almost instantaneously, I had another thought. *"Wait. That's not right. When I act on-camera, I always look more or less like myself. It's the* character *who changes from job to job. Why should voice acting be any different?"*

I felt like a huge weight had been lifted from my shoulders, and I grew a level in voice acting because I was able to relax and understand what type of voice actor I was. Darkstar, Cosmic Boy, and Ted Kord all *sound* like me, but each one is a fundamentally different character because of the way I *perform* them. I'm never going to be the guy who can do interesting character voices, but I *am* the guy who can create interesting characters using only his voice.

Whether on-camera or in the booth, we actors have to know what our strengths and limitations are. We have to know what types of roles we can reasonably expect to play so we can help our agents and managers put us into a position where we can compete for them. To be successful voice actors, we need to combine both *voice* and *acting* (wasn't it nice of them to work the job description right into the title?), but that doesn't mean that we can't be a little stronger with one than the other. And when we know what our strength is, we can focus our time and energy developing it to its full potential, instead of struggling to be something we're not.

~ WIL WHEATON, ACTOR

"PEOPLE TELL ME I SOUND LIKE SO-AND-SO ..."

Are there already established actors who have sounds and vocal qualities that are similar to yours? Perhaps someone has even told you how much you sound like so-and-so. Great! Knowing this is a good way to start narrowing down what your own attributes are. What are the qualities you associate with that actor? Maybe you're quirky and natural like Ellen DeGeneres, or maybe you have more of a raspy, sultry quality like Kathleen Turner. Either way, identifying a matching voice could help you find adjectives that illuminate the qualities you possess. And sounding like a celebrity might even help when you are marketing yourself to potential clients by giving them something they're already familiar with.

Take a look at what types of jobs that famous actor whose voice is similar to yours is booking, and point yourself in that direction. Lots of celebrities have regular clients and campaigns. Kaiser Permanente has featured Allison Janney, and George Clooney has been known to promote everything from water to phone services. Perhaps, if you're good at celebrity voice impersonations, you may even get paid to do those voices in a movie or video game.

You see (as we mentioned in the section about video games), sometimes, when celebrities aren't available or are too expensive but the client really wants them, the producer will hire someone who *sounds* like the celebrity, someone who can *voice match* that person. For example, Christopher Walken has had many impersonators (*come on, admit it, you do Walken, don't you?*), but one of those guys actually gets hired to sub for Walken's voice when he's not available. How cool is *that* job? So listen closely and brush up on your impressions.

Voice Matching...You

The art of voice matching is an interesting one and is not generally part of the career plan for many voice actors. For most it's something they stumble upon from time to time due to the simple fact that they happen to sound similar to an actor who needs to be doubled for a film or its trailer. Then, there is a much smaller group who actually do quite a bit of voice matching in various ranges of voice and form.

I happen to be someone who has done countless matches for celebrities, character actors, and classic cartoon voices. I honestly have lost track of how many voices I've matched, but highlighted ones would include Dick Van Dyke to David Spade, Ewan McGregor to Johnny Depp, Christopher Walken to Christopher Lloyd, Michael J. Fox to Jay Baruchel. All for different types of projects: movies, trailers, TV shows, video games, toys, commercials, etc. It's basically like being the stunt double for a person's voice. In fact, I have several friends who are stunt men who have done the stunt-doubling for an actor while I ended up doing the voice-doubling, and the on-screen actor was never even involved in the scene. A strange and unique job, for sure.

And after over 20 years of voice work, the best piece of advice I can give about voice matching is this: Don't lose your own identity in being someone who can do anyone else. You always have to maintain your own unique style and voice in what is becoming a very competitive world of voice acting. You may be the guy (or gal) who can match anyone, anytime, but do you truly know your own voice and what you can do within *it?* I've been very blessed to voice many well-known characters that are indeed just *me*, my *regular voice*. But I found that in some scenes I would get stuck as to how *I* (James) would do or say something without the restriction of sounding like someone else or of staying within another actor's acting beats. I finally came to the conclusion that my voice is, at times, an amalgam of all the various people and characters I have portrayed in my career. So it can be flexible. In fact, that is my primary selling point now: that I can pretty much go wherever I need to go vocally within a character whether I'm playing Obi-wan Kenobi or Fred Flintstone or Johnny Test. But the problem still remains that, except when I am voice matching, my voice must always still sound like *that* character, who is indeed just *me*.

Many of you want a career in voice acting to show everyone all the voices *you* can do.

But do you know *you*? And how to be just *you* in any scene or situation? I have to make a concerted effort to regularly explore my own voice by simply listening to recordings of me being *me*, and then use all the skill I've picked up from years of matching people to identify this actor inside of me. Because at the core of every good voice actor should simply be an actor, not a person who "does voices." Our voice is the only part of a voice actor's performance that is recorded, but we are more than just a sound. We must embody all of the character, and that's why voice matching can be tricky: you must become the other person, not just in sound, but in every beat and nuance of their character. There are many impersonators, but few can sustain all parts of the actor or character they're doing for extended periods, and in any situation. And perhaps even fewer can truly be themselves in any situation or scene. Practice, and know who *you* are before focusing on becoming someone else! Good luck in all your endeavors!

~ James Arnold Taylor, Actor

A HEALTHY VOICE IS A HAPPY VOICE

You want to be able to count on your voice to be there for you when you're working, so you can begin by keeping your voice healthy. Each person's voice is different, just like each person's fingerprints. You'll ultimately have to decide for yourself what's best for keeping your voice in top form. But remember, your voice is tied to your overall health, so when you get sick, your voice is generally the first thing to go.

You probably know yourself pretty well by now and have a good idea what works for you to keep you feeling good. Here are some things that we find work for us:

sleeping

hydrating

exercising

not smoking

Of course, we're not your parents, but these things have definitely played a part in how we stay healthy. Just know that, like an athlete, you'll have to put a little time every day towards preparing your body to work.

KNOW YOUR BOUNDARIES

As we've mentioned before, when you're creating a character, be careful that you don't come up with a voice that you aren't confident you can sustain safely over the course of a session or a season. It may sound cool at first, but if it blows out your voice inside of five minutes, nobody's going to think it's cool anymore, least of all you. Remember, you are enough. Let's say it again, because this is a valuable lesson that can be applied across all of your pursuits: *You are enough.* You already have the *perfect* voice naturally, and anything else you are able to bring into being with your vocal cords is a bonus. Who is enough? You are.

Get comfortable with your boundaries, as well as your strengths, so that when you walk through the door, you'll be at your best. Knowing your boundaries will keep you from injuring yourself, something which can cost you time, money, and potential future jobs. Remember, once an actor's voice blows out after a few lines, a client'll think twice about hiring that actor again. So take care of your voice!

It is very easy to hurt the little fibers/tissues/muscles that create your voice, and doing so can cost you a lot. Singers, actors, and many people in the business of talking or yelling a lot find themselves in danger of permanent harm to their voices. You'll want to train and strengthen your voice so that you can use it healthfully and productively for many years to come.

You don't want to develop vocal *nodes*, which are like small calluses that form on the vocal cords and can require up to six to eight weeks of complete vocal rest (not a sound!) to heal. Or worse, your nodes could turn into *nodules*, which are usually larger than nodes and often have to be removed surgically – with the danger that your voice will never quite sound the way it did before. The best things you can do are practice positive vocal health and treat your limits with respect. Always warm up your voice before a session and treat it with care.

What can you do to actually make your voice stronger? Any number of activities, from theatre and voice classes, to singing lessons, yoga, and even martial arts. These activities can teach you breath control and help you to use your voice safely and healthfully.

"I USE MY VOICE ALL THE TIME. HOW HARD COULD IT BE?"

When speaking (reading) dialogue, you will obviously be using your voice much like you do in real life. But the difference between normal everyday use of your voice and using your voice to make a career in VO will be noticeable in things like your control, your stamina, and your ability to meet any challenge the job might put in your way. Think of it like the difference between occasionally playing sports with your friends and playing professionally. You will sometimes be recording sounds and non-words (screeches, yells, screams, efforts) that might not be part of your daily routine. Making these sounds requires skill that will take practice to develop and hone.

CHAPTER 4
BEFORE YOU GET TO THE AUDITION

"The best job goes to the person who can get it done without passing the buck or coming back with excuses."

NAPOLEON HILL, U.S. AUTHOR, LECTURER

CREATING A CHARACTER –
THE *ACTING* PART OF VOICE ACTING

You may notice we haven't really gotten into the *So how do I go out there and book that job?* part yet. Well, that's part of our devious plan. There are several things that we think you should know before you start auditioning. One of these things is the importance of creating a strong character. We've noticed that the people who really succeed in this business are generally good *actors* first, good *voice-over* actors second. Strangely enough, when juggling all the balls of voice-over, one of the easiest to drop is the acting. Acting is where the most fun is, so who wants to drop that ball?

Creating a character is so much more than saying the words in the right order, or in a unique and interesting way. Creating a character is really about using your imagination to create the universe the character lives in, and then saying "yes, and…" to that universe. This *yes, and…* theory pops up a lot in improvisational comedy (improv) and theatre classes, so you may have heard it bandied about before now.

Put simply, one of the fundamental keys to good improv (and good acting in general) is agreeing to the scenario (*yes*) and then adding something (*and*) to take it to the next level. The more you say "no, but…" the harder it is to get to where you're going, and the less interesting it'll be for everyone involved. You'll find that when you're specific about the world your character lives in, the type of character that would reside in that world quickly becomes clear to you. The character's personality you end up creating this way will be real and honest, no matter how outlandish and wild the character's reality might be.

Who's to say that a talking sponge can't have friends under the sea and wear geometrically formed pants? We bet a lot of people said "no, but…" to this idea once upon a time, but the success of that show goes on and on, because the right people said, "yes, and …."

Bringing a character to life through your own creativity, truth, and ability is what being an actor is all about. You get to live different lives and have experiences totally foreign to your own. Showing how much you love this role (by committing to the character's reality) will not only be invaluable once you've got the job, but it's going to help you get cast. Being able to create an interesting character at an audition shows that you'll be able to create an interesting character if hired.

SURPRISE! IMPROVISE!

I do a lot of games and I love it. One director in particular just calls me in to record without telling me what I'll be doing. Usually, I'm shown a picture of the character, and sometimes, if it is an ongoing game (like *Everquest*), I'm played a sample of some other version of the same type of character (so I can see if the evil elves' British accents sound more like the Queen Mother or Sporty Spice). One day,

I showed up for a session and was told I'd be playing a Valkyrie. The picture was of a nasty looking winged warrior. No problem. Then the director said, rather tentatively, "Um, the producers would really love it if she could *sing* her lines – you know – like in opera?"

"Okay," I said, "Which ones?"

"All of them."

"I can do that," I said, and watched them relax a little. I had two things on my side. First – improv – I recommend it to everyone, but this was the closest thing to an improv setup that I'd ever been handed (*You are a winged beast in battle and you must sing all of your lines – go!*). My second advantage was classical vocal training. Who knew those arias would actually come in handy some day? I was excited to see what would come out of my mouth.

And, as with any improv, I didn't have time to think about it. The engineer said, "Rolling," and I went for it. I had recently been to see a Wagnerian opera, *Tristan and Isolde*, so I had the heavy, dramatic music in my mind's ear. And for a few minutes, I felt like a voluptuous woman filling a 2,000 seat theatre. I had a great time and have been back to work for that director many times since then!

~ DEBORAH SALE-BUTLER, ACTRESS

THE IMPORTANCE OF THE Ws: WHO, WHAT, WHERE, WHEN, WHY, AND HOW

Sure, these questions are important for reporters, but they're also important for you (assuming you're not already a reporter). They're the questions that help you make clear character choices. Luckily, in most cases you'll have a script to draw from, and it'll be chock full of answers to these six questions.

In some ways, acting is like being a detective. If you can find enough clues and put them together, things begin to make sense, and you don't have to *do* anything special. Thinking about reasons why your character says or does something (as indicated in the script) can often help you make creative choices that will help your work stand out and bring your character to life.

1. *Who* are you: what kind of a person/creature/thing are you? What is important to you? Who is the character you are talking to; what is your relationship to him/her/them/it?

2. *What* are you doing, what have you done, what do you plan to do, and what's going on?

3. *Where* are you physically, where are you usually, where would you like to be, and just where are you in the telling of the story?

4. *When* is this scene/story/moment taking place, and how much time do you have to do whatever it is you're doing?

5. *Why* are you doing/saying what you are doing/saying anyway? Why aren't you saying/doing something else?

6. And finally, *how* does your character choose to do what he/she/it is doing, and how is that different from how you, yourself in real life, might do it?

Often, pondering the differences between how *you* might do or say something and how the *character* does or says it will teach you something important about the character.

Between your imagination and the script, you should have more than enough information to flesh out a unique and real character. Actors often try to make choices because they feel an idea will be *interesting* or *cool* – regardless of the information they've been given. Try, instead, using your *yes, and…* powers to see what makes sense in terms of the story that the writer has given you. Would that Martian speak with a German accent just because it would be kooky and fun for you to do, or because the script indicates that the only interaction Martians have had with

Earth has been through German soap opera broadcasts?

And don't get caught up in thinking, "Well, I've never been to Mars. How am I supposed to know what a Martian sounds like?" Or something closer to home, like, "Well, I don't have a brother, so how am I supposed to know how that feels?"

Odds are, if you're interested in an acting career, you probably have a pretty active imagination. Use it. It's fun. Your imagination is like your voice or a fingerprint – unique. Using it will automatically make your take on a character different from anyone else's.

Even when you're dealing with sterile commercial copy, something as simple as, "Come in today for a great deal!" it can be easy to just say the words without even thinking about it (which isn't always bad). But try taking a second to get specific about what you're saying. Think of a person you know, and deliver the line as if it's just for that person. Imagine the circumstances under which you could be saying this line to someone. For example, what if you're telling your little sister who never listens; or what if it's a secret that you don't want to be overheard; or what if you're in a hurry to get the info out because the deal ends in fifteen minutes? Suddenly, this simple, throwaway sentence has taken on a whole life of its own, just in the time it took to ask and answer the Ws.

Specific choices and clear ideas on how you feel about what you're saying take your work to the next level. Sometimes things aren't clearly laid out on the page, and you can't ask the writers what they meant. This is where you get to make up some things, get your creative juices flowing, and harness that wild imagination of yours. This is where things really get fun.

Let's say the scene is between two brothers, and the only lines are the older brother saying, "I'm taking you to the zoo," and the younger brother saying, "Okay." The writer hasn't given you much to go on here, but nobody's keeping you from filling in the blanks on your own. Maybe the last time the younger brother went to the zoo he was attacked by monkeys, and he was left traumatized by the event. You'd better believe that's going to color how he says, "Okay."

Or maybe the older brother's never done anything nice for his little brother before, so the little brother's "Okay" is a suspicious one. Maybe the older brother's in the mob, and "taking someone to the zoo" has an even more sinister meaning.

In life, we're rarely indifferent about things. We almost always have an opinion or feeling towards almost everything we encounter, so why wouldn't our characters have their own opinions and feelings? Humor and drama come directly from our relationship to the things in our environment and from how we react to those things.

PLAYING WITH SPEED, PITCH, AND VOLUME

There are so many different elements that contribute to how a person sounds; if you can become aware of them, you can use them to your advantage to help you create some really fun, funky, and fancy voices for your repertoire. Start with the *speed* which is simply how quickly you're speaking: slow, medium, or fast. People often joke about Southerners (from the U.S.) speaking in a slow, meandering drawl, while folks from the northeast (U.S. again) are more fast-paced, clipped, and blunt. Play around with your speed to find fun patterns, not only of the words, but of the phrases and sentences.

Then move to the *pitch*. Generally a voice can be pitched high, mid-range, or low. Some examples of a high-pitched voice might be the aforementioned SpongeBob SquarePants, or the actress Ellen Greene, or yourself after sucking on a helium balloon. A low-pitched voice calls to mind James Earl Jones, Tom Waits, Ron Perlman, or Lurch from *The Addams Family*. The rest of us fall somewhere in the middle.

One person's mid-range pitch may be your low or high depending on how you're built, and depending on what sex you are: men naturally tend to have a lower register, while women's voices are usually higher. Play around with your pitch a little and see what happens. It can lead to touching moments, funny moments, and downright scary moments sometimes.

The final basic element is *volume*: loud, conversational, and soft. Perhaps a character speaks in a loud booming voice and is always being asked to quiet down (maybe thanks to working for years in an anvil factory). Or a character's voice is shy and whispery, and can't be understood (too many years as a librarian, perhaps). See how entire characters can develop out of how loud or soft you choose to speak?

Now look at these three elements: speed, pitch, and volume, and break each of them down into its low, medium, and high grades. The result is nine different qualities to mix and match in three dimensions. Imagine a giant 3-D tic-tac-toe board with each quality represented by its own dimension. It's kind of like a simplified vocal *Rubik's Cube of Choices*, with speed represented by height, pitch represented by width, and volume represented by depth (see diagram below).

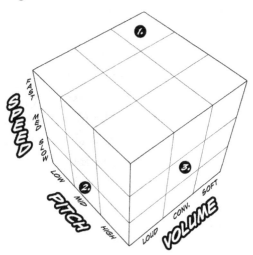

Now pick one of the intersections of these elements (a small cube within the cube) and see what combo you get. Here are quality groupings you'd end up with if you selected each of the numbered cubes in the illustration:

Cube 1: a fast, low-pitched, soft voice
Cube 2: a slow, mid-range, loud voice
Cube 3: a medium-speed, high-pitched, conversational voice

You can come up with a variety of other combinations simply by mixing these three different qualities. This doesn't even take into account any other flair you can add, such as attitude, accent, or age. The possibilities seem endless!

IMPRESSIONS AND TIMING

Oftentimes, an actor (or anyone, really) will attempt an impression of someone famous, or maybe even of someone they know personally who has an easily identifiable vocal mannerism. Unless you're able to do an exact voice match, what you'll usually get will not be a perfect imitation – and sometimes not even close. But what you *do* get is a brand new character voice for your bag of tricks – one that you don't even have to attribute to your intended target. You can take all the artistic credit.

The saying goes that in comedy, *timing ... is everything*. Well, it can be a pretty powerful tool when working on a character's voice as well. You need look no further than the two titans of vocal timing, Christopher Walken and William Shatner. The reason they're so often imitated is that they have oddly characteristic vocal rhythms. What are some of the things that characterize their speech? Oddly placed pauses? Stressing words that don't normally get stressed? Play with that for a little while. Do your best to imitate one of them.

Now experiment with a character that has similar rhythm patterns, but make this individual really soft spoken, with a high-pitch, and a fast delivery, for example. An interesting character, totally different from Walken or Shatner, suddenly pops up, and no one'll be the wiser as to who was your muse. *Hmmm.* Christopher Walken as muse ... William Shatner as muse. Ponder that for a while.

PROFESSIONALISM

In all the excitement of a voice-over career, professionalism can be the first trait to go. We cannot stress this fact enough: you will stand out from others by being a consummate professional. And you don't have to know anything about voice acting to act like a professional.

Do you think the most talented actors always get the job? Not if they're difficult to work with. You'd be surprised at how often actors will get the job just by showing up, doing the work, being decent to interact with, and then going on their merry way. Be one of these people. It doesn't take a lot of extra effort.

Be someone who is reliable, humble, polite, talented, and available. Being professional means you show up on time (or even a little early), ready to work, and ready to learn. You don't need to go to charm school for this, and it'll help get you where you want to go a lot faster, no matter how many *E! Entertainment* specials you see about *difficult* celebrities.

Be on time

Key to the whole professionalism thing is always arriving *on time* for appointments, whether they be auditions or work. If you can, show up a little early. Once again, this simple thing will set you apart from a great many actors, and will endear you to directors, producers, clients, and casting people. They have so many other things to worry about; don't let your being late add to that.

If for some reason you *must* be late (and it happens to all of us), show the proper courtesy by calling and letting the studio know. Otherwise, not only do you send a poor signal about your work ethic by not showing up on time, but you also indicate that you don't care about their time or the time they set aside to see you.

Being on time sometimes means being early, since *on time* might actually make you late by someone else's clock. In fact, we have noticed many successful actors live by the rule, "early is on time; on time is late." Think about it: if you're pulling up to the studio at 9 a.m. for a 9 a.m. session, and then you have to park, go inside, sign in, make yourself a cup of tea, head into the studio, chit chat with the director, and then have the engineer set you up at the mic, your session just started at 9:20. So take that stuff into account when you're planning your travel.

If you do get there late, don't make excuses about why you were late, how traffic sucked, how you forgot to wind your watch, or how you were attacked by ninjas. Just apologize and get down to business. Making excuses will always dig you a deeper hole, and will never get the project completed any sooner.

Be prepared

This maxim doesn't apply just to Boy Scouts, and you should put it near the top of your professionalism to-do list. *Do your work* ahead of time: read the script, warm up your voice, and make sure you've thought about whatever it is you're reading. A big pet peeve among casting people and directors is actors who show up and haven't read the script.

Sometimes it isn't possible for you to get the script ahead of time. In that case, do whatever *is* within your power to take control of the situation and get yourself mentally and physically prepared to walk into the audition, the recording session, or the meeting. Get there a little early to see if the studio has a script or sides you can look at. If something comes up at the last minute and you don't have much time at all to prepare, give yourself a quick mental checklist, a mantra, or a power pose that'll help center and focus you at the drop of a hat.

Most professional athletes have rituals or practices that allow them to focus and get psyched up. Come up with your own routine that you can do no matter how much time you have to prepare; or maybe create a short version to use when time is tight, and a longer, more involved routine for when you have more time. It can be as simple as crossing your fingers and saying, "I am super cool: I belong here," in your head before you walk in the door. The most important thing is for your routine to be one that energizes you, focuses and grounds you, and puts you in the right headspace to walk in confident, calm, and ready to work.

Now, with all that we've said about preparation, don't obsess over trying to prepare and control every little thing. Remember, there's no way you can possibly know what's going to happen in the room; so perhaps the most important trait of all is to be relaxed, open, flexible, and ready to roll with the punches.

Be a stand-up guy

Yes, being a *stand-up guy* goes for all you ladies, too. And if you identify as non-binary, same deal. Basically what we're saying is, don't be a jerk. Sure, we all have bad days, but when you walk into the work environment for a job, meeting, or audition, keep your doom and gloom to yourself and get down to business. Seriously. We mean it. When you're snarky and snap at your friends, you can apologize to them later. When you're on the job, you won't always have that chance.

You can go home afterwards and punch your pillow if you want. And who knows? If you're lucky, your session might help you exorcise your demons. A lot of video game recording sessions are really good for that. And sure, it's fun to gossip; but voice-over is a small town, and you never know who might be friends with whom, so you're better off not talking trash about anyone.

May we refer you to Aretha Franklin for a moment: *respect* personal space, *respect* other people's efforts and time, and just … *R-E-S-P-E-C-T*. And don't be a jerk. Because no one wants to work with a jerk. And sure, you might say, "Well, so-and-so is a blankety-blank-blank and they work all the time," but go ahead and trust us on this one: being a jerk will never get you anywhere. One more time, say it with us: *Don't be a jerk.* Capisce?

Take those NDAs seriously

NDA stands for "Non-Disclosure Agreement." You will often be asked to sign an NDA upon booking a job, sometimes upon *auditioning* for a job. It basically means, "Keep your mouth shut about this." Video games, in particular, prize secrecy to the extent that they'll fire and/or fine you if they catch you tweeting about what you're working on. We've seen it happen. We don't personally know anyone who's been fined, but we know plenty of people who have been fired after tweeting a photo of themselves in the booth or on a soundstage at a job because they think it doesn't reveal anything about the project. Fans are smart. They'll figure it out.

We know you're excited, but keep it to yourself for now. There'll be plenty of time to squee with your friends later. Honestly, it's probably a good policy to not talk about a project publicly even if you *haven't* signed an NDA. Better safe than sorry. If you absolutely must say something, then ask production to clear it first. You (and they) will be glad you did.

GIVE YOURSELF AN EDGE

Breaking into the biz, much like trying to break into *any* aspect of Hollywood, is not easy, but I think there are more opportunities in voice-over than in almost any other aspect of show biz. That doesn't mean a newbie is going to walk in and land a movie trailer narration and walk out with $5000. It takes a helluva lot of commitment and dedication to the craft to start booking jobs like that – and you may never get those specific types of jobs. Though there are always exceptions to every rule, you will want to give yourself every edge you can, and so you're going to want to get training. That is where you start, and that is where you stay for a long, long time. If you're reading this and wondering, "How do I get a hold of the casting directors? I just want to tell them I love this and want a shot," and you haven't put in the work – meaning you are not a trained actor – most likely you are not going to get anywhere.

But if you do get the training, and you get mic time, and you create a good demo, *and* you are a talented actor or voice-over artist, *then* you can get out there and try to meet the casting directors and producers who can give you a shot at an audition on something. And you can try to find an agent who can help get you auditions, too.

Andrea Romano, a renowned voice director, spoke at one of our voice acting workshops at the San Diego Comic-Con to a room full of voice actor hopefuls. She reminded everyone that in order to break in, you've got to compete against the cream of the crop – the best voice talent around. (And in fact, if you can't compete against the best, then why bother?) But if you really want this badly enough to keep you on track for as long as it takes, then you *can* ultimately make it in.

The most important piece of advice for an aspiring voice actor wannabe is this: there are a whole bunch of extremely talented actors working in the biz, and the ones I see in the studio time and time again – the ones I see get all the work – are the nice ones. The ones that you *want* to work with. Those are the ones *I* want to work with. The ones who make recording sessions enjoyable and pleasant. And on the opposite side of that – those who aren't so easy to work with, the ones with attitude problems – I don't see them as much.

Even if they are extremely talented. So the advice? Be one of the nice ones!

~ ERIC P. SHERMAN, STUDIO PRESIDENT

BE WILLING TO PLAY

When it comes right down to it, we do this – voice acting – because it's fun, because we get to play. But sometimes we can forget that. Remember to have fun, be personable, and enjoy what you do.

Fact #1: people like working with people who are having a good time doing what they do. We mentioned being flexible when we talked about being prepared. Showing that you are willing to play and experiment lets everybody know that you will be a positive force on the creative team. And that you play well with others.

Fact #2: people like working with those who don't take themselves *too* seriously (see earlier note about not being a jerk). There is, of course, a line which should not be crossed: nobody likes working with someone who is *always* goofing off or being a little *too creative* with the script. But you'll get the feel for it; don't worry.

The focus of this book is the actor. However, don't let this mislead you. The actor is only one piece of the puzzle. Acting is a profession in which teamwork or group effort is definitely key. In order for an actor to perform even the most basic of jobs, a number of different people must be involved as well: writers, producers, directors, engineers, editors, technicians, designers, animators, and developers, to name just a few (and that's not even counting the audience). So, always remember that you are a part of a fantastic and exciting team.

At the end of the day, when people have to make casting choices, there are a lot of things that come into play. Partly it is a matter of them thinking, "Can this person get the job done?" Partly, "How much time/cost will we incur by having this person do the job?" And maybe most importantly, "What will it be like having to spend a lot of time working with this person?" Be the person everyone will want to spend their time with.

FOCUS

We know it sounds funny to follow up a section on *playing* with a section on *focus*, but since we first wrote this book, we've noticed a tendency of actors to be on their phones during a session (and though we try to be good, we've even sometimes been guilty of this). Now we don't mean taking calls (although we've seen it happen), but phones today are a marvelous distraction, and everybody's got one. So in a dull moment you may find yourself sneaking a peek to see if you've got new messages; or checking to see what's trending on Twitter, or Instagram, or whatever's hip when you read this book.

We know it's hard to ignore your phone, but checking it is not professional. When you're in a session, try to remember a) how grateful you are to be doing this job, and b) someone has hired you to do this job, and c) the job they hired you to do isn't playing Candy Crush. Now some employers are less concerned with this, and sometimes in a session you, the actor, have a lot of legitimate downtime. And some actors are both talented and excellent multitaskers. But you *never* want to be the actor who slows things down when you miss your cue or a piece of direction because you're on your phone. In fact, it's become such a problem that some contracts now include a clause *specifically stating* that a performer can't be on a phone during a session.

Of course, it's totally acceptable to check your phone if you're waiting on a call from a doctor, or if your kid was just arrested and you absolutely need to be reachable; but let the director know ahead of time what your situation is, or ask for regular "bathroom" breaks so you can check-in.

FIGHT SOUNDS/EFFORTS

If you watch cartoons or play video games (or, like us, do both), you're probably aware of how much time is spent on action. And for action to come off well, certain sounds are absolutely necessary. You will be making a lot of these fight sounds and efforts, which range from grunting and screaming to the dying gasp. Some studios will actually have toy weapons for you to play with as you make these sounds to help you bring as much realism as possible to your work; but most will not, and you'll have to fire up your imagination on a regular basis.

Luckily, everyone's got an imagination. And the beautiful thing is that you can practice making sounds like these at home. Imagine punching, being kicked, blocking a hit, jumping, landing, or even dying. Listen to some of your favorite animated action series or video games, and take note of the types of sounds the actors have created. See what you need to do with your voice and your body to replicate them. Heck, take a martial arts class: there's no more organic place to develop your fight sounds.

YELLING/SCREAMING

Sure, we've all yelled or screamed at one point or another, whether it was at your brother, at a rock concert, or at a horror movie. Sometimes it leaves you hoarse, sometimes not. The trick is figuring out how to scream over and over again without hurting or losing your voice.

Strongly supported breathing is key when it comes to yelling and screaming. Animation and video games are filled with yells, shouts, screams, and pain sounds, so get used to making them. This is one of the reasons we really, really, really (did we mention *really?*) recommend doing vocal warm-ups and getting comfortable with your voice. Say, why not take singing lessons; no one learns how to protect their voice better than trained singers.

YOUR DIAPHRAGM AND BREATH CONTROL

You always want to fully support your sounds with good strong breathing, which comes from a good strong diaphragm. You'll be able to yell longer, louder, and most importantly, safer, if you become friends with your diaphragm.

Your diaphragm is a very powerful muscle that makes breathing possible. It separates your thorax (where your heart and lungs live) and your abdominal cavity. It's the thing that sometimes gets agitated and makes you have the hiccups, but it is also crucial for any and all effort sounds you'll be creating.

Imagine your diaphragm as a resilient partition of muscle and connective tissue beneath your lungs. When you inhale, it contracts and pulls down toward your toes; and then when you exhale, it relaxes back up, almost like a trampoline.

It's hard to actually feel your diaphragm itself, but try this: put your hand on your abdomen and take in a deep, long breath while thinking of filling your belly with air. You should be able to feel your abdomen pushing out against your hand. Now, when you breathe out slowly, keep pressing against your abdomen, and you should feel it sink back in. That out-and-in movement of your abdomen is a reflection of the diaphragm's movement down and up.

If you're having trouble feeling this movement, try the exercise again, but breathe only through your nose; or try it lying on your back on the floor. If you're not used to breathing this way (and many people aren't), this motion may feel very small or even non-existent. But fear not: practicing like this will bring more awareness to your breathing, strengthen your diaphragm, and help you develop better vocal control. And all of that helps enable you to yell and scream more safely and powerfully. Screaming well may seem like a funny skill, but better yelling can lead to a variety of voice-over job opportunities.

MIC SAYS: Practice better breathing by inhaling deeply into your belly; it will strengthen your diaphragm, and it feels good too.

BREATHING: JUST DO IT

Don't get too caught up right now with *how* to breathe; we'll discuss breathing techniques later. For now, just remember to do it in the first place. Suggesting that you might forget to breathe may sound ridiculous, but trust us, when you're nervous, the first thing to go is your breath.

Don't worry about your breath being picked up by the mic; just focus on breathing naturally and fully as you would when you are normally speaking. Nothing says *amateur* louder than actors trying to pretend they aren't breathing while they're recording, or worse yet, *actually* not breathing. You have to breathe to speak normally, so why would you stop breathing just to *act*?

REACTIONS

Another important part in many voice-over sessions is the *reaction*. The reaction might be a simple *noticing* sound such as *huh* or *ah* when your character sees or discovers something. Other reactions vary from gasps and breathing, to laughter and coughing, to the verbal response you make when losing your balance. In fact, reactions include just about any sound a person might make when reacting in life. Sighs and exhales can be used just like spice to help add flavor to the spoken dialogue of a character.

Start paying attention to those little non-dialogue sounds when you're watching a show or playing a game. They're there, we promise.

NO, SERIOUSLY – JUST DO IT

That sneaker company was right about one thing: when it comes to efforts, fight sounds, and screaming or yelling, it will always sound better if you *just do it*. Imagine yourself in that situation and go all out, as if you were reacting to something in real life.

How powerful is your imagination? There's scientific evidence that your body goes through real physiological changes even when you're just thinking about something. When you *imagine* performing a physical action, your muscles fire as if you were actually performing that action.

Sound far-fetched? Well, does your mouth ever start salivating when you imagine fresh baked, chocolate chip cookies, all warm and gooey? Have you ever gotten home late at night, you're all alone, and you have to grab a tennis racquet and walk around throwing open the closet doors and looking under beds just to get your heart to stop pounding? That's your powerful imagination at work. And you can make it work for you in your acting.

Many athletes practice visualization, knowing that by imagining physical actions, they are helping their bodies learn to do those movements better. Tiger Woods, the golf pro, plays through new courses in his mind before he physically plays them, and it seems to have worked out okay for him. Whether or not you believe this, the more *real* you make your reaction, the better it'll sound and the safer it'll be for your voice.

Holding back rarely sounds as good as letting go, and sometimes can even hurt you. Really commit yourself, and people will take notice. Our only caveat is, of course, don't let *really doing it* become about flailing around the booth knocking things over.

People will take notice of that too, but only so that they can avoid you in the future.

LET'S GET PHYSICAL – PCAP TIME

When is voice acting not just voice acting? When the client is interested in your full body performance as well. Time to bust a PCap in that, uh … audition.

Okay, so you have an upcoming audition for a video game and it's going to include performance capture. You may have already auditioned for the vocal part, and they narrowed the list down to the voice actors they felt were also right physically for the character. Now you're headed to an audition where you'll need to move around. You'd better be ready.

Before you go in to a PCap audition, make sure you've prepared the scene – which they will have sent you ahead of time because they want you to be as comfortable as possible working without a script in your hand. Take time to learn both the dialogue and the stage directions so you know exactly what's going on in the scene and can react physically. Get on your feet, practicing the scene in your living room like you'll do it eventually in the audition room. The better you know your words and movements, the less nervous you'll be in the room.

If the script says your character is crouching behind a car, holding a blaster, yelling at the enemy on the other side of the car, make sure you are prepared to do the scene with that physicality. Sure, you can pantomime the blaster (although sometimes they'll have one for you) or use your rolled-up script, but know that there is a high likelihood that you will need to be off book and on your feet, so the client can see if you're committed to making the character look and sound believable. Don't worry if there is complex choreography in the scene; the casting director will go over it before you start. Being flexible is especially important if, say, you've practiced the scene a hundred times in your giant living room, and you show up to the audition and the casting director's office is a tiny box with a folding chair in it.

Pro Tip: We don't care how many replica (or real) guns you own. Don't bring your own prop to an audition. It makes other people in the room nervous. And not in a good way.

You don't have to be a stunt performer or a fitness buff to keep yourself in tip top shape for opportunities like these. But exercising, or at the very least, warming up before you go into an audition, will help protect you from injuries and keep you comfortable working on your feet. (More on warm-ups in the next section.) Most importantly, work both the dialogue and movement for that scene (or those scenes) hard before the audition to keep yourself confident and relaxed in the room. And while the client often likes to see an actor off book, if you're ten times more confident carrying the script (even if you never look at it), carry that script!

WARM-UP TIME

Since your voice isn't accustomed to making all these fight/effort/ yelling sounds on a frequent basis, it's important to warm up your voice a bit first. Warming up your body as well can be a great way to get it ready for whatever you plan on asking it to do.

"What?" you say. "But I'm just using my voice. Why do I need to spend time warming up my body? It's not like I'm going to run a marathon or anything."

Well, the answer is simple: *Because we said so.*

No, wait, that's not it. Hold on; it's around here somewhere. Oh, here it is.

The answer is: *Because your voice is connected to the rest of your body, and part of warming up your voice is warming up the rest of your body.*

If you warm up only your voice, you're only halfway there –

especially if you are preparing for performance capture, but also when you're recording behind the mic. But don't worry: we like to have fun as we warm up. The exercises we suggest won't take long, and should be both painless and good for you.

First, though, before you begin any movement, listen to your body. What's it telling you today? Every day is going to be different. Some days touching your toes will be out of the question. Some days even getting out of bed is hard. But some days you'll feel like tackling a mountain before breakfast. Listen to what your body is telling you that day, that minute, that second. Work within your comfort zone, and never do anything that feels uncomfortable or painful, or anything your doctor would advise against.

Our favorite warm-ups include working the full body, face/mouth, breath, and voice. We'll now go through a few exercises that'll help get you ready to play. We like to start in a standing position so that we get the whole body working right away, but you can adjust as you need to for any time, space, or mobility constraints you may have. After your body begins to warm up, we'll move on to your face, your breathing, and then your voice, allowing time for each area to really begin to feel ready to get to work.

Body Warm-up

- Start by standing.
- Reach your *arms* up overhead and stretch as tall as you can. Lean left, lean right, lean back with your stomach out. Now lean forward and stretch gently as you try to touch your toes.
- Now bend your knees a little and roll up slowly back to a standing position.
- With your arms by your sides, shrug your *shoulders* up, back, down, to the front a few times, making little circles; then reverse direction.

- Put your hands on your hips and rotate your *hips* a few times, first one direction, then the other.
- Shake out your *arms* and *legs* to get the blood flowing (you should look silly doing this).
- Gently rotate your *neck* clockwise, then counterclockwise.

Facial Warm-up

- Warm up your *face* by massaging it with your hands, rubbing gently on the nose and sinuses, jaw, forehead, and temples. (Your sinuses surround your nose, from the forehead and along the sides of the nose to just above the mouth.)
- Scrunch up your *face* as if you just ate a whole lemon; then open your mouth and eyes as wide as they'll go. Do this back and forth a few times, exhaling as you make the open face, and even adding a sound if you want.
- Press the tip of your *tongue* against the inside of your lower lip and start tracing it around the inside of your mouth, like a propeller; when you get tired, switch direction.

Breathing Warm-up

"Breath work? But I breathe fine! I've been doing it all my life!"

We know; but we're going to teach you to breathe even better. The key to all voice-over work is having strong breath support, which is something that not all of us naturally provide for ourselves. Improving your support will help you speak for a longer time without having to take a breath, protect your voice when you're doing weird or loud stuff with it, and give you a better sound all around.

As we've already noted, your diaphragm plays an important part in all this. Over time, training to strengthen your diaphragm will actually increase your lung capacity. So practicing these exercises daily can help your breathing grow stronger and your breath last longer.

One great way to help strengthen your breath control and diaphragm is to practice breathing by inhaling and exhaling through your nose. Your nostrils take in and release air more slowly than the larger opening of your mouth, so it forces you to breathe less rapidly. And focusing your attention on breathing can also help you slow down as well. Breathing slower gives the lungs more time to extract oxygen from the air you've taken in, and that gives you more energy. Of course, you'll need to exhale through your mouth when you're vocalizing, but the rest of the time, breathing through your nose is a good habit to develop.

Remember, if you start to feel lightheaded or dizzy at any point during the following breathing exercises, take a break, and come back later. After all, we don't want you passing out and hitting your head. Even for your art.

- Breathe out all the air you currently have in your lungs. Inhale deeply while mentally counting to three, and then exhale while counting to three. Try to take in as much air as possible on the inhale, and push the air out for as long as you can on the exhale. Repeat this exercise a few times, and then try a few breaths counting to four, then five, and so on. (You should be able to see and feel your abdomen going out and in. That's your diaphragm working.)
- Breathing with vocalization
  » Try the above breathing exercise while hissing out like a snake: *sssssssss*.
  » Try again, only this time, make a buzzing sound: *zzzzzzzzz*.
  » Try panting like a dog (fast, short breaths, in and out): *uh-huh-uh-huh-uh-huh*. (This strengthens

your diaphragm by forcing it to repeatedly contract and relax.)

Vocal Warm-ups

Even more specialized than just warming up your breathing is focusing on all the tiny muscles and parts of your body that will create the actual sounds. You will want to make sure all these tiny parts are warmed up and ready to play.

- Begin by warming up your *vocal cords/folds*. You may notice when you first wake up that your voice sounds sleepy. Humming and feeling the resonance in your chest is great for getting the voice gently moving.
  - » *Hmmm*
  - » *Mmmm*
- After your voice starts to feel a little less groggy, begin to focus on *enunciation,* or the art of speaking clearly. Pay attention to the different ways the mouth must move in order to create the following sounds:
  - » *PTKT* pronounced *puh-tuh-kuh-tuh*
  - » *BDGD* pronounced *buh-duh-guh-duh*
  - » *Wewa* pronounced *wee-wah*
  - » *Trills* created by rolling your tongue on the roof of your mouth while saying *TR: trrrrr* or *R: rrrrrr*
  - » Rapid fire succession *ptkt-bdgd-ptkt-bdgd*
- Similar to enunciation, *articulation* relates to speaking distinctly. Let's call the moving and non-moving parts of your face and mouth that help you articulate words (lips, teeth, tongue, roof of the mouth) the *vocal creators*. Articulation is a function of how these vocal creators work together to make sounds. After practicing the enunciation exercises *ptkt, bdgd, wewa,* try to pull everything together for articulation by saying these rhymes

and tongue twisters:

> » "What a to-do to die today, at a minute or two 'til two, a thing distinctly hard to say, but harder still to do; for they'll beat a tattoo at a twenty 'til two, a rat-tat-tat-tat-tat-tat-tat-tat-tat-too, and the dragon will come when he hears the drum, at a minute or two 'til two today, at a minute or two 'til two"

> » "You know New York, you need New York, you know you need unique New York"

> » "Red leather, yellow leather, blue blood, black blood"

> » *"Brrrrr"* (a sound made by blowing out with your lips closed to create a motorboat sound, sort of like a raspberry without sticking your tongue out): this can get a little spitty, so watch out.

- And finally, you'll want to work on your *range* (the high-to-low pitches that you can take your voice to). Here's an exercise for expanding your range:

> » *Sirens* (sort of like the sound of a fire truck): *ee-eeeeeee* up and down in range, starting from low to high, and then high to low

Still feel like you need some more warm-up exercises? Check out the new appendix of this book! You'll find plenty more in-depth exercises to get you toasty. Okay, now that your face and body and vocal creators are awake, it's time to take them to work. Oh, wait, we can't just go to work. We have to get the job first. And that takes auditioning.

We've talked a lot about getting prepared for the audition. Now let's actually get to what's involved in the audition itself. It's where your magical journey continues…

SCRATCH TRACKS   **WITH TARA & YURI**

CHAPTER 5
THE AUDITION ITSELF

*"Always be a first rate version of yourself and
not a second rate version of someone else."*

JUDY GARLAND, AMERICAN SINGER, ACTRESS

THIS IS THE FUN STUFF

This may sound like common sense, but if you're going to embark on this quest to be a voice actor, you need to enjoy acting because *there's gonna be a whole lotta actin' goin' on.* And most of the acting you do will come in the form of auditions for which you won't be getting paid – in money. Acting is unlike most other professions in that, as much as you may be working, you'll still be interviewing for new jobs almost every day (if you're lucky).

Remember, though, getting to audition is getting to act, and that's the fun stuff, right? And if you don't think so, it'll be to your advantage to start looking at it that way because you'll be doing a lot of auditioning, and even the best actors are not going to get the job every time. As a matter of fact, the best actors aren't even going to get the job *most* of the time.

Sound depressing? Hey, it can be, from time to time, especially if you *really* want the job. But don't worry: with every audition you get under your belt, you worry less. And the more you can look at auditioning as a fun part of the job as opposed to an awful, evil trial you must suffer through to get the job, the better everything will go.

Remember, every chance you get to work (whether they're paying you or not) is an opportunity to learn and perfect your craft, and of course to play. And isn't that really what we want? To play? For a living? Relish getting auditions as much as getting jobs, since an audition is an opportunity to show the person hiring (the *casting director* or *CD*) what you can do. And it may lead to many more auditions, as well as getting you more comfortable, confident, and settled into who you are behind the mic. You're building a foundation with every audition; and every good audition you have and *don't* get the job is just as important as the ones where you book the job.

Casting directors are very good at remembering good actors. Good actors make their job easier. We've both been brought in for auditions (and sometimes hired) based on totally unrelated auditions we went on, sometimes years before. In fact, Yuri recently booked a job, and when he walked into the studio, the producer said, "Hey, man, so happy to finally meet you! We've been wanting to hire you for years, and we're glad this finally worked out." Yuri had auditioned for this company countless times over perhaps a decade! It's impossible to follow up and get notes on every audition, so just assume, that they always love you and they'll cast you as soon as it's the right fit.

EXPANDING YOUR COMFORT ZONE

We all have our happy places when it comes to acting. Some of us revel in playing the hero or heroine, while others feel perfectly at home twirling our moustaches as the villain. Either way, it's good to know where your comfort zone is and where you enjoy playing. It pays to know your strengths so you can take advantage of them and carve out a niche for yourself in the area to which you may be best suited But it's also good to be aware of your strengths so that you can take time to work on the areas in which you aren't as skilled. In this way, you expand your repertoire and make yourself a more versatile, interesting, and employable actor.

It's certainly not our intent to detract from the idea of doing one specific thing very well. That's extremely important. It's just that, if that one thing goes out of style, you want to have something to fall back on. And just because you're good at one thing doesn't mean you can't learn to do other things equally well. For example, our good friend, the otherworldly talented actor Dee Bradley Baker, is known far and wide for his creature voices, monster babble, and alien squawking, and that's what people tend to hire him for. But when called upon to do so, he also turns in a very moving, believable, *human* performance.

The best actors push their personal boundaries and continue to grow throughout the life of their entire careers – filling them up with memorable, interesting, and bold characters. If you feel you're having a hard time pushing your boundaries on your own, get into a class where it will be someone else's job to give you a friendly shove in the right direction. Classes can hold you accountable for your work in a way you often can't do on your own.

Use your auditions as a place where you always push your boundaries and expand your comfort zone a little. Open yourself up to all possibilities. Widen the circle you play in.

MAKING BOLD CHOICES

Bold choices is a catch-all phrase when it comes to acting. *They make such bold choices. You need to make bolder choices. I loved his bold choice.* So then the question is, "How do I make those kinds of choices?"

What constitutes a *bold* choice? Well, it all relates to how well you know your personal boundaries and how comfortable you are exploring them.

A common misconception among actors is that to make a bold choice is to do something crazy or intentionally weird. But making a bold choice relates more to being committed, specific, and imaginative in your approach to the character in the scene. Freaking out in an audition situation or reciting all your lines in a high pitched whine would be a bold choice, to be sure. But would you rather be a story that casting directors tell at parties, or would you rather have them call you in again because you stood apart from the rest – as a pro?

One way to make a bold choice could be to find the thing that makes the character personal to you and play that, regardless of what you feel would be the *right* way (the way that you assume that they want it). Remembering that there is never really a right way to do it can be so freeing. Sometimes the clients (or director) don't actually know exactly what they are looking for 'til they hear it. And the only way you can really set yourself apart from the rest of the actors who are also vying for the part is to be true to the person *you* are. There's only one of you, so when you're true to yourself, your performance is unique. As soon as you start trying to imagine what they want, you'll only trip yourself up.

Another way of making a bold choice might be to take a specific quality or idea and fully explore it in such a way that you make it real, no matter how outlandish and off-the-wall the idea is. Sure, you may decide that the character is suffering from an extreme bout of the hiccups, but you'd better know exactly what caused it, how long it's been going on, how it's affecting the other characters or environment, and how the character feels about it; otherwise it's just an affectation that will detract from the scene.

People love relating to things that are part of the human condition, things they can identify with; so sometimes making a bold choice simply means finding a creative and fun way to explore the humanity of your character. Case in point: the aforementioned Dee Bradley Baker. His creature work is very likely as compelling as it is because of the humanity he brings to something that most people would just call "noises."

YOUR GUT ALWAYS KNOWS BEST

When Fox Animation held auditions for the fish character in the pilot for their animated series "American Dad," the fish was written as French-speaking ("Francois?"). Since I had worked with Seth MacFarlane and knew the tone of Fox Animation as being pretty "wise-ass," I thought I should go for it and give them an offbeat choice – a German fish. Not what they asked for, but for me, I felt it was a better choice. I could speak German, and it would allow me to pepper in a little Deutsch to make it even more ear-catching and fun. My French read wouldn't have been nearly as fun or funny, and there were other voice actors who could better hit that accent, so I went with my gut, gave my strongest offer – and booked it.

They considered recasting the fish back to French after we finished recording the pilot, and my agent made sure I could re-audition with a French accent. But I decided I would leave them with my original audition, which was my best offer. I didn't want to leave them considering something that was half as good as my best solution for this project. Thankfully, I stuck with my gut and they kept me on. The stakes were high, but that doesn't call for a timid swing at the ball. Quite the opposite. You want a strong, specific offer that fits – and that stands out! I figured I had to give my best or nothing.

~ DEE BRADLEY BAKER, ACTOR

USING YOUR *REAL* VOICE

So many times we've run into people who say, "I do all these crazy voices; I should totally be doing voice-over."

Now this may be true, and there are certainly people who

have made great careers out of crazy voices, leaping effortlessly from screeching aliens to friendly giants to neurotic chipmunks; but crazy voices ain't always the way to the top. People who are known for specializing in those voices are just a small part of the VO community.

Then there are the rest of us. We can do some cool, crazy things with our voices, but more often than not (in our case, about 90-95% of our work), we use the voice we speak with naturally every day. We pitch it a little higher or lower, speed it up or slow it down, add an accent or dialect; but basically we talk as we normally do. And this is very important. Know your voice. Know how you sound when you aren't trying to do anything in particular. Know what the specific qualities of your voice are, and learn where a voice like yours fits in as far as what kinds of roles/ jobs are out there.

Don't ever fear that your voice sounds too *natural* to be interesting. Listen to the radio or TV ads. *Natural* is in: *Less announcery, more realistic, conversational, guy/girl-next-door.* Don't be afraid to just sound like you. Since each of us is unique, who's to say that you aren't exactly what they're looking for? Yuri had always hated the sound of his own voice, thinking it sounded "too much like a kid, not grown-up enough." Now he works all the time, playing kids and young heroes, and doesn't complain at all.

RELAX. IT'S NOT JUST ABOUT YOU

The best way to learn to audition is not by auditioning. That's the second-best way. The best way is by spending some time in casting. Through the process of casting, I learned how stressful and difficult casting can be, and I can relate to and identify with the casting directors and *their* needs in a much deeper way. As a talent, that awareness gets me out of my own head and my own *need*, and *need* is casting director repellent. In addition, I learned how many, and sometimes *most*, of the determining factors in casting a role have nothing to do with the quality of my audition. I can *let go* and have fun doing what I do best; and when I *let go*, I can *book*.

~ ZACH HANKS, ACTOR, DIRECTOR

TAKING DIRECTION

Okay. So you got the audition. You showed up, waited in a crowded room with a bunch of other actors, and it's finally your turn. You're in the booth, the engineering team signals that they're recording, and the director says, "Start." (All directors will, of course have their own way of saying *Start*. Only rarely will it be, "Action!" as that's more an on-camera thing – although you could very well hear that on a performance capture stage. Sometimes it'll be "We're rolling, whenever you're ready … ," and sometimes it'll just be, "And … Go!")

First, make sure you've read the script you have in front of you *before* you come in. Nothing makes you more nervous than feeling unprepared. And once you've read the script, hopefully you've made some sort of choice about it. For example, if you're going to audition for a commercial, make sure you know how you feel about the product you're trying to sell, and decide who it is you're trying to sell it to. You're going to talk differently to a forty year-old mother of three than you will to a six year-old boy. Be specific. Make that choice. Or come in with a few choices.

By making a choice you show the director that, in addition to having some skill as an actor, you've read the material, understand it, and have an opinion. Also, a director can better direct you if you've made a choice going into the audition. And then – this is where it might get confusing for a second, but stick with us, we're here for you – don't get too attached to the choice you've made.

Sometimes directors might like your choice, but often – and this *is* the job of directors, remember – they might ask you to do the scene a completely different way. This does not mean that your take on the character the first time through was not *right*. The CD may have loved your choice, and now just needs to see if you're directable.

Sometimes you'll finish your first read and the CD will say, "That was great! Now gimme something different." This can be annoying, but it happens, so it pays to have something *different* to give them. And if you don't, it pays to be good at improv. Of course, if you are having a hard time making a choice based on the material you've received, feel free to ask the CD for more information. But if you do ask, don't just ignore what the CD tells you: make sure you incorporate that new info into your work.

Listen to what directors have to say. Remember, they're not there to make a fool out of you. They want you to get the job. They want you to be good. It makes their job easier. If they've asked you to do it again, it means they already think that you *can* do it; they just want to see if you're *willing* to try it their way. And that's your job as an actor. Don't fight the director on interpretation or try to explain why your idea was better (even if it might have been).

Remember, *take the direction*. If you don't understand the notes the director gives you, ask for them to be repeated or clarified so that you do understand. Then take a moment to look over the material with this new direction in mind. The CD should be happy to give you this time. There is nothing worse than a director giving direction and an actor not taking it. All that shows the CD is that you might be difficult to work with and unable to do what the director requests. Neither of those are qualities you want to be known for; nor will they help you book the job.

Specs

Even before you get in to the audition room, you might be given some direction and not even realize it. This direction comes in the form of the *spec* or *specification*, a notation somewhere on the script (usually near the very top), that describes what the client is looking for in your performance. A few examples of what the specs might include are the particular vocal qualities, the feeling of the read, and the attitude of the character.

Or like a friend of ours, you may be handed a spec that says: *Someone who sounds like a REAL actor, not someone who is clearly a voice-over actor.* We know what they're TRYING to say (we hope, anyway), but it still feels like a little knife in the heart every time someone says, "Oh, you're a voice actor? Cool! Have you ever done any *real* acting?" Perhaps what the casting people were looking for was a natural quality, not an overly dramatic delivery. But what they *communicated* was that they did not appreciate the very real acting skills of voice actors. And that's not just the semantics talking.

Animation or video game auditions might provide specs that include artwork, a character sketch, a little background information, and a celebrity vocal reference to start you off, while a commercial spec might be: *Non-announcery, Ex. Bradley Cooper, Robert Downey Jr., Joseph Gordon Levitt."*

These guys are popular celebrity vocal references these days (and there'll be completely different ones in a couple of years, no doubt, as we used Justin Long in the last edition of this book), and what people mean when they reference these actors is not that they're looking for someone to voice match them, but that they're looking for their essence: someone cool, hip, laid-back, charming without being aggressive, with just a little bit of edge, but in no way mean. See? It's easier just to say, *RDJ.* Sometimes the casting people don't know how to word what it is they want.

They just know they want something like ... that guy.

Whether you get a lot of info or only very little, be sure you pay attention. It's like they're giving you a helping hand ... that is, provided they know what they want in the first place. We actually got a spec on a commercial spot recently that said, *Action hero read, but slightly pulled back, trailer voice but not dramatic, imagine "I'm gonna kick your ass" on every line.*

That said, we know a very successful actor who NEVER reads the specs. He just does what he does best, and it either works or it doesn't. This isn't vanity. This is showing the casting director who you are so that even if you're not right for this job, they know who to call for the jobs you may be right for. And because the client often doesn't really know *what* they're looking for, who's to say they're not looking for you? We've said it before, but it bears repeating: never try to guess what they're looking for. It'll only lead you astray. Try this experiment: when you get an audition, don't look at the specs before you do a take; then read the specs and do a second take. See how your two takes differ. If you're recording the audition at home, send both takes, but put your favorite take first.

WORKING WITH THE MATERIAL:
BE A DETECTIVE, A MINER, AND A GARDENER

Sometimes you get pages and pages of script; sometimes it's a single word on a piece of paper. But whatever you have, make sure you explore it to its fullest so that you can best do that thing you love: act! So now you're not only a detective, but a miner too, excavating the page for little gems of knowledge. Whether you have a line of commercial copy for a product you've never heard of, or a titular role in a new animated series, it is important to use all the tools at your disposal (the Ws and the vocal "Rubik's Cube," for example) to bring the material to life.

Make sure you understand what you're saying and why you're saying it. And if there's no one there to answer any questions you may have, make up your own answers to justify what's happening in the script. But above all, remember the material is your best friend and should have all the information you need to do your job (more, if it's well-written material). Even if you decide to riff on the material and throw some improv in, the script is always your starting point and should be honored.

Imagine, if you will (and we know you will, because you've got a wicked-powerful imagination), that the script is the fertile soil filled with creative seeds. Now rake it for details, water it with your imagination, and shine your energy and passion on it to grow and harvest fulfilling characters. Maybe not the best analogy, but see where our imaginations just took us?

Mining information from the page

Acting can be such a haphazard, chaotic, arbitrary endeavor, it's nice to know that there are life rafts out there for us; and one of your most important life rafts is the script. Whether your character has only one line, or all the lines; whether the page is mostly descriptions and direction, or only your lines with no context whatsoever; this is your gold mine. Now dig. Look for those Ws. Does the script tell you where you are? Who you're with? What's going on? Do the other characters talk about you? How do they talk about you? Paying attention to these things and answering the Ws will make your work (play) easier.

For example, if a character refers to you as a *scaredy-cat*, perhaps your character is quite timid or spooks easily. That's something for you to go on. If other actors auditioning for the same part have read only their characters' lines, then you're ahead of the game when it comes to knowing your character. You can make a choice that uses the information you uncovered.

If you're dealing with commercial copy or narration, perhaps the script contains description or backstory that will give you context; and knowing the context can't help but bring out a more solid and nuanced performance. If the scene takes place *at night in a bedroom with someone sleeping beside you*, maybe you're whispering so as not to wake that person. All of these things can seem obvious when pointed out, but the trick is training yourself to find this sort of information in the script when you get it. We sometimes get nervous when we're preparing for an audition, and concentrate too hard on *what* we're supposed to say. And while that's certainly important, just as important is what's been said *about*, *to*, or *around* us.

Never overlook something in the script because you don't think it's important. Writers spend countless hours writing, reviewing, and re-reviewing a script to make it perfect. Rarely is something in there for fluff, or *just because*. Use everything the writer gives you to bring life to your character. Why did the writer choose these words specifically for this character? Try to understand the reasons behind the writer's choices. Become a psychologist and a detective all wrapped into one (a *psytective ... detectologist*? Our list of jobs that acting encompasses seems to be growing ...). Scour the page for evidence of compelling relationships and human emotion so that you can bring these characters to justice! Or rather, so you can do justice to these characters.

Try this: Pick a *W*. Read through the entire script with only that element in mind. Then go back to the top, pick another *W* and go through it again, thinking only of that one. Repeat until you've filtered your script through each individual type of clue, and we'll bet you end up with a deeper understanding of the scene and your character, and ultimately, with a better audition.

"So what exactly am I looking for?"

You're looking for whatever'll help you do the job. Whatever will help you understand who the character is and what the story is. Your ability to be your own Sherlock Holmes and do some basic sleuthing for the Ws will allow you to make choices that flesh out the copy realistically. These choices allow your performance to shine because, even though everyone auditioning will get the same information at the start, each person will interpret that information differently.

You can tell 100 different people something as detailed as "They are in a fight with their big brother over the last piece of cake at their aunt's house on the first day of summer vacation," and you'd better believe that's going to mean something very different to each person because everyone is different, with a unique set of experiences, and quirks, and ways of thinking and seeing the world. And you'll get very different individual performances despite the fact that each actor has been provided the exact same information going into the audition.

Your job is to look for clues, so that you can fill in your character with the fun palate of *specifics*. And by specifics, we mean definite ideas about your characters, the environment he, she, they, or it's in, how the character is feeling when going into the scene, and how things or people might affect your character. Hopefully, reading the descriptive sentence in the paragraph above brought to life a scene for you and got your creative juices flowing. Remember, nobody else will do a scene exactly the same way you will.

Look for *hooks* that will help you make choices. Sometimes it'll be easier and sometimes it'll be harder. You won't always get as many *Who-What-Where-When-Why-hoW* details as in the example a couple of paragraphs ago. That's when you have to dig a little deeper, take what you find, and make it work for you. For example, if you are reading a piece of commercial copy that has no stage directions, see if maybe you can find some fun wordplay or alliteration that you can take hold of to make things your own.

You'll also learn when to look at copy and just tell it just like it is, without getting too flowery or trying to read too much into it. If the specs ask for a normal, friendly, or *non-announcery* quality, the likelihood is that the producer wants a straight read, as natural and as conversational as you can make it. Let this be a clue that they're probably not looking for an outrageous choice. Sometimes a straightforward choice is the best choice you can make.

"Where do I find these clues on the page?"

The best clues are found in descriptions and in the way other characters relate to your character. But sometimes a clue is as simple as the word *quickly*.

There are lots of reasons that something might need to be said quickly. For instance, others are about to arrive and certain information has to be communicated before they get here; or you are so excited about the info that you just can't say it fast enough; or you're running late and are in a hurry to get somewhere else. What other reasons can you come up with, just for that single word, *quickly*?

There can be a multitude of motives for anything you find yourself doing in the script. To make the material come alive, you only need to decide for yourself *why* you say something, or why you say it *quickly* or any other way.

And remember, don't get hung up on looking for the *right* way. There is no right way. There's just the way you came up with. Odds are, if you come up with *your* way, even if the person auditioning you doesn't agree with your take on it, they'll redirect you and ask you to do it again. As we've noted, casting directors love it when you come in with your own ideas. It shows them that you cared enough to work on the material before you came in.

"What's on the page, you know, besides my lines?"

We've talked a little bit about reading the script and looking for specific things that'll help you do your job, but reading a script isn't always like reading a book or magazine. Sure, you'll have your lines, but to make it easier to identify where you are in the script, and to give you some direction, the scriptwriter includes mysterious notations and cryptic numbers.

Let's go about translating some of those, shall we?

In pre-lay (original) animation, the scripts generally look like the kind of script that you would have if you were working on a play or a movie. The lines are labeled by the individual character's name so that you can tell which ones are yours. In addition, each line is numbered so that the director can easily refer to a specific line.

To help give you an idea of how to color your performance, there may or may not be descriptions in the script of what's going on in the scene. For example, suppose the script says, "With a thunderous roar, Roknar unleashes a salvo of rockets at Sam, obliterating the cliff she is standing on." The fact that an explosion just went off, and that you, Sam, may now be falling to your doom, might give you an idea of how you'll deliver your next line.

Sometimes, scriptwriters include very specific directions, like [muffled] or [whispering], before a line if they want the line delivered a particular way. Only rarely will they include specific *acting* notes, like [sad] or [angry], because hopefully, the writer trusts that the actor and director will come up with their own brilliant interpretation without having to have it spoon-fed to them.

ADR and dubbing scripts have their own set of notations; and while they may vary slightly from script to script, they'll generally be pretty much the same. Remember, because the performance has already been created (often in a different language), and the character has been animated, or the actor's likeness recorded to video or film, there will be very strict parameters for you to follow. You'll have to consider things like timing, rhythm, emotion, and volume, all at the same time. And because there are so many things to juggle all at once, you're sure to encounter a cryptic barrage of technical notations.

A technical notation lets you know that something very specific needs to happen in the *physical* delivery of the line, not in your character's emotional life. A good example is a pause – needed so that the line will fit in the time allotted, not because the character is feeling hesitant/confused/pensive/whatever. Some of these script notations might look like ^ *or* MNS *or* OFF, and we'll cover them in more detail in the "Mouth Movement" and "Hitches" sections of Chapter14, *Practice Makes Permanent.*

You'll know you're working with an ADR/dub script when, before each line, there's a string of numbers that may look something like this: 00:01:17:20. This notation is called the *time code* and it allows the engineer to start recording a line exactly where it needs to fit into the show.

Sometimes there's an additional time code notation to show where the line ends (00:01:17:20 – 00:01:19:20), so you know exactly how much time you have (in this case two seconds) even before you preview the line. All of these notations are in the script to help you synchronize what you're saying to the mouth flaps that are already there. Take a look at the sample scripts we've included in the "Animation Scripts" and "Video Game Script" sections in Chapter 14.

WHAT'S NOT ON THE PAGE: IMPROVISING AT AN AUDITION

We've talked about how important the script is, how a writer has been paid good money (hopefully) to create a brilliant master-work for you to read, and how you should pay close attention to the script for clues on how to create your character and color your performance. That said, what happens when you get a great idea that's *not* in the script? Can you just change the script? Start riffing? Add a joke here and there? What if the wording just doesn't feel natural to you? Can you change it until it does?

These are all good questions for which there is no absolute answer. But we've been in this spot many times, and here are our thoughts on it: in short, it depends on the situation and it depends on the actor.

First you have to decide how comfortable you are with making up dialogue. Some actors are very secure with improv and have no problem ad-libbing something funny on top of what's already there. There are other actors for whom ad-libbing is a downright compulsion: they can't get through a script without changing it. On the other hand, the thought of having to improv anything fills some actors with mortal terror. (There is actually a class taught here in L.A. expressly to help voice actors improve their improv skills.)

And then the question is *when* is it okay to ad-lib? In certain situations more than others, that's for sure. When you're dubbing a foreign film and an army of people has spent countless hours making sure that the lines are translated, and then adapted, and then written and painstakingly *re*written to fit the exact movements of the on-camera actors' mouths? No. Definitely not.

In a pre-lay animation recording session where writers are sitting in the control room proudly listening to you perform their masterpiece? Maybe. It depends on how well you know the people involved, how long you've been working on the project, and how good you are at improv. Some people are naturally funny, but not everyone's Robin Williams. You'll want to pick your battles, because even if you *are* funny, no one will put up with an actor who improvs *too* much.

How about in a commercial audition? Definitely, yes. Why? Because ad agencies will get hundreds, if not thousands of auditions for a single commercial spot. By the time they've listened to twenty actors, their ears will start to glaze over; and sometimes it's that one audition where something is just *different*, that wakes them up or makes them laugh unexpectedly. And they'll remember that. Sometimes all it takes is a *button* on the end of your audition – an extra comment, a punch line, a laugh, or a chuckle – to get your read moved to the top of the list. In examining the commercial jobs we've booked, we have definitely noticed that throwing in an extra little *something* has increased our chances of booking the job.

What about in a performance capture audition? Well, this can be tricky. Oftentimes the writer will be in the room and you won't want to mangle their work intentionally – that's disrespectful. But the team (writer included) loves nothing more than to see their character come alive and jump off the page, and that happens when you personalize it. Nolan North of *Uncharted* fame, is known for his ability to improv and bring a character to life through his commitment to the reality of the situation; and it is, in part, what makes Nathan Drake, Nathan Drake. They had obviously written Nathan Drake before Nolan came to read for the part, but the Nathan Drake we got (and deserve) is still around because of what Nolan brought to the role that wasn't written in the script. And in a PCap audition, sometimes it's not about the words you add, but the physicality you bring to it. Think about the world they're putting you in and really start *playing*.

In the end, there's no hard and fast rule about when to improv. It's one of those times when you've got to listen to your gut.

YOU NEVER KNOW …

I was auditioning for an in-house partner read (radio commercial), and my character ate food that didn't taste good. He then had to make a sound as if he wasn't feeling well and had to leave. I know that for radio commercials, the word "god" is not allowed, but I managed to improvise a little and quickly say, "Oh my god!"

Upon realizing that, I figured I would do my best to completely ruin the take so it could *not* be used. I followed "Oh my god!" with "Jesus Christ!" The booth director laughed and said, "I'm sending that one." The girl I was reading with seemed worried that maybe it would be bad to send that. Reasonable. I wasn't sure either. Two weeks later I got a call saying I booked the job.

~ ADAM BOBROW, ACTOR, COMEDIAN

ASK QUESTIONS IN THE AUDITION ROOM

Why? Exactly.

See, when you ask a question, even if you don't come up with an answer right away, your mind starts working, and that's going to come in handy for making choices about your character. Maybe you come up with *the* answer, or maybe not. More importantly, your brain will come up with *an* answer, and that's gold.

Your performance will be richer and your character more interesting the more questions you ask – and answer – about the material. If you get to the audition and you're still unclear about something, don't be afraid to ask the casting director or director. It's a perfectly legitimate request and shows them that you've prepared the audition material.

Now if the director or CD gives you an answer that you hadn't considered, that's fine. But they'll probably be more impressed if you've already asked yourself the questions and come up with some kind of answer on your own. Once again, it shows you care, and that will put you ahead of most of the other actors you'll be up against who are just coming up with a funny voice and reading the lines.

The director or CD wants you to have everything you need to do good work. Remember, as scary as they may seem sometimes, *they want you to get the job.* It means they can go home early. That said, don't ask them questions just for the sake of asking questions. They're busy and have a lot of people to see.

MIC SAYS: The questions will give you your answers: Who, What, Where, When, Why, and hoW.

AUDITIONING FROM HOME VS. GETTING IN THE ROOM

Modern technology has made it possible for the actor (that's you, kid) to audition for many VO projects from the comfort of home. There are many benefits to this, not the least of which are saving on gas and saving time – and, of course, being able to record in your underwear.

However, we have found that if you have the opportunity to go in to audition live, in front of an actual casting director, you always stand a better chance of booking, for several reasons:

1. You are a warm body that the CD can meet and interact with, giving you the opportunity to allow your glowing personality to positively affect your chances of getting hired or brought back for other projects.

2. You stand a chance of getting direction and extra information from the CD, a chance which you would not have gotten by recording your audition at home in your closet.

3. You are *showing up for yourself*, or *putting yourself out there*, and making the choice to physically go where the work is, which is a nice way of energetically aligning yourself with your future goals.

4. In a PCap situation, you are showing the team, and yourself, that you can embody the character in physicality and attitude, which, for this type of work, can make or break a booking!

5. If they're only seeing people in person, they can only see, maximum, maybe a hundred people in a day, maybe half that, maybe less. So your odds are much better than if they're listening through hundreds, maybe thousands of emailed auditions.

Sometimes, however, auditioning from home is your only option: the client is located somewhere else entirely, you don't have time to get there, or they are accepting only submissions from home. If this is the case, just do your best to lay down a solid, professional audition that will stand out from all the others that are undoubtedly being sent in by other actors.

There are benefits (besides the underwear thing) to recording at home. For one thing, there's no pressure, and you'll have more time to work on particular moments if you want. Of course, don't let this become a detriment by getting all nitpicky about your audition and belaboring the smallest details. And while it's nice to have CDs tell you what they want in an audition, when you're on your own, you're the boss, and that can be very empowering.

You'll get to direct yourself, make fun creative choices, and all the while be able to play to your own strengths. Only, be careful of falling prey to not really pushing yourself, and accepting tired or half-hearted work; or the opposite, trying to push yourself too hard. It's a fine line, and you need to develop the ability to be honest with yourself when you're alone in the booth.

Now if you aren't equipped to record auditions at home (more on that in Chapter 9, *Your Home Booth*), there's always the option of renting studio time at an outside studio. However, renting can quickly get expensive (especially if you have to do so every time you want to audition), and there's nothing like paying by the minute to make you nervous while you're working.

MOCAP & PCAP AUDITIONS

Because we're so excited about all the new science we're trying to drop on you, we went ahead and described motion capture and performance capture in Chapter 2, *You Really Want the Job, But Which One?* and somewhat prematurely got into PCap (MoCap) auditions in the last chapter under "Let's Get Physical." But we'll touch on auditioning again here.

Just like in the voice-over audition, you will want to bring all your preparation, professionalism, and ready-to-play attitude to bear in a PCap audition, only you'll have more space to play in, and you won't have to worry about staying on mic! And what if you land a VO audition and show up for it having prepared to stand behind a mic and read off a script, and you walk in wearing your tight jeans, and it's actually … a PCap audition? This happens sometimes, and take it from us, it can be nerve-wracking because you'll be thrown off your game and unprepared. You may feel like you have no choice but to go ahead with the audition, but that's not your only option. Miscommunications happen, and rather than just try to push through even though you're not dressed comfortably and you haven't had time to memorize the material, just explain that you understood this was a VO audition, and ask if you can come back later, either that day, or another day. They'll usually accommodate your request because they want you to be at your best, too.

Many PCap auditions are actually held at the soundstage where they will be filmed, so you'll get a first-hand look at the amazing technology that is involved in bringing a character to life in a game, a series, or even a film. One of your main challenges as an actor will be ignoring all this cool tech so it doesn't get in the way of your performance.

As with any audition, you'll want to take a little time to warm up so that you're physically ready to be flexible, move, react, and take direction. The PCap process is complicated, costly, and time consuming, and the whole team will be looking for talented people who can also help the work go as smoothly and quickly as possible without sacrificing quality.

Often, right before your audition, the tech person will attach a small wireless microphone to you to capture your vocal performance, and then will run multiple cameras to capture your physical performance for the team to review after your audition. You may also be expected to hold props and interact with set pieces, so hopefully you've become so familiar with your script that you can put it down and not have to worry about it. There may also be a whole bunch of people sitting behind a table, staring at you the whole time. They may introduce themselves, and they may not. Among them could be a casting director, a game director, a VO director, a game cinematics director, a development executive, an audio director, and a host of people there to make sure you're properly recorded. Don't worry about them. They'll introduce themselves if they need to. The only people you really want to pay attention to are, first, the person giving you direction and, of course, the person reading with you in the scene. If you're lucky, they'll have an actual actor reading with you, and only one person giving direction.

Ultimately, try not to let the space, the tech, and all the people psych you out. If you're prepared, have strong choices ready and are willing to laugh at yourself, you'll be ready to shine. Always remember to take direction and ask questions: providing you with answers is why the director's there. And most importantly, have fun!

SCRATCH TRACKS   **WITH TARA & YURI**

CHAPTER 6
THE BOOTH

"Give me a place to stand, and I will move the earth."

ARCHIMEDES, GREEK
PHILOSOPHER, ASTRONOMER

Hey! You got the job! Congratulations! Now what? Well, let's get you familiarized a little bit with where you're going to be spending most of your time working as a voice actor: the studio. But more specifically: *the booth.*

WHERE YOUR FRIEND (THE) MIC LIVES

The booth is basically an enclosed, soundproofed space with a *microphone* (mic) in it. Some booths are fancy, with contoured designs for optimum sound quality, and expensive LCD monitors for dubbing to picture. Other booths are much simpler, with just a mic and a stand to set your script on. Many have windows through which you can see into the control room, while some are nothing more than a padded closet. No matter which one you find yourself in, though, knowing a few simple things will make you feel more comfortable in an otherwise very odd place for a person to spend any amount of time. And the more comfortable you feel, the more professional you appear. As we mentioned before, that's definitely a good thing.

First off, we know the mic looks cool, and it's always tempting to touch shiny objects; but when in someone else's booth, never touch the mic without permission from the engineer or booth director/owner (odds are they'll never ask you to touch it, preferring to adjust it themselves). Mics are highly sensitive pieces of equipment and can be very expensive to replace, so the less handling the mic gets, the better. Besides, it's part of the engineer's job to make sure that the mic is positioned correctly in relation to your mouth, to get the cleanest sound possible; and they'll want to be absolutely sure they've got it set just right for each individual actor.

By the way, after the engineering team has adjusted the mic for you, be sure to thank them. Saying *thank you* may not help your performance, but it might help your relationship with your engineer, and that's the person who's helping to make you sound brilliant.

THE PROPER DISTANCE FROM THE MIC

As we just mentioned, the mic is very sensitive, so where should you stand in relation to it? The engineer might ask you to get a little closer or stand a little farther back, but here's a good place to start: open up your hand, palm up. Now, close just your three middle fingers (the index, middle finger, and ring finger). You're left with only your pinky finger and thumb extended, much like the popular surfing *Hang ten* sign or, if you hold your hand up to your ear, the international *Call me!* sign. The distance from the tip of your pinky to the tip of your thumb is about the distance your mouth should be from the mic. You can also put two fists on top of each other to measure roughly the same distance.

An exception to this mic distance rule is when you're working with a loop group doing ADR and walla. In that case, you'll be working in a larger room, moving around a lot with a group of people, and your distance from the mic will be much farther.

Now obviously, these rules may change depending on the type of sound you're trying to create. For example, if you're going for a whispered, or soft, sultry quality, you may wish to get a little closer in on the mic. For yelling and screaming you will probably want to back off so as not to blow out the engineer and whoever else may be in the studio.

When you speak, the sound comes out in a cone shape; so while a mic will generally pick you up no matter where you are in the booth, you'll always get your best sound if you're standing directly in line with the mic. And once you're in position, pay attention to where you are and how that feels. It'll be important for you to maintain a pretty consistent position throughout your session so that the recording quality matches from line to line and session to session.

How much freedom do you have to move around? The answer is … some. You shouldn't be worried about keeping your head stock-still. You have some play: about 15-20° to the right and to the left. The same goes for up and down. There's a stand in the booth to hold your script, so feel free to tilt your face down to read from it. The mic can take it, and so can the engineer.

You definitely don't have to memorize each line and then look up to deliver it, although some people might do this, particularly if they're looking up to sync with mouth movements on a screen. The trick is to do the looking with just your eyes, and not change the relationship of your mouth to the mic in the middle of a take. Moving your head will make a difference to how the recording sounds. So, before you say the line, decide how you want to place your face in relation to the mic.

Movement only begins to cause problems in two cases:

1. when the movement itself gets noisy, either due to your clothing/shoes or your flailing about and knocking into things

2. when your movement carries you too far from the mic or too close to the mic

Either of these cases can cause you to have to do another take of the line because there are limits to what even the engineer can compensate for.

P POPS, POPPER STOPPERS, AND BLOWING A TAKE

What if we said that you have to be careful of *plosives*? Would you duck and cover? Ask for a helmet? Well, before you do, give us a second to explain.

When you say something like *Peter Piper picked a pickled pepper*, or even the word *stop*, you are dealing with a plosive, a sound that is created by a burst of air that rushes from your mouth, primarily on *p* sounds, but also sometimes on *t, k, b,* or *d*.

Our knowledgeable friend *Webster's* tells us:

> *plo·sive* (plō′sĭv, -zĭv) *adj.* 1. Produced by complete closure of the oral passage and subsequent release with a burst of air (as `p' and `d' in `pit' or `dog'). *noun* 1. A consonant produced by stopping air at some point and suddenly releasing it.

So don't worry. Plosives are perfectly natural. As a matter of fact, why don't you try *plosiving* now? Hold your hand up in front of your face, a couple of inches away. Now say, "puh," or "potato." Do you feel the puff of air? Now see what you feel with "karate," or "toenail." Surely less than with the *p* words, but you may still feel a small puff of air.

Where this can *pose* a *problem* is with the delicate instrument that is the mic. Sometimes plosives can *pop* the mic, or distort the sound because of the air being blown into the sensitive mic mechanisms, or *micanisms* (okay, you caught us; we just made that word up). Sometimes, if you hit that *p* a little too hard, it'll spike the engineer's levels, you'll literally *blow* the take, and you'll be asked to rerecord.

Fear not, though. Most mics are outfitted with a clever little accessory often called a *Popper Stopper* (although this is actually a brand name used to refer to the more generic *pop filter* or *pop screen*, much like *Xerox* is sometimes used to refer to making a photocopy). It is basically a metal or fabric mesh screen that is positioned between your mouth and the mic to catch the stronger puffs of air before they reach it. These are mostly effective and help keep you from obsessing over plosives. But if an engineer says, "Hey, be careful of your *P*s, or "Watch your *p pops* this time," there are things you can do to minimize the *poppage* and once again endear yourself to your engineer.

One way to fight those pops is to break up the flow of air by holding a pencil or your finger in the groove under your nose and blocking your lips, almost as if you were going to *shh!* someone. Try some plosives again, with and without your finger/pencil in place. Do you feel the difference?

Another way to lessen a *p pop* is to try slightly swallowing the sound, thereby eliminating some of the air you release; but make sure that in doing this, you don't cause the word to become unintelligible.

A third method for taming plosives involves a little something called going *off-axis*. To do this, you'll just need to point your mouth a little to the left or a little to the right of the mic so that the air isn't going straight into it. Be careful, though: you don't want to turn *so* far off-axis that the mic doesn't pick you up well enough.

MIC SAYS: A finger or a pencil can help stop a pop.

WATCHING YOUR VOLUME

Some of the techniques for minimizing plosives can also be used to keep from blowing out the engineer's levels when you're going to be suddenly, and without warning, LOUD. If you're going along at a very conversational volume, and then all of a sudden you scream or shout, odds are you're going to take the engineer by surprise, and a surprised engineer won't be able to bring the recording levels down in time. So, if suddenly you realize that you're going to be loud and the engineer might not see it coming, throw that loud stuff a little off-axis, by turning slightly off-mic (for you Beatles fans out there, a little *Twist and Shout*), or by backing off the mic a foot or so to compensate for the sudden boost in volume.

This is a lot to be thinking about right now, so don't become obsessed with this stuff when you get in the booth. We're telling you most of these things to help increase your general awareness, comfort, and confidence; not to have you create a list and memorize it.

The bottom line is that you'll pick up these behaviors and techniques as you work, and the engineer will be there to tell you if you need to adjust anything as you go. The info we've given you is all just stuff for you to keep in the back of your mind, so that when it does come up, you won't be completely caught off guard. Know that, as many years as we've been doing this, we still pop and blow takes at times.

MOUTH NOISES: CLICKING, SMACKING, AND GURGLING

We keep telling you that the microphone is a very sensitive instrument. What we haven't mentioned before – but what you may very well be aware of – is that your body makes noises, sometimes even when you don't want it to, and your good buddy *Mic* hears every one. Many of these noises you've learned to hide from the public at large, and some noises you may not even hear yourself. But you can be sure of one thing: the mic will pick them up. Picking up sound is what the mic was designed for. Let's talk about some of the more popular sounds that occasionally creep into a recording.

Clicking (a mouth click) is the bane of a VA's existence. Mouth clicks happen when your mouth becomes too dry and the mic begins to pick up the sounds of your lips, cheeks, and tongue. Sometimes this is called *being smacky*. A swig of water can help with this sometimes, but saliva is your best lubricant, and water can actually dry out your mouth even more if you already have dry mouth; or, just as bad, make you *splashy* or too *wet* sounding.

But fear not! There is a magical cure. To help an actor with a severe case of *clickiness*, most studios will have on hand this cure: The Mighty Green Apple. And by green, we mean Granny Smith, not Golden Delicious; let's just be clear about that. One bite, and the clicks disappear as if they never existed. Why does this work? Why only Granny Smith apples? It's a mystery. (And by that we, of course, mean magic. Yuri thinks it has something to do with little apple elves who erase the sounds as you make them; but then again, that's our Yuri.)

Actually it's the tartness of the Granny Smith's juice that does the trick (so if you've got another tart fruit, like pineapple, for example, that'll also work), because it causes your salivary glands to lubricate your mouth. In fact, you don't even have to *eat* the apple to get the benefits. Simply biting and sucking will suffice. And once again your engineer will thank you, because if there's anything worse than clickiness, it's having to listen to super-amplified actors chewing and swallowing and trying to clear their mouths of apple bits.

Tara once had a session in which, between *every single line*, it was necessary for her to take a bite of apple since she was recording a quiet, whispery character. She was in really close to the mic, and *everything* was being picked up. So it was a trade-off: no more clicks, but the engineer had to listen to her munching apples all day – in addition to hearing the burbling, gurgling sounds that her stomach made as it fought to digest the onslaught of Granny Smith!

One way to minimize this kind of trouble is to make sure that you're staying really well hydrated at all times. Basically, drink water as often as possible. This will keep your vocal folds/cords ready to work, and your mouth well-lubricated and ready to talk. And don't wait until you show up to work. It takes time for water to truly circulate throughout your body after you've ingested it. Drink water starting the night before so that your voice and body are ready to stand (or sit) in a dry booth and talk (or scream) for several hours at a time.

We actually have a (not particularly clever) mnemonic that helps us: ADW – Always Drink Water (we know, we *told* you it wasn't particularly clever). This means that if anyone at all ever offers you water, you have to say "yes" *and* drink it (unless you suspect that they might be trying to poison you). Drinking more water every day may have serious side effects, though: improved health, vitality, and a serious need to go pee more often, have been known to result from hydrating. But don't confuse *hydrating*, with *drinking liquids*. The latter may not necessarily mean the former.

Beverages such as alcohol and coffee (or any caffeinated beverage, really) actually dry you out. You might want to avoid drinking them right before a session, or even the night before a session. Warm herbal teas (without caffeine), on the other hand, can have the opposite (and positive) effect of soothing and warming up the voice. Add a spoonful of honey and you're good to go.

And while we're on the topic of foods, try to avoid dairy products right before a session. They make you phlegmy, which, in addition to just sounding gross, can also choke you up a bit and make for bad recording.

MIC SAYS: Green apples keep the clicks down.

NOT JUST YOUR MOUTH:
SHUFFLING, RUSTLING, AND SQUEAKING

Let's assume for a moment that the noises from your mouth are coming out exactly the way they're supposed to: you're not out of the woods just yet. Hey, if all you had to do was move your mouth, you'd be fine. But, what with all the acting you're doing at the same time, it's hard to keep the rest of your body still; trust us. And moving body parts = more noise.

Like what, you ask? Well, let's start from the top and move our way down: first, ditch the baseball cap. If you *must* wear it, turn it around so that the brim's in back. A baseball cap will actually change the sound quality of your recorded voice because of how the sound waves bounce off the brim. Satiny shirts, or jackets made of crinkly or otherwise noisy material? Definitely a no-no. Same goes for pants, and that includes corduroys. And anything jingly that you have hanging off your clothes or appendages. And finally, your shoes: squeaky soles or squeaky leather will get picked up every time.

Sure, you look great in all your stylish finery, and standing there in front of the mirror you don't hear a thing. But in the booth, you move whether you like it or not. Hey, we've all gotta breathe. And as we've said already many times before, the mic is built to pick up the slightest sounds. Do you really want to be self-conscious about breathing and rustling and squeaking when you should be concentrating on having fun?

Tara once learned the hard way that fashion and VO don't always mix when she went into a session with a beautiful new skirt. It was bright and had an overskirt with little mirrors all over it. Little did she realize how noisy hundreds of little pieces of glass clinking together could be – until the sound was amplified in her headphones, of course. She sounded like one of those bead curtains from the 1960s. It got so bad that she had to roll up the top layer of the skirt and tie it behind her so that the rustling and jangling wouldn't be picked up on the recording. Boy, did she feel like an amateur. She never let *that* happen again.

Once, in another session, Yuri had to lend another actor his hoodie because she had to remove her noisy shirt and had nothing else to change into. At least, that's his story ...

So before you leave the house, dance around a little first. If *you're* hearing something, the mic's *definitely* going to hear it. Ditch the noisy article(s) of clothing and move on. You can be fashionable later. Your ideal voice-over wardrobe is going to be comfortable, soft things like tee shirts, jeans, and sneakers. It's always good to have a sweatshirt or something long-sleeved with you as well. Sometimes even when it's hot *outside*, the booth can be like an icebox. You want to be prepared, and you definitely don't want to catch a cold.

And not just your clothes, either ...

Now that you've gotten a handle on your noisy wardrobe, we're going to give you one last thing to keep quiet: your script. Unless the studio has set it up so that your script is displayed on a screen in the booth, or on a tablet you can swipe quietly, your script will likely be in the form of pages on a stand in front of you. And you're likely going to have to turn those pages at some point. And the mic will hear that. So as you're standing in the booth, take a moment to see if you can arrange your pages in a way that allows you to read as many as possible without having to fiddle with them, thereby eliminating noise. If you must turn pages while you're recording, that's perfectly all right; just make sure that no one is talking as you do it – not you or anyone else. As quiet as you think you're being, odds are that mic is going to hear the page turning, and the engineer's going to ask for another take.

FULL OF HOT AIR

While working on a show for Hasbro I was asked to schedule a female VO actress to do a simple pickup. In order to spare her blushes,
let's call her "Jane." It happened that Jane was working near the
studio, and had just finished her post-lunch session. As she only had
one loop to pick up, she offered to come over immediately.

Now ... it just so happens that the male VA who was working in
the booth, let's call him "John," had eaten a spicy lunch, thinking he
would have *single occupancy* of the booth for the whole afternoon.

When Jane arrived, John seemed very shy about letting Jane into
the booth, and if memory serves me correctly, he was a little more
animated than usual – you know: waving his arms around a lot.

When we finally enticed John out of the booth, Jane ran in ...
only to run out again a moment later shouting, "Oh my god. It
smells like something has @*%!ing died in there."

It took ten minutes, a lot of wafting, and a personal appearance in
the booth to convince Jane that it was safe to go back in the booth.

And so you see the old phrase is right: comedy is all in the timing!

~ MARK A. TODD, WRITER, DIRECTOR

"WHAT'S THAT STUFF IN THE BOOTH WITH ME?"

Every booth in every studio is going to be a little different. Some
might be bigger and some might very well be the size of a small
coat closet. Some booths may be stacked to the gills with equipment, and some you may share with only the mic. So rather than
list specifics, why don't we just paint a general picture of what a
typical sound studio or recording booth might have in it. And, as
always, technology advances at a lightning pace; so who knows
what'll be in the booth when you finally step in to work.

The stand, the cans, the mic, and you

Hey, look! It's some of your old friends: mic, mic stand, and pop
screen! The old gang is back together again. These guys'll almost

always be there, in one form or another, no matter what studio you're recording in. Remember, though, as familiar as you've become with these guys, don't get *too* familiar and go moving them around. That's still the engineer's job. Besides: it gives the engineer an excuse to come in and chat with the actor for a minute while adjusting the position of the mic for you.

Now, the mic stand isn't the only stand you'll encounter on your journey. Your *script stand* (usually just called *the stand*) looks like a music stand (and more often than not, is one). The script stand is where you'll rest your script while you read from it. (We may not have mentioned it thus far, but one of the perks of voice acting over on-camera or stage acting, is that you will rarely, if ever, have to memorize your lines. You'll always have your script open in front of you – except when doing performance capture.)

Some studios these days have all but done away with a printed script, opting instead to present your script on a monitor or screen which is visible from where you're standing in the booth. Sometimes there'll be a tablet (usually an iPad) to display your script, and if so, it'll still be on the script stand – which is generally fair game for you to touch without making your engineer nervous. But remember, depending on how high or low you set the stand, you can actually change how the mic picks up your voice. So if you're going to adjust the height of the script stand, do it before the engineer comes in, or while the engineer is in the booth setting up for you.

That reminds us, when they're adjusting the mic to the right height for you, be sure you're taking pretty much the same stance as the one you'll take while you're recording. Yuri has a tendency to settle into an *action pose* over the course of a session, and if he doesn't stand that way when the engineer's setting the mic at the beginning, the engineer inevitably has to come in to correct the mic position later on in the session.

This seems to be a good place to mention standing versus sitting. When you're recording, you can usually choose between sitting and standing. It's a matter of personal preference. Some people always sit and some always stand. We each sit sometimes and stand sometimes. Tara finds that standing helps her keep her energy up, which for certain shows or games can be extremely important, especially if there's a lot of action. On the other hand, if she knows she's going to be in a narration session for four hours, she'll do the session seated.

We talked about movement in the booth at the beginning of this chapter. The same rules apply whether you're sitting or standing. Keep your face in that sweet spot and the engineer will appreciate it. If you don't, then both of you will be doing extra work.

Oh, wait! Here's a new friend. Allow us to introduce to you a booth companion that may be familiar to you from your outside life: the *headphones*. Odds are, unless you're a DJ, *these* headphones (sometimes called *cans*) will be a little more heavy-duty than the ones you hook up to your smartphone. But they work pretty much the same.

These headphones will allow you to hear both the engineer and director when they're speaking to you from the control room, as well as hear the sound of your own voice when you're recording. Usually they're plugged into a headphone amplifier, a little box with a volume dial on it. You are, in fact, allowed to touch *this* dial, so feel free to adjust the volume to a level that is comfortable for you.

Some voice actors like to keep the headphones over both ears, while some like to leave one side off. Once again, this is a personal preference. Experiment with them both ways, and see which feels better to you. In some sessions you might not use headphones at all, the director preferring to use *talkback*. Talkback simply means that there's a speaker in the booth, through which the director and/or engineer will communicate with you. (Sometimes the term *talkback* is also used to mean communicating from the control room through *either* the headphones or a speaker system.)

Try practicing with the headphones all the way on, all the way off, and one-on/one-off. Your voice will sound different to you depending on the configuration of the headphones, and you want to choose the one that's most comfortable for you whenever possible. We know some actors who prefer wearing both headphones so much that, even when there are no headphones in the booth, they cup their hands around their ears to simulate the way they hear their own voices when the headphones are on.

Don't worry if you get into the booth and there aren't any cans. Some booths are set up to have talkback engaged through in-room speakers, so there is no need to use headphones at all. Don't get too accustomed to using them or not using them, so you can be flexible no matter what type of studio you're working in.

"WHAT'S THAT SOUND?"

Don't worry. You're not hearing things that aren't there. That beeping sound in your headphones? That's a more specific way of saying, *We're rolling.* It's an audio cue for you to begin speaking. As we mentioned in the section on dubbing, more often than not, the cue you hear will be The Three Beeps: *beep ... beep ... beep ...* after which you will begin, as if on the imaginary fourth beep. This can be very important for timing, particularly in the case of foreign language or ADR dubbing. The director wants your dialogue to sync up with the already existing mouth movements, so the engineer sets up the beeps to help you start on time.

The Three Beeps are equally spaced apart. The reason there are *three* is that three's the perfect number to give you an opportunity to get accustomed to the timing. So, you'll hear: *beep ... beep ... beep ...* and when the *fourth* beep would come in, you start speaking. Once again, this is most important when there is a timing issue, such as in dubbing. Otherwise, you may just hear the director saying, "Okay, we're rolling. Whenever you're ready, go ahead."

So you're standing or you're sitting; you've got a script on a stand in front of you or you're reading it off a screen; you may be trying to time something to a video image; you've got your headphones on (or half-on/half-off); you're waiting for beeps; and you're in your stance. That's a lot of stuff to be thinking about all at once, and increasingly tricky as soon as you remember that you also have to be *acting* at the same time. (It may sound a little like patting your head and rubbing your belly at the same time, while also spinning in a circle, eating an ice cream cone, and composing a symphony; but it gets easier.) After a little practice, the balancing routine will become a part of your magic act and you'll find yourself able to focus on your performance while the rest of the stuff just takes care of itself.

"WHAT ABOUT PERFORMANCE CAPTURE?"

It's probably obvious that when you are cast in a role that requires motion capture or performance capture you'll need plenty of room to move around; and you won't be recording in a sound booth – at least at first (you may go in later for additional recording due to things like new dialogue, rewrites, or technical issues with the audio recorded on stage). Check out Chapter 8, *The Soundstage*, for what it's like to work on a PCap soundstage.

BE A CONSCIENTIOUS CAMPER

One last note on the booth. Treat it like a campsite: always leave it in a better state than you found it. Clean up after yourself, and if the actor before you left a half empty water bottle or other trash behind, toss it on your way out. It may seem like a little thing, but it shows respect for your space, what you do, and the people you work with.

People often joke about how voice actors can go to work in their pajamas if they want because it doesn't matter what they look like. While we've never actually seen anyone show up in their PJs, we've both seen many an actor show up to work in comfy sweats and a well-loved tee shirt. Make sure they're not *too* well loved, though. Remember, another actor's going to be in that booth after you leave. You don't want to become associated with the smell you leave behind. That goes for strong perfume or cologne, too. The person who records after you might be allergic or just plain sensitive. So this might be the only time you *don't* want to come in smelling like a rose. Or anything else for that matter.

But the booth is a small place, and only part of where you'll be working. So what goes on beyond that door? Let's take a look....

CHAPTER 7
THE STUDIO

"*The way a team plays as a whole determines its success.
You may have the greatest bunch of individual stars in the world,
but if they don't play together, the club won't be worth a dime.*"

BABE RUTH, U.S. BASEBALL PLAYER

"HOW'S THE STUDIO DIFFERENT
FROM THE BOOTH?"

For our purposes, let's define a *studio* as anywhere you go to record. The booth is part of the studio. But, wait, there's more. In the studio, for every booth, there's a control room, where the director, engineer, and possibly others (engineer's assistant, director's assistant, clients …) are working hard at the same time as you. Remember, like most creative endeavors in the entertainment industry, the actor's job is just one part of the whole.

We've worked in all kinds of studios, but the basic setup as far as you, the actor, are concerned, is the same. There will always be some type of control room and some type of booth. Some studios will consist of nothing but those two areas, while others might have a fully stocked kitchen and catering department. Some studios might be housed in a massive compound with multiple rooms, while some might be only the garage at someone's house.

But don't let size fool you. As long as you've got a good director, engineer, and equipment, you're ready to rock ... and *roll*.

DON'T PSYCH YOURSELF OUT

There will be times when you're in the booth recording, and you've just laid something down (i.e. just recorded something), and the folks in the control room are working. If you're in a studio that has a window between the booth and the control room, you can see those folks; but often talkback is turned off while they work (usually to spare you having to listen to them). This is totally normal, and you'll have to learn not to obsess over what they're talking about in the control room. Due to the tenuous and often stressful nature of our business, actors can have a tendency to suspect the worst in a given situation.

So think about it: you're working, you're working, the director's making jokes, you're all laughing, everybody's happy, then abruptly the line goes dead and you're cut off. You can see that it's suddenly serious in the control room. The engineer's talking to the director, the director's talking to the client, the client's talking to their boss in Brussels over the phone, and you can't hear a word of it. All you hear is your breathing and every other little sound in the booth, amplified in your headphones. It's enough to rattle anyone.

They've got to be talking about you, right? *Right?* Well, the truth is, probably not. Remember, there's more to this process than just you, and odds are they've cut you out of the discussion so they won't bore you with technical stuff.

Also, turning off the talkback is the director's way of protecting you from all that outside stuff that might get in the way of your acting process. A good director knows when to let you listen to what's going on in the control room and when not to. Directors check in with the client occasionally to see if things are going in the right direction, and they should leave you out of that discussion. Most of the time, producers and clients don't have a clue how to communicate with actors. The director knows this, and would much rather interpret the information from the client, and communicate it to you in the best way possible. Sometimes the director is working with the engineer because everyone really liked your performance, but they need to do some technical tweaking to make it perfect.

In other words, if you can't hear what's going on, take a deep breath, relax, and assume the best. No news is good news. If the director and/or client want something different from you, they'll just ask. In the meantime, I usually stare at my script, pretending that I'm studying it, just so I don't even make eye contact with anyone in the control room until they're back on the line. And remember, think twice before grabbing your phone. And speaking of phones…

Some sessions are directed via *phone patch* because the director or the client is off site somewhere, meaning not in the same building or even the same country! Ah, the wonders of modern technology … In a phone-patch session you'll have to be even more comfortable with silence and waiting, as the client in Montreal may be talking to the engineer in the control room who may be talking to the director in New York who may be talking to any actors working opposite you who are actually in another studio downtown because they couldn't make it over to where you're recording. So enjoy the silence. It's golden.

It's All in Your Head

So here's a story I've told so many times that we decided it deserved a place in this book. I was in the studio to record a tag for a TV commercial. It was literally six words. I thought I'd be in and out in fifteen minutes tops, even if they had me do it several different ways to make sure they had their bases covered. Almost half an hour into the session, I'm sweating. They've had me do it what seemed like a thousand different ways, so obviously they're still not getting what they want. I'm alone in the booth and they've cut the talkback, but I can still see them through the glass.

I try to focus on the script, the floor, anything to keep myself from obsessing over what they might be talking about, but it's no use. I see the director talking heatedly to the client. They go back and forth. The engineer turns around to give his two cents. I don't know what they're saying, but it's not good. *I can tell.* "I'm about to get fired," I think. An assistant reaches for a phone.

I figure at that point they're getting on the phone to do one of two things: 1) Call my agent to complain about how bad an actor I am, or 2) Get another actor in to replace me. Maybe both. What was I going to do? My life was over. Word would get out that I couldn't hack even six words of commercial copy and I'd be back to temping, working in an office where I'd – the talkback clicked on. They must have seen my pitiful face looking out from behind the glass.

The director says, "Hey, sorry for the wait, Yuri. We totally got it, you're brilliant, thanks. We were just arguing over what we were going to get for lunch today. You want us to order you something?" I learned two things that day: 1) Never assume you know what they're talking about on the other side of the glass, and 2) If you are going to assume, assume it has something to do with Thai vs. Mexican.

~ Yuri Lowenthal, Actor

"WHAT DO THOSE GUYS/GALS DO ANYWAY?"

Just what do those people across the glass from you do? Any number of things, but generally they fall under the headings *director, engineer, producer,* or *client.* Each one is responsible for a different part of the process, and together, with your help, they assemble like the Voltron lions to form a mighty project.

So which is which? Not always easy to tell at first glance, and you might not always have everyone on this list in the studio with you, but odds are, whoever talks to you *most* will be the director. The engineer will also be pretty easy to pick out. That's the person who comes in and makes sure that your mic is set correctly, and is also working the control panel and instruments. The engineer may have someone sitting close by, either assisting, or keeping track of the script and the preferred takes as you move forward. All those other faces are up for grabs: producer, client, ad executive, writer, game designer, or maybe even the client's nephew. And you may or may not be introduced to these people.

If all goes smoothly, the director and engineer might be the only two people you talk to while you're in the booth. Communication with anyone else should go through the director, although occasionally, for a moment, the director will turn over the talking to a producer, writer, or designer who knows the show/game/product best.

We know that this is a lot of different people to remember, but the most important thing to keep in mind is: none of these people are against you, and everyone is rooting for you. Sure, you'll occasionally encounter someone having a bad day; but just remember to take it in stride, and never let your work be affected by someone else's having gotten up on the wrong side of the bed that morning.

THE DIRECTOR

It's the job of voice directors to know the script and the story (or product) and work with the actor (or cast) to create a performance that best serves the project. They will give direction or adjustments directly to the actors to keep them on track, and may experiment in different directions to capture the best performance possible. Skilled directors will be able to communicate their vision to an actor without resorting to a *line-read* (e.g. "Repeat after me." ... "Say it like this."), and will work *with* the actor to create the performance. But if you get a line-read or a frustrated direc-tor, just take a breath, relax, and work through it. Line reads get a bad rap, but may not even be that bad, provided the director has let you take a few cracks at the reading before giving you one. Plus it insures that the director and client are getting exactly what they need; or, in many cases, they realize that your way was even better than what they had in their heads.

You also must remember that, besides dealing with you, the director has to answer to the producer or client (who may even be there in the same room), as well as work with the engineer to make sure that your performance is recorded and useable. Since directors serve as your connection to the rest of the team, forging a solid and trusting relationship with them should always be a priority when starting a project.

This doesn't mean working hard to become the director's best-est friend ever. Rather, the best way to foster a good relationship is to listen, ask questions when you need to, and be responsive to the direction you are given. Keep in mind that a director who likes working with you on one project will likely bring you in on future jobs because they are familiar with your work, know you're easy to work with, and know you can get the job done.

If you have worked with the director before, and feel com-fortable occasionally asking for an extra take or to try something different, go for it. But once again, remember to pick your battles. An actor who wants take after take to get it *perfect* even though the director was happy with the first take, slows everything down, and may stop getting hired after a while.

FROM THE DIRECTOR'S CHAIR

I'm probably considered a cranky director. I want actors to take their jobs as seriously as I take mine. Whether interactive games or series animation, a lot has to be accomplished in a short amount of time.

So I'm not a big fan of playtime ad nauseam. If the actor comes in for a gig, I want them to already be acquainted with the material in advance so we can just "go"... no table read. Questions or story problems are worked out at the top of the session, and we basically "rehearse on tape," taking whatever is working for the print, and doing pickups or adjustments after we complete a run. So the more prepared people are, the faster we can get to making our magic! I ask *a lot* from actors. I rarely settle, and I thrive on getting every option out of a read.

In a recording session, direction may change and often does. So being flexible is a must. And *listening*. The other side of the glass is often a mixture of writers or producers working out their business. Actors should never think it's "them"! And, the person directing may not always be a great communicator or "an actor's director." It doesn't hurt for the actor to be a patient mind reader, or even a clever "second guesser"! When the timing is right, *input* from the actor can also be helpful ... Someone might have an idea for their character or a line rewrite that can make a scene better.

I often talk in *CliffsNotes*. Once the actors have, hopefully, done their homework, I can just give them the essentials before a scene or line ... not talk it to death, losing all freshness in their delivery (or mine). Just remaining open to everyone and everything creatively in a session is crucial. I'll never stop appreciating the wonderful talent that has come my way for decades now. The ones I revere are *not* celebrities. Yet. They should be.

~ GINNY MCSWAIN, CASTING DIRECTOR, DIRECTOR

Direction from near, direction from afar

When you are in the recording session, there are two ways that your director will communicate with you. The first and most common way in animation or video game work is for the director to be physically in the control room (most likely sitting next to, or at least near, the engineer and sometimes the producer), and using a *talkback button* to communicate with you through the glass. This is just a button that, when pushed by the director, allows you to hear what's happening in the control room (through headphones or a speaker – as we've already discussed). Having the director physically there is great because, even when the talkback button is off, the director can still *see* you through the glass; and *face time* with directors – if they like your work – can get you hired again.

On the other hand, sometimes (most often in commercial or promo recording sessions) you will find yourself alone in the booth, and the only other person on the other side of the glass is the engineer ... while the producer, director, and client are on a phone line talking to you (we've mentioned this before). The callers are then patched through to your headphones so they can hear you and direct you – even though some or all of them may be physically halfway across the world. Frequently, the ad execs are located in Chicago or elsewhere, and the work is recorded in NYC or L.A. The phone patch makes it possible to get everyone together *in the room* in spite of great distances. And, of course, if you're recording from your home studio (we'll get more into that in Chapter 9, *Your Home Booth*) the only person in the studio is you!

For all intents and purposes, a phone patch will *feel* the same to you in the booth as when you're using talkback with the director in the room, as all the info will be coming through your headphones or speakers. But with a phone patch, you won't get face time with the director/client. You could go years working with the same people, and never even know what they look like.

Translating some directing terminology

You will, in your VO journey, encounter some unfamiliar terms. Some of them may sound familiar but then end up having totally different meanings than you're used to. Here are examples of a few of the more common expressions:

"Gimme a *slate*" or "Slate your name."

This basically means that the producer and director want you to say your name (usually right before you begin an audition) so that they can record it; then they'll have it with your audition tape so they can keep track of whose audition it is. You will often follow your name with the name of the character you're reading for. You can keep it as dry as saying:

Yuri Lowenthal, Cowboy Number Three.

Or you can give it some character:

Howdy, this is Yuri Lowenthal, and I reckon I'm reading for the part of Cowboy Number Three, yeee-haahh!

During a recording session, the engineer usually records a different kind of *slate* between each take for keeping track of the takes for later. To lead into this slate, the engineer says something like this: "We're rolling on Take Forty-Two," or "This is Take Seventy-Four." That's usually your cue to start speaking your line. Of course, if you are dubbing, the engineer's slate will be followed by the three beeps before you chime in.

"Can I get an *ABC take*?"

Directors sometimes like for you to give three takes of the same line, one after the other with a little space in between, so they can pick the one they like best. The implied direction is that they would like you to *change up* (modify) each read a little, so that they have options from which to choose their favorite. So mix it up a bit.

"On this next one, gimme a *series*."

This direction is also a request for multiple takes of the same line, but it implies that you just keep going until they say to stop. This might happen, for example, when you're recording efforts for a video game. You're recording *light bullet hits* (*Hunh! Aggh! Oooh!*) and they'll want a few to choose from, so they ask for a series.

"Just gimme a couple more, *wild*."

Often, because directors don't want to spend time slating a new take number, or maybe because they feel you're on a roll, they'll ask you for *a few more, wild*. That just means that you don't have to wait for them to slate again. They're going to keep recording. You just let 'er rip for a few more takes or until they tell you to stop. This may also come up if you've been recording something *to picture* (perhaps dubbing something that's already been animated, or recording efforts to already designed gameplay). The director may ask you to go ahead and give a few more reads *wild*, rather than recording them against the video reference.

"Can I get a *safety*?"

This is not a football reference. It refers to one more take for the director to have just as a backup, or maybe for another choice, or just in case the first one had a technical glitch. It usually means that your first take was fine and the director just wants an extra for good measure. Basically, they're covering their bases (to use an *actual* sports reference).

"Gimme a little more *level* on the next pass."

Level, in this case, refers to *audio level*, so this essentially translates to, "Louder on this next one, please."

You know who really cares about the level? The engineer.

MIC SAYS: Facing a little off-mic might save you from *blowing* the take.

THE ENGINEER

From where you'll be standing, it will, at first glance, look like the engineer's job is just to hit *record* and *stop*. Nothing could be further from the truth. Engineers are the ones who will make you sound good, and who can make it easier or harder for you to do your job; so be sure to stay on their good side. The more you work *with* them, the more pleasant your job will be.

Engineers can often fix or adjust a recorded line that would otherwise be unusable, by compressing, stretching, or adjusting levels to make the line work. Or they can ask the director to have you do it again. And again. Until you give them something useable. Treat the engineers with respect, and they're more likely to be willing to fiddle with what you've given them to make it work. Sometimes, there's nothing they can do to save a line – it's too loud, too soft, you've blown air into the mic, whatever – and you'll have to do it again anyway. Don't get impatient. Just work with them until it comes out right.

The engineer you'll be working with is only the first of several engineers who might be working on the project. But the engineer in the room, the *recording engineer*, will probably be the only one you'll see. The others will take what you've recorded and begin the lengthy editing and mixing process to distill all of your work down to the final product. That's also where sound effects and music come in, but that's for another book. *Written by another author.*

On rare occasions, the director and engineer will actually be the same person. This happens sometimes when a person with an engineering background gets into directing or vice versa.

AN ENGINEER'S TWO CENTS

Do not try to *work the mic* like a singer might do. We see a lot of music videos where a singer almost makes love to the microphone. In voice-over, it is the microphone that loves you. A VO actor must allow the engineer to bring the volume to you. You do your performance. Engineers are simply there to *capture* that performance. They are constantly working the fader to maximize every nuance that you give.

The veteran VO actors are consistent in their microphone proximity. They read to the copy – not to the mic. Newer VO actors sometimes look at the copy for most of a line and then look up at the mic at the end of the line. That changes the mic proximity, and so their sound changes.

Also, seasoned VO actors know what they sound like and can make minor adjustments as the director demands. The highs and lows in volume within a line are in a vocal range that is acceptable range technically. Sometimes new VO actors are too dynamic – that is to say, they are too loud in the first part of a line, and then too soft in the second part. The engineer struggles to capture their performance, because there is no baseline, no sweet spot.

On *Mass Effect 2* the recording spec is: mic proximity is 12"-18" from the mic to achieve an on-camera type sound, and we use NO compression. For an engineer, that is like working without a safety net. If we get too loud and distort, we simply do another take. That is a luxury that we try to minimize in other situations like *full cast animation* recording sessions. The trick is consistency. Whatever you establish for a character – the volume should be in a confined range.

When we get to action material, the pros also warn the engineer that it is going to get louder. That is helpful, because we are always working together to make sure we're on the same page so that your performance does not take the engineer by surprise.

Headphones: most voice actors are used to working with them, and some are not. Voice actors can be fooled by what they hear in their headphones. When actors get softer in volume, the engineer pushes the fader up to get more presence. The actors hear themselves fine and then get even softer. That is a problem. Some directors do not even allow headphones. They do not want actors to *listen* to their performance because they are constantly monitoring what they hear and forget to perform as they normally would as an actor.

~ ELLIOT ANDERS, AUDIO ENGINEER

THE PRODUCER

The producer is in charge of making sure the project comes together just as the client or creator has imagined it. That can entail everything from hiring people to finding a studio to writing the lines you say. Producers sometimes might also be the clients, themselves, since many creators also come on as producers because of their vested interest in the project.

Producers have to make sure things stay on track from start to finish, and often they won't be in the actual session because they are handling some other aspect of the production. Remember, the recording is only one slice of the whole pie, so producers must often be master jugglers. If they don't seem to be paying attention to you, don't worry. They're probably dealing with a million other things at the moment.

As a matter of fact, if they're not paying attention to what you're doing, it's usually a good sign. It means they trust that this part of the process is going well, and they can move on to worrying about something else. If you get the chance, when you're done working, thank the producers and let them know how much you enjoyed working on their project. It's possible that they had the final say in casting you in the first place.

THE CLIENT

The client is the person or people for whom the project is being produced. They've usually hired a producer or an ad agency to take care of hiring people like the director, the recording studio, and you. Clients will only rarely be present at the recording, but will still have the final call on the end product since it is their vision (and they're paying for it!). In most projects, the final product that reaches the public will have been approved by, at least, the director, the producer, and finally the client.

Two good tricks to remember when dealing with the people across the glass from you:

1. Jot down their names on your script so you remember who's who.

2. If one of them gives you direction, or asks you to do something (within reason, of course), remember: don't argue with them, or explain why you did it the way you did it, or tell them why their idea sucks. Just do it. What's one more take? Right or wrong, just do it. They're the boss. Which is not to say that you should take abuse, or forget that it's your work that's going to be heard; but you must enter into this relationship with a fair amount of trust.

THE PERFORMANCE CAPTURE STUDIO

As we noted in the previous chapter on *The Booth*, your work in motion capture/performance capture will not take place in a standard recording studio. But there will be plenty of people for you keep track of there, too. So keep reading and we'll cover what you need to know about the PCap soundstage and MoCap team in the next chapter.

SCRATCH TRACKS   WITH TARA & YURI

CHAPTER 8
THE SOUNDSTAGE

*"Great things are not done by impulse,
but by a series of small things brought together."*

VINCENT VAN GOGH

As we've mentioned before in this edition, times have changed. Once upon a time, if you were working on a video game, you inevitably stood behind a mic just like any other VO gig. Not necessarily so, these days. As we voice actors get hired to lend more than just our voices to a project, the more likely we are to find ourselves showing up at a studio that looks less like a glorified closet, and more like a cavernous motion picture soundstage… with some very specific differences.

While motion picture soundstages are crammed full of sets and props and lighting equipment, a performance capture soundstage is generally jam-packed with… mostly nothing. It's one of the reasons some people call the space you work in "the void." On a PCap soundstage, the sets, the props, the lighting, the special effects, the costumes, the makeup and, in fact, the faces, are all created using the magic of technology, long after the actors have gone home – usually. Depending on the setup where you're working, you might even be able to watch some of that magic in real time – as computers deftly turn you into your character quickly enough for you to watch it happen. It's definitely a trip to be standing there in your skintight spandex suit, festooned with reflective balls, looking down the length of hardware store PVC pipe in your hand, and then to look up at the monitor and see a stately knight in plate mail, holding aloft a flaming sword.

MORE THAN A TALKING HEAD

So now that we've gotten you accustomed to the strict parameters of standing behind a mic in a tiny booth, we're going to blow all that up for PCap and put you in a cavernous space where you'll be required to run wild. Okay, well, not run wild entirely, although depending on the game... But while we certainly don't believe voice acting in a regular recording studio is about being just a "talking head," you'll definitely inhabit your body a lot more for performance capture. There will also be some physical boundaries you'll need to be aware of, but they're sort of, well, imaginary. Don't worry; we'll explain what that means in a moment. But for the time being, start warming up, because we're about to get busy.

On a typical voice acting gig, you can review your script in advance (if they allow you that luxury) without having to worry about memorizing it. But when doing PCap, you're going to be on your feet, moving around, so knowing your lines is imperative. If you've got a script in your hand, you may not be able to grapple with that Orc, or cook that curry (yes, this was a real scene).

If you have a theatre or film/TV background, you might be a little more comfortable with preparing and memorizing a script, but for many of us, the thought of having to memorize anything fills us with dread. Regardless, with PCap, memorizing lines is a must. You'll have enough to deal with when you're performing on the soundstage, so be sure to use the time you have with the scripts beforehand to prepare, prepare, prepare. You want to be ready to go when they say "Action." And while some actors may fear over-rehearsing a scene, you definitely don't want to be the one holding up a busy day because you keep forgetting your lines. We've seen it happen. Nobody wins.

Most productions will get you the scripts well in advance, but sometimes rewrites may come in the night before, or even the day of. In fact, we've even heard of one instance in which the project was SO secret, the actors didn't see scripts until they showed up for work that day. So just be as prepared as you can while staying flexible.

Some cushy jobs will have a day scheduled for rehearsal, but most won't have it in the budget, and will just rehearse a few times on the day of shooting. You may or may not have *pre-viz*, which is a roughly animated *pre-visualization* of the scene that animators have assembled to show how they hope it'll come together. With or without pre-viz, flexibility is key because things change so fast when you're working on the stage. Blocking may not work as planned; the dialogue may get cut or rewritten because it's not feeling right. Any number of things could happen, but if you come prepared, and remember to breathe, you'll be fine. If something's not working, feel free to offer a potential solve, but remember that there are a lot of moving parts and things to consider when putting together a game, so if your idea gets denied, let it roll off your spandex-covered back. Remember, it's not all about you.

MIC SAYS: PCap can be hard work! Be sure to do at least a light physical warm-up when you get to the stage to keep your body (and your job) safe.

VOICE-OVER VOICE ACTOR

THEATRE OF THE MIND

Let's get it out of the way right here: Unless you're a legit superhero, everyone looks ridiculous in a spandex suit. And (most) superheroes don't have to deal with the added indignities of being covered in reflective balls, weird makeup, microphones, batteries, and still save the day with a camera strapped to their heads. Also, as we mentioned before, the set you'll be acting on will be mostly empty, with only suggestions of the things you'll be interacting with. (Yep, that pole with the tennis ball on the end of it is a dragon.) Hardly the well-manicured and detailed set of, say, *Titanic*. And it goes without saying that your surroundings will look nothing like the lush jungles and ruins of *Uncharted*. This is where those imaginary physical boundaries we mentioned come into play. Here is where your powerful actor's imagination and cutting edge technology marry in the most delightful way. Out of this cold and unreal environment, the actors and the production team make magic happen. Your movement in a world you've created in your mind and your reactions to this imaginary world can bring reality to a gamer's experience. But you've gotta commit.

Okay. So you're on the soundstage. It's empty except for two parallel ropes on the floor in front of you, a large box with a length of PVC protruding from it, a stack of wooden boxes ("apple boxes" in the common parlance), a smaller piece of PVC pipe on a music stand, and another actor in a suit just like yours preparing to shamble. Not particularly exciting, right? Well, your job is to bring the excitement. Close your eyes.

Let's work with the aforementioned imagination for a moment. Imagine you're – oh, wait, you probably closed your eyes at the top of this paragraph because you're a good student, didn't you? Hm. Maybe read through this and *then* close your eyes and try it.

Now, imagine you're walking in an abandoned subway tunnel, following the tracks lit by the dim flickering of failing emergency

132

lighting. A rodent of uncanny size runs across the tracks inches in front of you, and you have to duck under a collapsed support beam blocking your way. You climb onto a ledge, squeeze into an alcove, and start to flip a switch that will hopefully light the rest of your way. But as you're reaching for the switch, you're suddenly attacked by a zombie! Aaaaand cut!

So that's a huge part of your job, using your imagination to bring all that stuff to life despite your meager surroundings. The other part of your job is more technical, and coincides with all the stuff we said about professionalism: be prepared, warm up, pay attention, take direction, stay safe, ask questions when you need to, remember it's not all about you, and have fun.

PROPS, PROJECTION, AND PARTICIPATION

Much like the sets on a PCap stage, the props there leave much to the imagination. Props may even be so different from their imaginary counterpart as to be distracting. For example, a smartphone may be represented by a block of wood much bigger than your actual phone, with reflective markers stuck to it to help the computers working with the data recognize it as a phone. Take a minute to get used to holding it so that it doesn't throw you in the scene.

Other times you may be re-holstering a gun or re-sheathing a knife, for example, and will have to avail yourself of the "magic pocket" because you'll have the prop, but your suit won't have the place to put it. You'll either pretend to put it in a holster and let it fall to the floor, or a kind crew member will surreptitiously take it from you. Because the crew member is not wearing all the gear you're wearing, it'll be like that person is invisible to the computer.

On one of Tara's first PCap gigs, she had to grab a gun from the back of her pants halfway through a scene, but there was no place to tuck it! So there was an unmarkered crew member standing in place in the middle of the set, holding the prop gun; when Tara crouched down, the crew member pressed the prop gun into her back, and she reached back and drew it as if it had been on her the whole time.

Have we ruined the magic for you yet? Hopefully not. In fact – if you'll allow us – there's a comparison to be made to traditional Japanese *Bunraku* puppet theatre, where the puppet is controlled, in part, by masked puppeteers clothed entirely in black: the *kurogo*. The presence of the kurogo is evident at the beginning, but our brains begin to tune them out as the performance goes on, fading them into the background where they become, for all intents and purposes, invisible.

Projection is something else that can trip you up if you're not familiar with working on a soundstage. You're standing in what is, frankly, a cavernous room, and the production team might be sitting behind screens that are pretty far away. The natural inclination – especially if you come from the theatre – is to PROJECT (as much with your face as your voice) so that those in the cheap seats can hear and see your genius. But remember, you've got a bunch of cameras on you, and likely more than one microphone picking up every little thing you do and say. So give yourself the freedom to *not* project, and instead make the scene as intimate and personal as is called for. Unless, of course, it's a battle scene: then cut loose and feel free to yell and scream (safely) as needed.

Most importantly though, remember to always really go for it. Never worry about looking stupid or feeling self-conscious. We've been over this, right? You already look ridiculous in that suit: let's move on. Everyone on the stage (and some beyond) is in the same boat – working to make the project come to life in the best way possible. So the more you're willing to participate and play, the easier everyone else's job is. Your director and members of the tech team will let you know if what you are doing isn't working. Remember you were cast for a reason, so trust your instincts and have fun!

"THERE IS NO JEEP"

Motion capture (or performance capture as it is sometimes called when it tends to include facial capture and audio as well) is, I believe, the most *freeing* form of acting. Legendary director Gordon Hunt would relate the MoCap stage to a giant sandbox – where we as performers have the opportunity to become children again and truly PLAY. It's true with all acting, but this medium particularly *depends* on the performer's imagination. The more you allow yourself to let the drab-colored walls and cage of cameras on the soundstage dissolve and make way for a Dwarven tomb, say, and actually *see* in your mind's eye that cave troll crashing toward you with a giant spiked club, and *hear* it filling the space with its roar striking fear into the hearts of you and your companions, not only will you have the best damn time being a kid again, but your performance will be the most genuine and fulfilling – not just for the project, but for yourself.

I have been fortunate enough over the years to work both behind the MoCap cameras as a crew member and in front of them in a marked-up suit as an actor. This unique journey has taught me so much, but this is the main thing I'd want to share: be your lovely, professional self. Show up early, off book and ready to adapt to possible script and scene changes. Be kind to everyone on the stage: with any luck (and your work ethic appreciated) you will see them again. The person getting your tea for your tired throat may be an actor as well – and they just might be learning from your example!

There's a fun story that has gone around for years involving Gordon Hunt while shooting the very first *Uncharted* game with creator and co-director Amy Hennig. After finishing a scene using a real-life 4x4 Jeep that they drove unto the stage, Gordon called to have the Jeep struck (i.e. removed) from the volume (the soundstage) so they could move on to the next scene. "It's all right Gordon!" he was told. "We can just tuck it in the corner and start shooting the next shot!" Gordon, perplexed, responded with something like, "But it's in the volume! It's in the scene! We need to strike it so we can move on!" The response he got was, "But it doesn't exist Gordon. Not in the digital scene. The MoCap cameras can't see it. There is no Jeep." From then on Gordon got a complete grasp as to the amount of freedom his performers could have with their work. If a prop or piece of furniture or vehicle that is physically in the volume for the actors to use does not have markers on it to reflect data back to all the cameras on stage, then it is invisible to the computers. Gordon (and any director) can be right there on the stage as close to the performance as he feels he needs to be. "There is no Jeep" has become a helpful, wonderful mantra for Amy over the years...and they are words I tend to remember while on the stage whether as an actor or as a Key Set Production Assistant.

So remember when the stage crew needs to build up or tear down the block sets and vehicles that represent the world your character is living in (we build the Jeeps now out of heavy duty boxes and a steering wheel) – they don't exist. It's your job – with the help of the director, writer, and animators – to help make that world exist and feel as real as possible for the audience. And it is so much damn fun.

~ Walter Gray IV, Actor

THE MOCAP TEAM

We've talked about how empty the inside of a PCap stage is compared to a motion picture soundstage, but there's always a trade-off. You see, on a movie soundstage you may have about one to three cameras capturing the action; but to record all the data required to tell the story in a video game, a *bunch* of cameras are needed to capture everything you do from a bunch of different angles. In fact, for a game we're currently working on (see how afraid we are to say what it is, even though by the time this book comes out, it probably will have hit the street months, if not years ago? NDAs, man...), the studio is ringed by a large number of specialized cameras to capture data, in addition to three traditional video cameras set up to record reference footage of the actors.

Suffice it to say that, even though so much is left to the imagination, there's a lot going on. And a lot of people in charge of that stuff that's going on. It can be a tad unsettling to walk onto a stage and see all those people hard at work, and have no idea what they're up to. Let's start by identifying some of the team members you're probably familiar with at this point, and work our way to the rest.

The Director

Much like in any acting scenario, you will find yourself working with a *director* who has been hired by the production team to oversee the performance of the actor(s). The director will give you insight into the project that you may not be aware of, and will act as liaison between the development team (sometimes "dev team") and the actors, to make sure they're getting the performance they need.

For video games, you may have *several* directors present on the stage: a performance director (in charge of directing the actor), a cinematics director (in charge of directing the non-playable story scenes in the game), an animation director (in charge of animating a given scene), an audio director (in charge of overseeing the audio), and a project director (in charge of making sure the overall game is as good as it can be). While you should make it a point to become familiar with all these people, it is generally only the performance director you should take your cues from. If things are going as they should, any of the other directors would give their thoughts to the performance director to relay to you. It doesn't *always* work that way (so don't tell a project director to shut up and tell it to the performance director), but it usually runs smoothest when it does.

The Producer

There may be more than one *producer* on set, and/or the *project director* may serve in this capacity. However the team is set up, the producer will oversee the entire project and will have a serious investment in making sure that things happen in a timely and safe manner, leading to the highest quality project possible.

The Writer

The *writer* of the game or project will often be on set during performance capture days to help handle whatever changes may come up. As we mentioned, once the team tries to take an idea from the printed page and convert it into the reality of a performance, adjustments often need to be made. The writer will approve or suggest changes, and is extremely helpful in providing context to the actor when the rest of the team loses track of where they may be in the story. Sometimes different writers cycle in, depending on what part of the project you're working on.

The Audio Engineer

Cleanly capturing every sound you make is the purpose of the key figure known as the *audio engineer*. This person will record all dialogue during takes (and sometimes in between, so be aware, catty actors…) and will ensure that everything sounds as good as possible. Even with the best sound engineer, though, things can happen during a take that make it unusable (I'm talking to you, Velcro.). Don't let it cramp your style, though. The engineer (and probably audio director as well) will be listening and will let the team know if a certain take needs to be re-recorded wild at the end of the day, or picked up in studio at a later date. Pickups are just part of the game of making games!

The Makeup Team

Performance capture may well be the only "voice-over" job where you need to worry about your makeup! But unlike beauty makeup (save that for your red carpet photos at the BAFTAs), you may be covered with tiny dots along key facial muscles so that every grimace and smirk is captured perfectly for your character's reactions. If you're working more than one day on a project, a *makeup artist* may take reference photos of your makeup set so that they can accurately replicate them next time you come in.

The Camera Team

The HMC (*head mounted camera*) *team* will be responsible for setting up and keeping an eye on the camera that will be attached to your head, capturing your facial expressions. The camera uses a fisheye lens to capture your whole face, so don't be dismayed when you see your image in the monitor. Again, *everyone* looks ridiculous from the head cam's POV. And because the camera is fixed to a lightweight helmet you're wearing, when you move your head, your face stays in the center and the world moves around behind you, so don't get disoriented.

Usually, there will also be a *reference camera team* present for traditional scene coverage, with more conventional video cameras to cover the movement in the scene. Some of the cameras may move to follow the action during a take, while some may stay locked off. Don't worry about playing to a camera unless specifically directed to do so. The camera team has your back. Or your front. Actually, both.

The Stage Team

The talented crew of folks known as the MoCap *stage team* is employed by the soundstage as opposed to being employed by a specific game company; they work on whatever title is currently shooting. They have a familiarity with the stage, and are in charge of things like building the sets from scene to scene, providing props, getting you in and out of your suit, making sure you're correctly markered and captured throughout the day. They may even be the ones who hire the audio, makeup, and camera team, and could be involved in casting and payroll as well. Getting started in the morning, these are the first people you see. Treat them well. They're just as important as anyone else on stage, and you'll be spending a lot of time with them.

The first step (hopefully after a delicious breakfast: don't eat TOO much) will be to get you suited up. This can involve some poking and prodding and yanking as they apply markers. The team will be as respectful as possible, but do let them know if you're particularly sensitive to the touchy-feelies around the waist and hips, especially since they may have to readjust you throughout the day. They'll take great pains to make sure you're comfortable. Once they've got you in your suit and markered up, they'll take you through a process called *romming* (in this case, ROM stands *not* for the common "read only memory" or less common "Rom the Spaceknight," but for "range of motion"). Being rommed entails moving through a specific sequence of motions, kind of like a dance routine (turn your head left and right, stick your arms out in front of you, reach to the left/right, squat down, etc...), with the camera capturing your information as you go. Think of it like a personalized full-body calibration for the computer.

Now, when you're working on the stage that day, the computer will be able to recognize you and keep you separated from any of the other actors on stage. You'll do a rom routine at the beginning of the day, and sometimes after lunch, just in case your markers shifted while you were on break. A cool aspect of this is that, once you've been rommed, you'll be able to watch your character in real time moving around the computer-rendered sets and even see your character in costume! It never seems to get old, watching your character move in time to your movements, and it usually leads to dancing (and lewd gestures…).

I guess what we're trying to say is that there will be *a lot* of people on a set like this, ensuring that everything you – and the stunt performers – do is perfectly captured. Wait! Did we say stunts? Why, yes, we did!

STUNTS

As you've likely noticed, video games get more exciting with each passing day. Producers are always looking for great actors to bring those exciting and highly cinematic scenes to life. Often, however, the best actor for the role might not have the exact physicality for the character, or the skills that are needed to fully flesh out the character and the action. That's where a stunt performer comes in. Sometimes an actor may do certain stunts, if they're simple and safe. And some actors may even get movement training to appear more believable as, say, a soldier, or a creature. But having the actors do their own stunts can be time consuming and sometimes dangerous, so it ends up being easier, faster, cheaper, and safer to bring in a specialist: the stunt performer. In addition to stunt training, stunt performers often bring combat, martial arts, dance, creature movement, and acrobatic abilities that are going to make the characters look so much better than the actors could do on their own.

Yuri has been working on the *[UNNAMED MARVEL SU-PERHERO] PS4* game for [UNNAMED DEVELOPER] (and may still be working on it when this book comes out), and as much as he keeps in shape and *wishes* he were [UNNAMED MARVEL SUPERHERO], let's just say he's more [UNNAMED NERDY ALIAS OF MARVEL SUPERHERO]. But there was a stunt performer named Ross Kohnstam (and other talented stunties when Ross was too busy filming *Deadpool...*) whose extraordinary tricking abilities came in handy when doubling Yuri for all the web-slinging...uh...that is, all the [MARVEL SUPERHERO SIGNATURE MOVE], kicking, and backflipping. Working in tandem, the two were able to bring the character to life in a way that created seamless gameplay and storytelling. As a result, the game features such a believable character that the whole team was happy – with the happiest of course being Yuri because Ross made him look SO cool.

This is how it *should* work. But it's possible that you may be asked to perform an action that could make you feel physically uncomfortable or unsafe. In that case, you should ALWAYS tell the director. This is not a place for pride or the time to be a hero (other than the one you may actually be playing). No one wants you to get hurt. That would slow things down and create paperwork no one wants to do.

GO FOR IT!

The cool thing about motion capture (wearing those spandex suits with the silver balls at all the joints) is that the world is almost entirely in your imagination. You are in a huge empty space with a box for your desk, spaceship, car, or whatever the virtual set is. You move and act in your mind. Sometimes we capture the motion before the voice-over. But usually the voice-over is captured first. Have you ever watched someone lip syncing to a song? Like perfectly in sync with the beats and pauses? Head motions and gestures? So flawlessly that you forget for a moment they aren't the ones actually singing? That's what we do a lot of the time with motion capture in video games.

Those of us who are stunt performers are given the scene. We are given our blocking. And then they play the track of the voice-over, already recorded by the VO actors. With all this information, we act out the scene, beats, fights, blocking, and all. This is where fantastic, nuanced voice acting is a gift. Each hitch or hesitation by the actor, we can play with in our motions. Each change in direction of emotion and each heart-felt beat we can hear and enhance with our movements. And with the voice, the movement, and the animation, all three artists create one beautiful performance. Like Voltron, we combine the unique skills we have into something so much greater than ourselves.

There was one time we were working on a game and the main character of the game was voiced by a famous actor. However, this actor didn't know the specific skills needed for VO acting, and while he was fantastic on camera, his VO performance came off flat and uninteresting. The challenge we faced was how to make this work for the motion capture and the game. Does the motion capture actor match the VO performance and risk a flat overall performance in a medium that now demands quality performance? OR does he physically show what the VO performance was lacking? If he chose the second option, would this enhance the performance, bringing it up to where it needed to be? Or would it come off incongruous and false? The team opted for the second option and the game turned out wonderfully. Once again showing how, at each level, if we support each other's talents, we provide the best possible outcome!

~ AMERICA YOUNG, ACTRESS, STUNT PERFORMER

ACTING NATURAL UNDER
UNNATURAL CIRCUMSTANCES

As you can tell, the work of performance capture is not always an easy thing to wrap your head around. Our good friend and PCap director, Jamie Mortellaro has always described it best, and so we'll let him describe it here:

"I don't think there is a more creative space in any medium than motion capture. In one day I had an actor perform as a dominatrix, a 300-pound sumo wrestler-bodyguard, and a 65-year-old blind man. How interesting it is for a director to watch an actor evolve into these unique characters in one space in one day. This amazing creative space captures an actor's performance in 360°: they are not confined by camera, lighting, or an audience. Just pure freedom. This incredible freedom gives me, as director, the opportunity to work out scenes quickly, without the restrictions of a live-action shoot, but with all the details and nuances of a feature film.

All this is done in the bleakest setting: a solid white room. I always say motion capture is the most natural performance an actor will ever give in the most unnatural environment."

Thanks, Jamie. We couldn't have put it better ourselves. Obviously!

LIGHTS, CAMERA, ACTION

You've studied your script, you got to the stage on time (i.e. early), the MoCap team has gotten you suited up, markered up, made up, rommed in, and maybe even attached a camera to your head. What's next? Well, honestly, probably some waiting around as all the technical details are worked out. Then you will likely rehearse the scene a few times, depending on how complicated the action is.

During this preparation time, you'll be shown what's known as a neutral pose to be used at the beginning and end of the scene. It may be called a "T-Pose" or "A-Pose" or "Z-Pose" depending on which studio you're working with. Each pose looks more or less like its name (T or A or Z) as shown in the illustrations below:

T-Pose

A-Pose   **Z-Pose**

Think of these poses as "bookends" for the data that is captured for the performer. They let the computer know you're starting or ending a scene. Make sure you're not standing directly next to a piece of scenery or another actor, as that can confuse the computer.

When everything's ready, you'll hear someone call, "Picture's up!" and it's go time. Here's generally how it will play out:

- Someone will call "Places!" – your cue to head to the place where you'll be starting the scene.
- There will be a call for "T-Pose" (or A-Pose or Z-Pose) – the signal for all the actors on stage to hold the same neutral start pose (which you should keep holding through the following several callouts).
- "Roll Sound!" – alerts the audio team to begin recording

sound; they will respond with the affirmative, "Sound speeds!" or "Sound speeding!"

- "Roll Cameras!" – is sometimes met with several separate responses because of the different cameras in play: "Face Speed!" or "MoCap Rolling!"
- Someone calls out a scene and take number (ex. "Scene 21A, Take 3!") – identifying the scene and take for later editing.
- "Mark!" – cues someone to loudly clack a slate with the scene and take numbers written on it; the sound and visual together give audio and camera a shared reference point which will help the editors later.
- "First positions!" – signals the actors to drop their T-, A-, or Z-Pose and take their starting positions. You'll always have time to get from your start pose to exactly where you'll need to be to start the scene.
- "Aaaaand... ACTION!" – prompts the team to start the scene. This is when you relax and do your thing: that thing you're so good at that they hired you to come and do it for money. And after you're done, stay in your final position until you hear...
- "Cut!" – indicates that filming of the scene is finished. But, remember, you're not done yet!
- Someone will probably call, "Z-Pose!" (or A-Pose or T-Pose) – signals you to get back into your neutral starting and ending pose. This will let the computer know that you're done with the scene.
- "Clear!" – is said when everything is complete with this take. NOW you can relax. At least until they ask for another take of this scene, or you hear someone say, "Moving on!" which means they're happy with what they got, and they're moving on to the next scene.

You did it! You survived your first scene on a PCap stage. And hopefully had a little fun at the same time. Or a lot.

SCRATCH TRACKS   **WITH TARA & YURI**

CHAPTER 9
YOUR HOME BOOTH

"There is no fate but what we make for ourselves."

JOHN CONNOR, FUTURE FREEDOM FIGHTER

Thanks to modern technology (see *The Internet* or *Flying Cars*) you can actually set up a recording studio in your *own home*. You can do it cheap or you can do it pricey, but the power, these days, is in the hands of the people. *Psst*: that's you.

"HOW DO I SET UP MY OWN STUDIO? WHAT DO I NEED?"

There are probably a million different ways you could set up your home studio, but no matter how you do it, you'll need at least four things:

1. a computer (or a tablet, or even a smartphone!)

2. a microphone

3. computer software (or an app) for audio recording

4. somewhere to record

Odds are that you've got a computer or a tablet, or a smartphone. Perfect. One down, three to go.

Your easiest choice for a microphone is to go with something called a USB mic. You can order one on line, or you can ask for one at your local musician supply store. This mic will plug into the USB port on your computer (most computers sold in the last 25 years or so will surely have at least one USB port). If you're using a tablet, or smartphone, there are mics that plug directly into those, as well.

Next, you need a computer program that interfaces the mic with the computer, allowing the sound going into the mic to be recorded digitally. Sometimes this program (or software) comes with your USB mic. Sometimes you already have software like this (such as Apple's *Garage Band*) installed on your computer.

If not, you can download free programs/apps or *shareware* that will allow you to record sounds to digital files, which you can then manipulate (edit, make louder or softer, add effects). Here's a quick overview of recording software ranging from free to cheap. (Thanks to our audio guru Juan for the wisdom!)

Free

Garage Band (Mac only) is included with OSX (but even if you have to pick it up as part of iLife, it'll run you less than $50). It's easy to use, and many people are using it these days for semi-pro production. Drawbacks: setup can be confusing with some audio interfaces.

Audacity (Mac, PC, Linux) is the reigning champion of freeware audio recording software. It's compatible with all major computing platforms (even older systems) and offers an incredible collection of editing tools. Drawbacks: no true multi-tracking (recording of sounds on separate tracks for later combination), and, well ... it's not the prettiest program.

WavePad (Mac & PC) is super simple and super basic, offers single-track editing only, but it's a fast way to get in, record, trim, and export a piece of audio. It's also the lightest on computer resources, making it a perfect fit for older systems.

Twisted Wave (iPad/iPhone: iOS only) is intuitive, easy to master, and allows you to export to different formats and send your audio files from your device.

Retail

Sound Forge Pro (PC) is still one of the most comprehensive audio editing suites around. It includes multi-track recording, but it's designed for editing *one* piece of audio. Drawbacks: heavy on resources, so make sure your computer meets (preferably exceeds) Sony's system requirements for a smooth experience. It's also a little pricey for a single-track editor these days.

Pro Tools (Mac & PC) is an industry standard for a reason. If you do studio work, chances are you've encountered it. It's incredibly flexible, and is used for a variety of production environments. Drawbacks: it can be a little overwhelming for beginners, and must be used in conjunction with a USB device called an iLok, which means cost of entry is higher than many other solutions.

Honorable mentions

Reaper, Adobe Audition/Soundbooth, Logic, Sonar, GoldWave, Traverso, Acid, and *Ardour.*

Depending on how complicated you want your system, you can get interfaces like mixers and compressors in addition to the mic and the computer, but we're going to stay simple for the purposes of this book. If you want to be an audio engineer, that's a different book (one not written by us).

So you've got your equipment and your software, and you've followed the directions that came either in the box or off the Internet, and you're ready to get set up. Great. What else do you need to know? Well, even the best equipment and the best software won't help you if you don't create an environment in which you minimize external sounds. You know, like the cat, cars driving by outside, your next door neighbor who likes to sing opera at odd hours … This may seem like an afterthought, but is, arguably, the most important part of the process. You don't need a powerful, expensive computer; you don't need an expensive mic (under certain circumstances the mic in your phone may work great); and you can get by just fine with free recording/editing software. But if you don't create a space that's sonically conducive to recording, it doesn't matter what fancy equipment you've got.

We've achieved some of our best results in the closet. Wait a minute. That doesn't sound right. Oh, well, it's true. Got a nice walk-in closet with clothes hanging in it? Perfect. That means you won't need to put expensive acoustic foam on the walls to keep the sounds from echoing around and reducing the quality of your recording. Don't have any extra room in your closet? Find the quietest room in your house/apartment and experiment with furniture, towels, packing blankets, pillows, and other objects that might help reduce the echo in the room. Speaking into a couch or a u-formation of fluffy pillows sometimes sounds great! Test a few setups where you live until you find something that works for you (and is easy to arrange).

See how easy that was? You're ready to roll.

MIC SAYS: Empty egg cartons and moving blankets can tame echoes on the cheap.

"SO WHAT'S *YOUR* HOME BOOTH LIKE?"

Good question. We recently, after many years, decided to upgrade to a more "professional" setup and ordered a stand-alone booth; but, honestly, for over a decade we had done very well by ourselves in a very simple home booth, aka a coat closet. We took all the shelves out of a hall closet and covered the walls in acoustic foam (some scavenged, some bought). We had a decent Audio-Technica mic on a mic stand with a Popper Stopper. The mic was connected by a cable to an interface called an Mbox which was connected by a USB cable to our computer (an Apple iBook laptop). The Mbox allowed us to adjust levels and listen to the recording through headphones.

We would use a program called Pro Tools LE (which comes with the Mbox) to do the actual recording and editing on our computer. With the same software, we could convert a recorded audition to MP3 format (a common digital audio format that takes up little space), attach that file to an email, and easily send it off to an agent or a prospective client. Total cost of our original booth (minus the computer, which we already had)? About $700.

By reinvesting some of our hard-earned VO money, we finally paid for an upgrade: a fancy new booth from Studiobricks, a new Mac Book Pro, the latest version of Pro Tools, an Apogee Duet 2 interface, and a Sennheiser 416 that Yuri uses for promo work. And guess what! *The closet sounded better.*

We had made the assumption that by buying all this fancy new stuff, it HAD to sound better. But it didn't. It took a lot of trial and error and calling in experts to figure out how to "tune" our new space. We learned that not every device plays well with your computer, and not every mic is perfect for the space you've created (or bought). We're happy we finally came out of the closet, but it wasn't easy. There were months of crying and gnashing of teeth until we finally got it sorted. Or as a wise person once said: "Mo' money, mo' problems."

So keep it simple to start, and don't beat yourself up about it. We know people who have spent thousands of dollars putting their home booth together and people who have spent under $100, and all of them are working voice actors.

SETTING UP A HOME BOOTH: MAN IF I HAD A NICKEL ...

See, how to create a home recording booth is a tricky question because there is no *one* magic setup. Different voices, in different rooms, with a near infinite number of gear combinations, is enough to make even the most seasoned engineer's head spin. I like to think about home recording in three general tiers: practice, auditioning, and session-grade.

Practice is easy. You likely have a phone or computer that can record your voice, and you can easily find some rudimentary tools for editing. Practice should be free.

Auditioning is when we need to start spending money. Your main objective is to capture an accurate sample of your voice, free of any distracting elements or noise, as efficiently as possible. This tier should *not* hit the wallet too hard, and as much as you consider microphones, you should also start thinking about sound treatments on your walls.

Lastly, session-grade is just that: a pro-level studio, necessary for the talent because of work commitments. You're working so much, you *need* to have a production-ready facility in your home.

Generally, my advice for most folks is threefold.

1. Set a budget!
Set a dollar amount you *refuse* to go over, then *hold to it*! This stuff

gets expensive *fast* (especially if you're a collector like me). This should *not* be a *max out the credit cards* budget either, but something comfortable. Some of my favorite recordings have been done on less than $250 worth of gear (minus computer of course).

2. Know your limits!

My first coaching gig had nothing to do with performance, but was with a fantastic VO actress in tears after spending thousands getting all the *right* session-grade gear: nice mic, compressor, mixer, interface, preamp. She now had a mess of knobs and cables that she was not prepared to deal with. She was very upset over not being *smart enough* to handle her own equipment. This obviously wasn't really the case. She just bit off more than she could chew for her first home setup.

I let her borrow one of my USB mics, showed her how to do some basic recording, and she booked her first gig from home a week later. All she needed was equipment for her home auditions.

3. Give it time!

And I don't mean time sitting around collecting dust, I mean time using this gear *every day*! Just because setting up a USB mic is easy (uh ... plug it in?), that doesn't mean you will know how to record competitive auditions. Don't start sending out audio right away. Practice with it *a lot* first. After you're feeling pretty comfy, once you can set up, record, edit, and send without having to think out each step, *then* send some samples out to qualified individuals for some feedback (preferably us engineers, but agents and other VO talent can help too).

You won't need to get a degree in audio production, but you *will* need to learn a little about how recording works: a *very* little, as most recording programs now use commands similar to word processors (drag to select, cut, copy, paste, make font/volume bigger or smaller, etc).

Who knows? You might just find you like your time behind the mixer as much as your time behind the mic ...

~ JUAN C. BAGNELL, DIRECTOR, AUDIO ENGINEER

GOING REMOTE

Remote recording is very likely nothing you'll have to concern yourself with when just starting out, and we'll cover it in a little more detail in the next chapter (Chapter 10, *Home Away From Home: Recording Remotely*). But we wanted to address it for a moment to make you aware of what to expect as your career takes off.

You've got your home booth set up. In that booth you book an amazing promo job for which you'll need to be ready at a moment's notice to record promos for a hit TV show. There's no time to get to a studio when the call to record comes in. You're going to have to run the real-time session from home, which means being able to listen to direction from the client and send high quality audio files instantaneously as you record them.

The simplest method for doing this is to have the client on the phone or Skype while you record; but this entails recording to your computer and then sending the files to the client after you're done. In the meantime, there's no way for the client to monitor the actual recording to make sure it's how they need it. This means you have to be a good engineer, too, so you can tweak the recording if necessary.

But many clients will want that audio as you're recording it, and no later. For a long time, the only way to do that was to install in your house an expensive ISDN (Integrated Services Digital Network – a fancy way of saying a dedicated line to simultaneously transmit voice, video, and data). An ISDN also comes with a monthly subscription fee. This technology is on its way out, but is still used by many voice actors.

ISDN is now being replaced by other methods that use the Internet to transmit data. Solutions like SourceConnect and ipDTL (Internet Protocol Down the Line) have become more and more popular for their cost efficiency. But you'll still want a fast Internet connection to use them effectively, and they can still come with a hefty monthly fee: so don't get 'em if you don't need 'em. We didn't have this technology until recently when Yuri booked a promo gig and we started using ipDTL which creates a simulated ISDN line or "ISDN bridge."

But, again, technology changes fast (see next section), and you'll figure out all this stuff if/when you need it. Until then, put it out of your mind.

CHANGING TECHNOLOGY AND THE FUTURE OF VO

Since technology changes at the speed of … technology, it's important to remember that even as you're reading this now, somewhere, someone is developing something to make things run faster, better, and cheaper. A good bit of advice, whatever your career, is do your homework and research technology related to your industry (in this case, VO).

If you need to buy a microphone, for example, jump on the Internet or drive down to your local audio equipment store and ask around. Check out what has just come on the market and see if it has the capabilities that you need to do what you want. Sometimes it's better to go with a time-tested device that's already had all the bugs worked out, while other times it can be fun to be the first kid on your block with a new toy. Either way, do your research. In today's world, with information so readily available, there's no excuse to do otherwise.

Is it time for you to build the perfect home studio now? Well, the beauty of it all is that you can start small and upgrade at your own pace. If you're just starting out and basically messing around to get used to recording VO, don't spend a lot of money. Get a cheap mic, plug it into your computer, tablet, or phone, and away you go!

Then maybe you'll get to a point where you want to be recording auditions and sending them out. Make sure you've created a space conducive to recording. Maybe get a better mic and down-load some free sound-editing software. Wanna start recording your own projects and really get into some serious editing? Invest in a really good mic and buy the equipment that you need.

Think about it: just a few years ago, almost no one had a home recording studio. Equipment was too expensive, and what could you really achieve at home anyway? Then suddenly, as things started moving more quickly in the industry (thanks in part to the Internet), actors realized they could get a jump on things by recording themselves at home and sending their auditions di-rectly to the people who were in charge of hiring. Computers became cheaper and so did audio equipment.

Now, most of the VAs we know have home studios, or at least professional recording equipment of a certain caliber and a space to record good clean sound. And the market follows suit. At least one of Los Angeles's largest voice-over agencies now insists that its talent record all their auditions from home rather than coming into the agency to record them.

Of course, some argue that, with technology advancing as fast as it is, soon there may be hardly any need for live voice-over ac-tors. Look at how skillfully computer generated imaging (CGI) is replicating the human form in films today, for example.

We choose to believe differently, preferring the argument that there will always be some things that humans will do better than computers, and that voice acting is one of those things. That is an-other reason your skill as an actor will serve you in this business, regardless of changes in the technology itself.

We wrote the previous paragraphs a decade ago, and we still stand by the words. Do your work as an actor and let the tech-nology take care of itself. Even where we are with creating CG characters, it's still cheaper and faster to record real human be-ings than it is to program/animate them from scratch. And while publishers may never listen to the argument that real actors are "better," they definitely do understand "cheaper" and "faster." So jump into the *uncanny valley* and get to work. You'll be fine until the *singularity* arrives; and if that happens after this book comes out, then *all hail our benevolent robot overlords!*

CHAPTER 10

HOME AWAY FROM HOME: RECORDING REMOTELY

*"The secret of success in life is for a man to be
ready for his opportunity when it comes."*

BENJAMIN DISRAELI, BRITISH STATESMAN, NOVELIST

L et's face it, as much fun as this work is, you can't spend all your time sitting at home auditioning and waiting for those bookings to roll in. You have to just live your life, and that means doing other stuff, getting out of your house, and traveling. And sometimes, you may even have a VO job, a good one, but it requires you to be sort of on call, always ready to record with very little notice: the "golden handcuffs" job. But that doesn't mean you need to live your life worrying, or that you can't be ready to seize opportunities when they come in. There are salves for your worry, and we're going to talk about them here.

YOUR TRAVEL RIG

Who says you can't take it with you? Technology has sufficiently advanced to the point that we may not yet have PCap suits that make going to the bathroom easy, but we definitely have ways for you to travel with your studio. These methods can be as simple as talking into your phone, or as complicated as your needing a little suitcase to carry your rig in. But we've opted for the old KISS adage: Keep It Simple…Silly.

If you're just starting your VO career, having a travel rig may be less essential than later on. However, it's definitely worth thinking about because you never know when the work will start to pick up, you'll book a cherry gig with an unpredictable schedule, or a client will want you to be able to record no matter where you are.

We have both recorded jobs and auditions in such glamorous places as hotel room closets, deep inside a blanket tent, Tara's old bedroom in her parents' house, and even inside parked cars during breaks in filming on location. Once, Yuri even threw a coat over his head in an airport terminal to record pickups that the client needed right away for a job he had done. You may be required to get very creative, but you're an actor, and using your imagination is squarely in your wheelhouse.

So what do you need to remember to assemble your travel rig? The same things we talked about when putting together your home booth: computer, mic, software, location. Only here, we're balancing that stuff with *portability*.

You may be tempted to buy a used microphone, but *caveat emptor!* Mics are very sensitive instruments that don't show their wear and tear. Only buy if you can verify that the mic is in good condition.

So how much stuff are we talking about? And how exactly do you determine your recording needs? Let's break it down:

Your Computer

You want to start with the smallest computer you can get away with. Laptops are perfectly fine, but you may want to consider a tablet or even a phone, depending on your recording needs. Will you need to establish an ISDN bridge with a client? Bring a laptop. And make sure you've got everything you'll need to connect to the Internet.

You'll need to be able to send your files or run your session whether you're using an Ethernet cable plugged directly into a modem or have access to Wi-Fi; or if your Wi-Fi accessibility is dicey, then you'll need your own portable Wi-Fi signal generator or hub. (Many smartphones function as a hot spot which will allow you to connect to the Internet, but be sure you'll be in network and that you have enough data on your plan!)

Will you be recording just auditions? You may need only your phone, or at most a tablet. Again, jump back, KISS yourself. Let your needs determine if it's necessary for you to lug that laptop around.

Your Mic

How to choose your mic? Well, you may need only a small travel mic like the ones mentioned in the previous chapter. See if you can test some mics under various conditions. Every mic plays differently in different spaces. Run a test in your car, in a closet, in a pillow fort. If you're working with a client who is used to a certain mic, you'll have to travel with that one so your recordings match what you've done before. If that mic is not available, the audio engineer may be able to manipulate your recording in post production and make your recording sound more like it sounds on another mic, but you want to endeavor to be the actor who makes the job easier, not harder – for everyone.

Your Interface

If you're not using a USB mic or other mic that plugs directly into your device (laptop/tablet/phone), you will also need some sort of interface (sometimes *preamp*) that allows the mic and your recording device to connect and talk to each other. For example, you may be using a mic like the one we use for work when we travel. It has only XLR output (3 pins: most studio mics have this). There are several interfaces, and most of them look about the same: a short cigar-shaped device into which you plug the mic at one end, and then plug the cable attached to the other end into the USB port in your laptop. You may also want to have handy a short length of XLR cable to give yourself a little slack between the interface and the mic. It'll allow you to move around more.

The interface device generally will have a headphone input, volume control, mic level control, and 48v phantom power for your mic if need be. We use a CEntrance MicPort Pro, but we know people who like the Shure X2U. There are others, but these two consistently rank among the best.

Your Software

Regarding software, go with what you're comfortable working with that makes editing easy, allows you to export different formats of audio files (mp3, wav, aiff), and in the case of apps you may be using on your phone or tablet, even allows you to send the file without leaving the application. If you're using a laptop, this becomes less important because you can always save the audio file to your hard drive and then rely on whatever system you normally use (email attachment, file transfer service, or ftp) to send the file. And be sure to test the software in a non-critical situation to make sure all your settings are where you like them, and that your computer is playing nicely with your mic.

If you need to run a session with a client in real time, you should consider subscribing to a service that will allow you to establish either an ISDN bridge or a similar simultaneous data transfer such as the more popular ipDTL or SourceConnect mentioned in the last chapter. Again, a fast and trustworthy Internet connection is essential. Make sure you have a reliable connection, and be sure to test this process before you really need to run a session for real. Any new setup takes getting used to, and almost never works exactly right the first time.

Your Space

Last, but just as important, practice throwing together a suitable place to record. Think of the kinds of places you might be when you have to record. The aforementioned hotel room and parked car are good examples. Do a dry run in your bedroom. Under your comforter, into some couch pillows, in a coat closet. Where do you put your mic? Do you hold it? Are you reading scripts off your phone? Can you hold both the mic and the phone/script comfortably? (Our travel rig contains a Dinkum Systems 3013 FlexiMount so we can attach the mic to something and go hands-free; Stage Ninja makes a slightly cheaper version that is similar.) Do you feel most comfortable using headphones? Then make sure you pack them as well.

"GOLDEN HANDCUFFS"

They call promos "the Golden Handcuff." It's good steady work when you can get it, but you are completely on call, and usually can't leave town. Obviously this is changing with wireless technology, but I remember a few years ago, I packed up the family and drove to Utah to visit my brother-in-law and his family.

We had everything planned. We would leave after my promo

gig on Friday and stay the weekend, I would record remotely from the hotel on Monday morning, and then we would start the drive back home. We confirmed the hotel had Internet and were on our way.

When we got there, we got the unfortunate surprise that the hotel did not have its own dedicated Internet, but instead was using a shared wireless ATT hot spot. I did my test connections and it quickly became apparent that my plans to record from the hotel would not work. The speed was horribly insufficient, and I had no control over any of the firewall ports.

Panicking slightly, I looked up studios in Utah. There were 2 with ISDN (a communications network that would make it possible for me to send my voice files to the client). One was booked up, and the other studio's line just rang and rang – not even voicemail.

So after trying for most of the weekend to find another connection option, we ended up packing up the car Sunday evening and driving all night from Utah to California so I could be home in time for my Monday a.m. promo. The Golden Handcuff, indeed.

The silver lining of this experience is that it forced me to find my own mobile connection method. I have since added a mobile hot spot to my travel gear, and it's worked beautifully. The first time I tried that out was on set filming a guest stint on a TV show when I had to sneak away from the set to record, and blamed my need to return to the trailer on some dodgy morning drive-thru. Sometimes the logistics of on-the-road recording are more of an adventure than the job itself!

~ JOSH KEATON, ACTOR

THE LAST RESORT: RENTING A STUDIO

Now that we've given you the lowdown on assembling your travel rig, we want to let you know there's an option that avoids all of that, and that could even save you from building your own home studio: *studio rental*.

Now, obviously, this comes at a cost, and won't be as flexible as having your own recording equipment, but we wanted you to have all the options. And what if you've got your travel rig all packed up, you get to your destination, and suddenly realize you forgot a key piece of it at home? Or the Internet connection where you are isn't strong enough to support your ISDN bridge? Or you just decided not to travel with your rig at all? Or perhaps the thought of setting up your own studio at home makes your eyes cross (though we hope we've shown you that it's easier than you may think)? Well, then you might have to start researching studios.

The benefit of going to a professional studio is that someone else will take care of running and engineering the session. This could be a great option for you if you're just starting out and are trying to limit your investment until you know whether VO is for you, or if you'd just rather entrust the quality of your recording to a professional. The downside is that, over time, it could cost you. Make sure to inquire about rates before you book time with a studio. In locations like Los Angeles where there are plenty of voice actors, some studios may offer special rates for auditions, charging you in 15 minute increments as opposed to by the hour, and you can often get away without paying too much.

We were once both working on a TV show that shoots in Hawaii (not *LOST*, the other one), and Yuri got a call from our agent saying that a client needed him to record the following day. Because we were dubious of the recording quality we might achieve with our travel rig at the hotel, our agent quickly researched local studios and the client booked Yuri (*Book 'em, Danno*) a session that didn't interfere with our shooting schedule. And in that case, we didn't even have to pay for the session: the client picked it up!

So remember, you *can* record just about anywhere, and if you take all of these things into consideration *before* you leave home, you can record remotely with maximum quality and minimum stress. Now get out of the house!

SCRATCH TRACKS   **WITH TARA & YURI**

CHAPTER 11
WHAT TO DO TO GET STARTED

"Everyone who got where he is has had to begin where he was."

ROBERT LOUIS STEVENSON, SCOTTISH NOVELIST

BE PREPARED: THE WAY OF THE BOY SCOUTS

"So what's the next step?" you might be asking yourself. "I'm thirteen, I'm still in school, I live in Wichita Kansas," you say. "I'm an on-camera actor living in Los Angeles who's looking for another source of income where I still get to act." Or, "I'm forty, I'm married, I work eight hours a day in an office."

Have no fear, no matter what your situation, there are things you can do. If you've read this far, then you already have a pretty good idea of what kinds of voice-over jobs are out there, the type of work each entails, and generally how things work and who you're dealing with. So how can you take that information and translate it into a wildly successful career in the voice-over industry?

Well, we've said it before, and we'll lay down the caveat once more for good measure: as with any art or creative industry, the path to success is not a straight one in this business. Nor does it come with a map. You can be phenomenally talented and still have to work hard. You may work hard for a year or for ten years before you feel you've *made it.* In fact, you may work for twenty years, be wildly successful, and *still* feel like you haven't made it. So make sure you're having fun. The only thing you can truly do (besides having fun) to create the best odds of succeeding is to get prepared and stay prepared, so that when the opportunities that you create pop up, you can take full advantage of them.

IMPRESS YOUR VOICE DIRECTOR AND PRODUCERS

Get to know the material before your session. If the script is not sent to you in advance of the session, make sure to have your agent request it. Voice-over sessions are unique in the fact that sessions move quickly and there is rarely time (or budget) for rehearsal. More often than not, there is very little time to work with the director on the nuances of a particular character.

Whether working alone or with a cast, be prepared to bend and shape your character and performance beyond your original instincts. There is always the possibility that the directors/producers will want to "tweak" the performance even if they liked what you did in the audition. Or they may want you to match the character you created in your audition. Producers and directors depend on the VO talent to bring their characters to life. If you can help them achieve this, they will remember you when they are casting their next project.

~ JAMIE SIMONE, STUDIO PRESIDENT

Luck

They say that luck plays a huge part in getting anywhere in this business. *Ya just gotta be at the right place at the right time!* We agree, but we also have a slightly different definition of *luck*. Our friend Merriam – you may know her: *Merriam-Webster* – defines luck as:

> *1 a: a force that brings good fortune or adversity*
> *b: the events or circumstances that operate for*
> *or against an individual*

We don't like that definition because it makes it seem as if we have no control whatsoever over getting what we want: if the mystical force that is luck is feeling *off* that day, we're screwed. The mid-1ˢᵗ century Roman philosopher Seneca said, "Luck is what happens when preparation meets opportunity," and that's how we'd rather look at it.

To take this a step further, instead of *luck*, we prefer to substitute the word *success* in Seneca's definition. We end up with the equation: *success = preparation + opportunity*. This is much better than relying on luck because you can take action to prepare yourself, and you can take action to create opportunities.

We do our best to be prepared and to create our own opportunities, and that's when we've found success happens most often for us. So what they say *is* true: luck plays a bit part. But you can get yourself to the right place, and if it's the right time and you're prepared, then boom!

But imagine what happens if you manage to get to the right place at the right time and you're *not* ready for it: the, uh... opposite of boom.

MIC SAYS:

~~Luck~~ Success = Preparation + Opportunity

READ MUCH?

For some people, reading aloud can be a scary thing. To make it as a voice actor, you'll have to overcome that fear. Take a class in reading comprehension to hone your verbal skills so that you're more comfortable. If you have dyslexia or a medical issue that makes reading difficult, do whatever it takes to increase your confidence when reading.

You could have someone read the copy or script into a recorder and work with it that way, memorizing it as best you can. But this will limit the types of jobs you'll be able to work on since some types of voice-over are so fast-paced, and the script changes so frequently, that often there isn't time to have someone record things for you in advance. We do know an actor who is legally blind, but is still a successful working voice actor because he's figured out a system that works for him. So nothing is impossible. Just examine your strengths and weaknesses, and take steps to exploit and improve them wherever you can.

Here's an exercise you can try while reading out loud: take only a quick look at the following sentence, then look up from the book and try saying it aloud from memory:

Hey there, Bob. I thought I heard you come in. Your coffee and paper are on the table.

Were you able to remember the line? Did you leave out a word? Try it again. How about this time? Better?

You can do this exercise while reading anything. *Pulling the lines off the page* like this is a skill that'll come in quite handy. This is especially true in dubbing, where you have to watch the screen to match the character's lip flaps. But it'll also be helpful when recording pre-lay animation, allowing you to make eye contact with the other actors while you're reading.

MIC SAYS: Read aloud or mimic your radio to get free practice.

START SMALL

We've given you a lot of things to think about, and it can easily become overwhelming deciding what to do first. You don't have to move to Los Angeles, get into a class, and record a demo today. Start with one small thing, and when you feel that you've accomplished that or have comfortably worked it into your routine, add another thing. Nothing'll crush your spirit harder, and paralyze you faster, than thinking you have to do it all at once. Make a list. Pick one action that sounds fun (you'll be more inclined to do it that way), and start there.

You can begin with something as small as warming up your voice in the shower, or reading a news article aloud, or making sure you drink two extra glasses of water that day.

There's a saying: "What you practice every day is what you will become." And what's the best way to stay on target with your practice? Create a routine.

YOUR ROUTINE

Creating a routine helps you actually *do* things. Plan out a time every day or every couple of days for working on something specific, even for just fifteen minutes at a time. In addition to whatever you may choose to work on, there are practice scripts in Chapter 14, *Practice Makes Permanent*, for your study and pleasure. But also see what you can find on your own.

Scour the Internet for scripts and advertising that you can pull, or go through magazines and tear out interesting ads. Put together a book of your own practice copy, and take it out from time to time when you want to exercise your skills. Or better yet, get some friends together and record each other reading, then listen to the playback and talk about what you sound like.

One of the best ways to grow is to take a look at what you're doing and learn from it: what you like about it, what seems to work, and what you can experiment with in the future. Practice dubbing your favorite show (*not for sale or public viewing, of course; we're not endorsing anything illegal here*).

Watch cartoons and mimic the voices you hear. *Come on! How many study plans ask you to watch cartoons? Isn't this great?* Practice doing the work you want to be doing so that your body and mind start to get used to your new skill, and then get better at it. Record yourself and listen to the playback so that you know what other people are hearing when you speak. And *don't be judgmental.*

If you find (or already know) that you have an actual speech impediment, say a lisp for example, don't give up right away. There are two obvious paths open to you:

1. Embrace it. Many people have become famous *because* of their *impediment*. However, know that this will limit you as a voice actor, because you might get cast only as characters for which a lisp works.

2. The better path (in our humble opinion) is to find a speech therapist to help you overcome the impediment. Sometimes this therapy is offered by schools for free. Yuri used to have a lisp when he was younger, but has since corrected it through speech therapy classes that were offered at his school. Eliminating his lisp has definitely opened up the number of roles that he's eligible for.

The same goes for accents. If you have an accent, use it to your advantage whenever possible. But to avoid limiting the types of roles that you'll end up playing, make sure you can also read and speak in whatever dialect rules where you're working.

Let part of your routine include a physical and vocal warm-up. Warming up your body will not only put you into a ready physical state for working, but can ultimately become part of your ritual to prepare yourself for auditions or jobs. To get you started, we have included several warm-ups in Chapter 4, *Before You Get to the Audition*. But whatever you do, create a warm-up routine that works for *you*.

The radio is your friend

Listen to the radio and start mimicking what you hear. Pay attention to the vocal qualities or attitudes of the actors who have been hired to sell products. You'll hear all types, from newscasters to DJs to commercial actors to public service announcers.

Use this free (did we mention *free*?) resource to begin to recognize who's out there and what they're getting hired to sell. We noted earlier that *hot* vocal qualities change with the times. You'll want to stay up to date with what's really going on out there. If everything you are hearing on the radio happens to be *wry* or *matter of fact*, perhaps think about strengthening those qualities in your own repertoire.

The same goes for TV. Watch it. Listen. And learn.

Get your mouth moving

Practice reading aloud because, trust us, you're going to be doing a lot of it. Get your favorite book, magazine, or whatever's lying on the coffee table, and start reading out loud. Just get your mouth accustomed to reading and vocalizing.

Try different types of material (newspaper articles, short stories, children's books, advertisements) so that you get comfortable with any type of VO copy that may come your way. If you're waiting at the bus stop, pick up that pamphlet on the bench next to you and start reading, or take a stab at the poster on the wall next to you. Get your mouth and mind accustomed to reading unfamiliar material and making sense of it on the fly.

CLASSES, CLASSES, CLASSES

Get into a *voice class* (for singing, breath, voice-over, or vocal placement), or an improv or acting class that will get you on your feet working with other actors. Dance, martial arts, gymnastics, parkour, and the like could get you in shape for the PCap stage. Classes will build confidence and help you learn as much as you can about yourself, your body, and your voice. Each of these different classes will, no doubt, have something unique to offer. So make sure you research a class before you commit, to see what you should expect. Get recommendations from people you trust who have taken classes you are interested in. Just putting yourself in a situation in which you get to work on your craft with other like-minded individuals often can lead you to wonderful things. Don't have money for classes? Audition for local theatre and comedy groups. Who knows, it might even end up with *them* paying *you*.

EASY AS 1-2-3

I got into voice-over completely by accident. I didn't take a class until I'd appeared in several episodes of original animated series and done a few recurring/regular roles on anime series, a handful of video games, and more than a few radio commercials. The class I took *should* have been taken at the beginning of my work in VO.

Example: I went in to record a series of radio commercials for a theme park in Salt Lake City, and the engineer said to me, "This take, give me an 'ABC,'" which means to do three different takes of the same line. But I didn't know that.

So, he told me we were rolling and slated me. When he pointed at me to record, I proudly said, without missing a beat: "A, B, C."

A huge laugh came from the control room, the phone-patched producers, and the actors in the booth with me. Ahhh, yes. Another lesson learned ... the *hard* way.

~ HENRY DITTMAN, ACTOR

THAT SHINY, HAPPY THING WE CALL THE DEMO

If you're serious about this whole voice acting thing, one item you'll need eventually is a sample of your voice and your acting: your *demo*. On-camera and theatre actors, to put themselves out there professionally, need a picture and résumé. Voice actors need a demo, which is sometimes also called a *reel*.

Some voice-over classes actually offer demo production as a part of their curriculum, and some classes are even dedicated purely to creating a demo. Remember, this will be your calling card in the beginning, your *first impression* on many of the people who could potentially hire you. As with all first impressions, you want your reel to be as good as it can be. So don't rush to throw together just anything. You don't want your demo to sound cheap or unprofessional.

That means you're going to want to spend a little money on it. The best demos have a variety of sounds and styles on them, but are also succinct and clear, as well as professionally produced and mixed. More on creating your demo in the very next chapter: Chapter 12, *The Demo*.

STAYING PREPARED

We've covered some of the ways you can prepare yourself for work as a voice actor, but how do you *stay* prepared?

Getting prepared involves breaking out of your comfort zone, learning new and exciting things, and strengthening muscles you didn't even know were there. Staying prepared is like keeping your engine revving after all that preparation, so that when the starter's pistol goes off, you're ready to go. Really, what would be the point of spending time, money, and energy on classes, or a demo, or your routine, if you're going to stop making an effort the minute the class, activity, or job is done? We mean, *really*.

Just as an athlete plays practice games in preparation for a competition, or doctors or lawyers attend continuing education classes to stay on top of the latest developments in their field, your job as an actor is do what it takes so that you are always ready for the job or audition around the corner. You hope an opportunity happens soon and comes often, but you never really know when an audition or job is going to pounce. That means you need to stay warmed up so that when it does, you're ready. Get into an acting class that is ongoing; do a play from time to time. Something, anything, that'll keep your creative acting juices flowing.

Stick to the routine you've developed. Continue to do warm-ups just as you did to strengthen and train your voice in the first place. Maybe change up your routine here and there to keep it from getting boring. And interact with others who might be doing the same thing you're doing. Social networking has become invaluable to this profession and has made it much easier for you to access information. Often, your best teachers are the people you encounter in your everyday life.

Make sure you are treating your voice right. If you do find yourself in situations that may be unhealthy for your voice – screaming at a concert, lacking sleep and following that up with a ton of caffeine to compensate, hanging out in smoky clubs – then do things that you know will help get your voice back on track. Hum to get your vocal cords lubricated and warmed up; give yourself a self-imposed vocal rest if you need it. (It is said that actor and comedian John Leguizamo will often maintain long periods of silence while working on challenging vocal performances, simply to keep his vocal cords in a state of readiness.)

There are many schools of thought as to what may affect the health of your voice for better or for worse. Suffice to say, different things work for different people in different situations, so experiment a bit and see what works for *you*.

READY, SET ... GO! (NO, SERIOUSLY, GO)

If you've done all the things you can wherever it is you live, and you still find yourself in love with acting, and you're chomping at the bit, hie thee to where the work is (especially if you're far removed from a major voice-over hub or you have dreams of working on a performance capture stage).

Yes, in theory, VO can be done from anywhere there's a recording booth. But we've learned that a lot of places want you to come in and audition live for them; and if you get the job, they might want you in the studio later that same day or at nine o'clock the next morning. You know how expensive plane tickets are if you buy them the day of the flight? Whatever they cost, we're betting it's more than what you're going to make doing the job under most circumstances.

And think about it for a second: with millions of people in the world who call themselves actors, what would happen if a job were open to all of them at the same time? The casting people wouldn't have enough time to listen to all of the submissions. So for the CDs, it's far easier to limit the pool they're choosing from – and that's where you want to be swimming. Dive into that pool. Go where the work is.

THE BIG DUB-OUT

It was another hot, sweltering, summer day in 2001. It was already 10 a.m., so we dressed quickly and dragged ourselves downstairs to the second floor of the hotel, only to discover we had missed breakfast once again. I needed coffee, *bad*. So, we hustled across the street to our local neighborhood deli. I had been there the night before, and enjoyed the similarities to a Smilers in NYC, or a 7-Eleven in L.A. Only, this was Italy. No, not Little Italy. *Rome*, Italy. Ya know, the country shaped like a boot in the Mediterranean Sea? And I was far from my home in Hollywood, CA.

Hello, I said, *Hello*, with no response from the guys behind the counter. *Hello-oo, Ciao, Buon giorno, Hello-oo?* Over the glass, I saw two very hot, young, Italian hunks. They were both, tall, dark, and very handsome. *Hello, Helloo-oo* they called back at me, playing with their vocal tones, trying to copy my voice with their *hellos*. Laughing, I said *hello* back, and then we all started laughing. *Hello, Hello-oo, Hello-oo* ... all of us just laughing away.

"Do you know what she does for a living?" my friend asked with a mischievous smile. "She is on *Digimon!*"

All of a sudden, the Italians came from behind the glass counter, repeating, *Digimon, Digimon, Digimon!* They kept saying it, like a mantra, as another Italian hunk came out from the back. *Digimon, Digimon, Digimon*. Each of the three hunks kissed me on both cheeks (did I say how much I love Italy?), and had me chant with them. *Digimon, Digimon, Digimon*. The Italians were thrilled to discover a Hollywood animation star, right in their little deli. They all knew the series and wouldn't let me pay for my grub. I felt pretty good drinking that hot coffee. Ah, the perks of celebrity.

Later that day, I went to the largest flea market in Rome. It was gigantic, the biggest flea market I had ever seen. I started going down the aisles, one by one. On one of the long tables, I spotted "Patamon," the character I voiced on *Digimon*. Oh wow, my first talking toy of a character I created, right here in Italy. While out of the country, I had gone "International." Isn't show business grand? I was thrilled and quickly bought my first "Patamon" (who desperately needed batteries).

It was a hot, sweltering day. As I unpacked my suitcase, I finally got the opportunity to check out "Patamon" in his Hollywood home. I opened up the little guy, and noticed he was made in China. Carefully, I put the batteries in. I pressed the button and listened intently as this little voice said, "Bueno, bueno, bueno." Oh wow, oh wow, it wasn't me ... My voice had been dubbed ... in Italian.

~ Laura Summer, Actress

TOP VO CITIES

It doesn't matter where you live. No matter what country you call home, there are likely to be certain cities where the entertainment industry – VO in particular – congregates. In most countries, the larger cities offer more work. For example Paris, France; London, England; and Vancouver, Toronto, and Montreal, Canada, all have thriving communities of working voice actors.

In the U.S. (where we're most familiar with things) there are several hot spots. The major U.S. hubs for VO work seem to be:

1. Los Angeles, CA

2. New York, NY

3. Dallas, TX

4. Chicago, IL

5. Nashville, TN

6. Atlanta, GA

We made the above list when we wrote the first edition of this book, and we feel it still holds up. Atlanta has been building a huge infrastructure for filmmaking over the past decade, and they have a growing need for VO and motion capture work. But the juggernauts L.A. and NYC still top the list. For now. Texas is also a huge contender, with work in both Dallas and Austin, and there continues to be work in Chicago and Nashville as well. We have also heard from VAs working in Seattle, San Francisco, and Philadelphia, but we aren't as familiar with those cities. We recommend doing your research on the particular market you are interested in based on your specific goals.

There are other cities in which voice-over is recorded, and they can be a great training ground as you begin. But to really be in the thick of it and have the best opportunity to make a living at

VO, it is best to locate yourself in one of the major cities. We're based in L.A. and have found some measure of success here, and we have friends in other cities who are also doing quite well in their respective markets.

Sometimes, when voice actors achieve a certain level of success, they can move away from the hustle and bustle of the top cities and let the work come to them. We worked with a well-known actor who lives in Kansas City and records everything from home, coming into L.A. only on very rare occasions to put in face time. But remember, you'll have to establish yourself first. So get in the game!

PAY-TO-PLAY SITES

Another option before moving to a VO hub would be to take a look at the "pay-to-play" sites available online. These sites charge a fee to account holders in exchange for hosting the actor's profile and demo reel on line, providing access to auditions, and allowing the actor to submit for roles on line through the site. Full disclosure: we have not ever subscribed to any of these services, so don't have experiences we can share. However, from talking to friends who have used them, we have gleaned this:

- Some sites are better organized than others
- There is a fair amount of competition because, essentially, anyone in the world can submit an audition
- The jobs are all non-union
- The jobs are generally not very well paid
- Some sites are less than scrupulous, so, again, do your research before signing up

That said, the fact that we don't have experience with pay-to-play doesn't mean you shouldn't look into it to see if it could be a good proving ground for you, especially if you're just starting out. Just be careful, and walk away if you feel you're being taken advantage of.

CHAPTER 12
THE DEMO

"You will never get a second chance to make a first impression."

WILL ROGERS, ACTOR, HUMORIST, COWBOY

YOUR CALLING CARD

As promised, we've arrived at the *demo*, or demonstration, of you and your many talents. It's not enough to record yourself just doing all the crazy voices and impressions you can do into a tape recorder (or even into *Garage Band*, as the kids are calling it these days). You need a demo that will be competitive in order to open the right doors and get you noticed by the right people. And this means that, as tempting as it may be to get your second-cousin-twice-removed-the-wedding-DJ to record you in his garage, you might want to consider getting your demo professionally produced. It is, after all, going to be the professional world's first impression of you and what you have to offer. You don't want to give them any excuses not to fall in love with you.

Your demo reel can be geared specifically toward a particular area of VO work. For example, actors who focus primarily on commercial work don't always have an animation demo. Promo or narration folks sometimes stick to their areas of expertise and have a demo that showcases only their talent for that kind of work. Some people have a different demo for each type of VO, while others just split their one demo into separate tracks that highlight the different areas. Your demo can be as specific or diverse as you want. The most important thing is to do it well.

FAKE IT 'TIL YOU MAKE IT

"But I haven't done any work yet! What am I supposed to put on my reel?" you may ask, your brow furrowing in panic and dismay. Relax that brow. A demo reel doesn't have to be from actual work you have already done; more often than not, everything on a demo is totally fabricated. As a matter of fact, even if you do have some real material to put on your reel, you may want to put made-up stuff on it anyway. This will allow you to focus the demo and highlight the qualities that you want to showcase. After all, *demo* can also mean *demonstration* of what you *can* do, not necessarily what you *have* done. Trivia: Tara and Yuri still use the commercial demos they created before they had booked any real work!

Now here's a thing that's going to highlight the weirdness of the entertainment biz: all agents know that actors make up most of what's on their demos, especially when just starting out; but they still want to be fooled. So that's what you've gotta do. Fool 'em as best you can. Let's see how you can do that.

What are you going to record? Well, first we're going to caution you against copying things directly from other commercial spots you hear or shows you see. The reason for that is this: as big as you think this world is, people are paying attention; and with people like casting directors and agents, it's *their job* to pay attention.

You don't want to record yourself doing a McDonald's spot you heard on the radio or shouting out the catchphrase of a popular animated character, and then send it to an agency whose client actually *did* record that spot or character. Your demo will immediately be outed and possibly *thrown* out. That's not to say it's definitely going to happen, but we feel that in this situation, it's better to be safe than sorry, especially when there are easy ways to cover your tracks.

This seems like a good place to mention something else that we feel is important and will serve you throughout your long career in this business: *don't lie about the work you've done.* There might be a temptation to say that you worked on things you didn't work on so you seem more experienced to a possible employer, especially in the beginning when you don't have any credits to speak of. *Don't.* Don't do it.

We're not saying you should open every conversation with, "Okay, now, I just want you to know that I have never done this before." If they don't ask, let 'em think what they want. But if you didn't work on a title, don't put it on your résumé. You'll be working in a very tight circle of people, and if people reading your résumé didn't cast it, odds are they know either the person who did or the director. Being caught in a lie is a great way to get remembered for all the wrong reasons. Don't get caught up in trying to make people think you're much more experienced than you are. If they like you, they're going to want to be the one who *discovered* you. Let 'em discover you.

After reading the last few paragraphs, you may be saying to yourself, "Hey, first they're telling me to fake it and now they're telling me not to lie. What gives?" Sure, our advice on these two issues can be seen as inconsistent, but trust us on this one. Acting is a business of illusion, and bending the rules in this world with fake copy on your demo *is* accepted. Taking credit for things you did not do, not so much.

Now that we've hopefully made that clear, let's get back to making your demo sound as legit as you can. "But if I can't copy real things, how am I supposed to know what to record?" you may ask. Well, here's another place where we're going to ask you to employ that powerful imagination of yours. Look at some real stuff … and then mess with it.

To create commercial copy for your reel, go pick up a magazine and flip through the ads. Print ads are written differently than radio or TV ads, so you won't ever have to worry about someone already having recorded this exact spot. Now mess with it, rewrite it a bit, and make it your own.

Do the same for animation and video game bits. Watch, listen, play, take notes. Then mess with it, riff on it, make it your own. If you really hate writing, find friends who are good at it and see if one of them will help you. Before you know it, you'll have scripts to record. And you don't need many.

Let's say you've recorded your demo as professionally as you can. Now, you'll want someone (an audio engineer) to spend time mixing it and *sweetening* it with effects and music, so that it sounds as if the spots were pulled from actual shows or commercials. The engineer will work with each clip you've recorded as if it were a real spot, and make it sound as good as possible; then you'll work together to pull your favorite section of each spot.

You'll want your demo to run about sixty seconds total, so you'll have to pick only the best part from each spot. Agents and casting directors are busy people. They're not going to have time to listen to a five-minute demo, so you gotta hook 'em quickly and leave 'em wanting more.

Another trick that engineers often use to help the demo reel sound more *realistic* is to change the recording levels and settings between the different spots. This way, even if you record them back-to-back in one session, the sound quality will be slightly different from spot to spot, just as if you had recorded each spot at a different time in a different studio with a different engineer. You can even help the engineer achieve this effect by changing your position slightly from script to script. It may seem funny, but sound is a finicky thing; and little things, even moving an inch back from the mic, or an inch left or right, can drastically affect how your voice is recorded. That's why, if you record at a certain studio regularly, you may notice the mic setup is always the same in order to maintain consistency in recording.

All of these things will add up to a professional sounding demo, which will be key in helping to open the doors that lead to work. Don't be afraid to spend both time and money on your demo, but also don't be afraid to shop around. If a deal seems too good to be true, make sure it isn't by first doing a little research on your own. If the Internet's good for something, it's research. Well, research and cat videos.

MAKING IT YOUR OWN

When I first had aspirations of becoming a voice actor in college, I paid a voice-over teacher to coach me and help make my demo. We worked through different voices she felt would be good, and pulled bits from a stack of copy she had. Years later, when I became a producer and had to cast a few shows, I was surprised to hear other actors with some of the *same* bits of copy on their demos. It was embarrassing. That's why I encourage people to write their own stuff for their demos. That way it will be guaranteed to be original, and you'll never have to worry that any agent, producer, or casting director has heard that same bit over and over again.

~ STEPHANIE SHEH, ACTRESS, DIRECTOR, WRITER

PLAY TO YOUR STRENGTHS

We talked earlier about *finding your voice* and the adjectives that best describe it, and suggested making a quality list. This is particularly important when creating your demo. To market and promote yourself most successfully, you'll want to be comfortable with and aware of the strengths and weaknesses of your voice. As you plan and execute your demo, knowing these attributes will help you zero in on what will best showcase you.

Let's narrow it down a bit. Using the list below, see which adjectives best describe the main qualities of your voice. Think honestly about which ones would be a stretch and which ones are right in your wheelhouse. Also, for your own reference, see if you feel any of these qualities describe a trend you are currently hearing on TV or radio. If you think of adjectives that are not on this list, add them. This is not the be-all end-all list of adjectives.

wry	calm	perky
honest	open	cut-to-the-chase
sarcastic	happy	clipped
giddy	haughty	innocent
secretive	emotional	bored

MIC SAYS: Leading your demo with your strongest voice ensures that even listeners with short attention spans will hear you at your best.

THE COMMERCIAL DEMO

We've already noted that there are several different types of demos. Let's start our discussion with the commercial demo.

A solid commercial demo usually has a mix of several kinds of spots: a hard sell, a soft sell, a partner-read/dialogue spot, a PSA, an upscale sell, a legal disclaimer, and sometimes a character spot. You already know that you have about sixty seconds to cover these spots on your reel.

There is no absolute order in which the different spots should be placed on the reel, and no rule about whether you need to include every kind of read. Just try to keep the sounds different from spot to spot. In other words, if your upscale sell has a similar vibe to your soft sell, break them up by putting one of the other spots in between. Also remember that the people listening to your demo may have very short attention spans, so put a couple of your strongest reads in first and second position. If you have only fifteen seconds to grab them, make sure you're really showing them who you are.

But don't load your demo up with different examples of one *type* of spot, even if you believe that it's what you do best. Having a good mix on your demo will show that you're proficient in an array of different types of copy. Let them know that you'll be able to handle anything that gets thrown at you in the booth.

The *hard sell* or sometimes, *high energy* sell, is just what it sounds like: a forceful and direct attempt to convince a consumer to buy a product. You've heard this type of spot before: "You need this! Buy now, while supplies last! Be the first one on the block to own one! We're almost giving them away!" There's been a noticeable decline of the hard sell, but it's still out there. You'll notice it a lot in ads that are selling to kids. When we first wrote this book, we suggested you check out the ads for cereal and toys in between cartoons on Saturday morning. But we're very sad to report that Saturday morning cartoons have gone the way of video stores. Still, no matter where or when you watch your cartoons, you can still pay attention to how they advertise. Unless you, like, watch them on Netflix or something and there's *no* advertising. Okay, how about you just go to YouTube and search "toy commercials."

A *soft sell* spot is essentially the opposite of the hard sell. The soft sell is a more subtle approach, giving potential customers just enough indirect information to get them to come to the conclusion themselves that they need to buy whatever it is you're selling. Often these spots use comedy to get you feeling good, and then associate the product with the good feeling you're experiencing. Your brain does the rest: *Ha ha ha! ... I feel good ... Maybe if I get this product, it'll make me feel good!* The soft sell will likely be less energetic than the hard sell, and more natural and friendly – stressing the personal, intimate connection with listeners rather than trying to convince them to buy something.

For the *partner read* (also called a *dialogue spot*), the material can be either high energy or low energy. What is most important is to have at least two distinct voices (you and another actor) talking to one another. In the partner read, you two will be discussing something and joking, arguing, or learning about the product. This spot will help add texture to your demo by having someone else's voice bring contrast to your own. Always try to get someone of the opposite sex, or at least a very different vocal quality, to record this spot with you; we don't want the listener to become confused as to whose demo they're listening to. Doing dialogue spots for your demo can be a great way to collaborate with friends who are also interested in VO and may be able to use the spot on their reels as well!

A *PSA*, or *Public Service Announcement*, is a little different. We're sure you've heard many PSAs. They are primarily geared towards causing a strong emotional reaction in the listener, and most often promote issues of health and safety. Common PSA topics are anti drug use, pro seatbelt use, and support for charitable causes. They can be shocking, bring tears to your eyes by uplifting you, or make you feel sad and wistful: "One out of every six children is diagnosed with a learning disability..." The vocal quality of these spots is generally low energy and intimate, sometimes no louder than a whisper.

The *upscale sell* is often referred to as a *perfume* or *car sell*, and we sometimes like to call it the *sexy voice*. This read is most often used to sell luxury products geared toward a very elite crowd, and positively drips with wealth and comfort. No matter what the copy says, the upscale read communicates a subliminal message: *Hey, I'm part of this secret club and you're part of this secret club. We both know what's best, don't we? And if you're not a member yet, buy one of these, and I'll pull you out of the riffraff.*

We say it's *sexy* because upscale spots tend to have a sultry or suggestive voice cooing and purring seductively about the product. The implication is that the product will bring you wealth, power, and sex. It's kind of a cross between the hard and soft sells when it comes to the approach, but the delivery is soft, intimate, and sensual. If you're younger, or have a younger sounding voice, you might consider leaving this read off your demo. A younger voice trying to sound adult and sexy may just end up making the listener feel uncomfortable ... and that's not what we're trying to do here.

The *legal disclaimer* (sometimes referred to as just *the legal*) is also kind of optional on your demo, but it doesn't take up much time and does come up a lot in commercials. It can also be fun, so give it a try and see what happens. The legal is that bit at the end of the spot that often ends with "Prices and participation may vary," and which goes by so fast you almost can't tell what's being said. This is done intentionally, partly because the client would rather not draw your attention to the legal jargon, but also because there is only so much time to cram everything into the commercial. Some people are really, *really* good at this, so if you're not, no worries. Concentrate on getting the jobs you're good at.

Whatever you do, don't have an engineer speed up your voice to sound faster. Even if you fool people on your demo, one day you'll get asked to do it for real, and then you'll be in a pickle. Pay attention to the legal next time you're listening to a commercial.

(Usually you'll hear it on radio spots because in TV spots the legal can be flashed on screen in small print near the bottom.) Listen to the actor's delivery. Try to repeat it. Heck, try to say, "Prices and participation may vary," three times – *fast*. It's not easy.

And finally the *character spot*. The character spot is one with which you might get to play a little more while creating your commercial demo. This is *not* your average girl/guy-next-door read: you may be using a totally unique delivery to characterize a talking lemon, or a squirrel, or a robot.* Have fun. The character spot might be a great place to showcase your dialects or an oddball voice that wouldn't fit into any of the other spots. If you haven't had an opportunity yet on your demo to show off something fun that you can do well, this may be the place.

*This is not to say that any of these characters wouldn't be just as interesting in your own normal voice. And if you actually *are* a talking lemon, a squirrel, or a robot, the authors apologize for this apparent discrimination.

THE PROMO DEMO

Promos are similar to commercials but have their own specific feel, and some people have made entire careers in promo VO. Remember, promo is short for *promotional*, so you're going to be promoting something. What's a promo sound like? Well, movie trailers are good examples of promos: "In a world ... where a person's voice is the only weapon he has ... one man must defy all odds to become the ultimate warrior ..."

Of course doing VO for movie trailers is highly coveted work and hard to come by. But there's other promo work out there, such as the ads you hear promoting different networks or programs: "ABC tonight! You'll never believe the trouble Tara's gotten herself into this time, on TV's hottest new reality show, *Tara Uncensored!* Tonight at 9:30/8:30 Central, after *The Wild and Wonderful World of Yuri*, on ABC!"

Promos can be found wherever you watch or listen to your favorite shows. Unless, again, all your favorite shows are on Netflix.

The *promo voice* was traditionally a very specific official-sounding voice, but as times have changed, so have promos. On a network like E! you may hear a very high-energy promo voice which is very different than the low, dramatic quality of the typical movie trailer delivery. And much like in the commercial world, the tone of many promos has become wry or conversational as if the person doing the promo is a friend of yours telling you what a great show it is, or in the case of sitcom promos, as if the person is in on the joke.

A promo reel needs to have a variety of examples. Listen to some different promos to see where your strengths may lie before creating your own (as we said, not everyone can be the movie trailer guy). Perhaps you'll hear a trailer for your favorite TV show, announcements for an awards show, or even the voice of a company when you visit its website. Your promo reel might have spots of differing lengths since some promos can be quite short while others are much longer. Feel free to mix it up a little, but keep in mind that you don't want the listener to get too much of any one thing.

In general, the rule for any demo is *shorter is better*. Agents and casting directors will thank you for it.

THE ANIMATION/VIDEO GAME DEMO

Once just a humble animation reel, now it's called an animation/video game reel. Obviously, we have a special place in our hearts for animation and video games. For this reel you should really feel free to let yourself play. However, as we've mentioned before, it's not just about coming up with crazy cartoon voices. Lead with your strengths, as in other reels, and make sure you include some characters that sound like you *without putting on* a voice.

There are a lot of *normal* characters in video games and animation. Soldiers, spies, doctors, and princes can live in the same world as dragons, dwarves, and aliens. Just make sure that you put them in interesting situations when you're writing words for them.

If you are better at some voices than others, make sure you use longer clips of the best ones. Don't feel as if you have to include every voice under the sun on your reel. Pick your best.

If you want to showcase dialects, this is the place to do it. But make sure you're *really* good at the dialects you lay down. If you need to, practice with a dialect coach before recording your demo. Nothing turns off an agent or casting director faster than a poor, or even mediocre, dialect.

All animation clips you create should, of course, be sweetened with effects and music to sound as real as possible.

And once again, try to remember that those listening to your reel don't need to hear an entire show or even a full scene. They simply want to hear enough to tell two things:

1. What do you sound like?

2. Can you act?

If you're incredibly versatile – a man or woman (or robot) of a thousand voices – that's great, a bonus. But first establish the two things most cared about: your sound and your acting skill. Only then should you go for what's in your back pocket. You don't even necessarily have to use complete sentences: feel free to cut things in the middle. It is always better to leave people wanting more than to give them enough to get tired of.

The animation section of a demo can be a wonderful opportunity for you to create fun copy for yourself. Think about the kinds of characters you'd love to be playing. Now you get to create them, tailor them to exactly what you want, what you like. Cast yourself! How empowering is that!?

Also consider whether or not you need an additional actor to read some dialogue opposite you in a scene. If you say "I'll get you," and "Oh, yes I will," wouldn't it be fun to have someone interject, "No, you won't," between your lines to add more depth and realism to the interaction? Remember, don't pick someone whose vocal print is close to yours. After all, we don't want the listener falling in love with your *partner's* voice. *Of course, if they do, make sure to ask your partner for your 10% commission...*

With your animation/video game demo in particular, make sure to include action in some of your clips. There's a lot of fighting and jumping around in cartoons and video games, and these days, directors are asking for movie-like realism. As a matter of fact, to put the actors in the right frame of mind in one VG recording session, the director actually had us listen to battle scenes from the movie *Black Hawk Down* in our headphones while recording. Show them you can throw down in the booth. Give them a little laughing, a little yelling over gunfire, a little getting hit in the gut. No animation is complete without these sounds. Creating believable efforts is a valuable skill, and if you're good at it, people will remember you. Trust us.

THE NARRATION DEMO

Narration can be for fiction or non-fiction material, for film, TV, or audiobooks. Because of that, we recommend mixing it up a bit on your reel. Throw in a little narration for a documentary or nature special: "The mother polar bear is particularly protective of her cubs, but as you can see, they can be quite a handful ..." But also include a little narration from a children's animated movie or a fantasy epic: "Once upon a time, in the land of McMukmuk, two churlish dwarves began a quest that would not only test their skills, but their friendship as well ..."

There is a cornucopia of styles to choose from: history books, children's books, medical or legal tomes, and many more. Try some plainer texts, and then if you feel adventurous, move to stories that will require you to play a variety of different characters. On the other hand, if you find that your voice (and you) tend toward a specific type of narration, don't be afraid to focus on that in your reel.

These clips are expected to be a little longer than others because it's going to be important that the listener hear you maintain a tone and pace over time. Still, a few sentences or even a short paragraph per sample should be plenty. And for the narration demo, don't feel compelled to create your own material. Feel free to read aloud from not only different genre books, but also anything from self-help to textbooks and technical writings. You might also try children's books and classical literature to give your demo a nice variety. This is easier than having to write something yourself, and you can get all your material for free at your local library.

Make sure that, with any copy you read, you know the correct way to pronounce every word, especially if the copy is technical, medical, or full of tough words. If you're unsure, find something else to read. You don't want to sound unqualified or unprofessional simply because you don't know how to pronounce something correctly. With narration, especially for non-fiction, it is absolutely crucial that you sound like you know what you are talking about. Even if you don't.

PCAP DEMO

Let's take a moment to address a question that has come up recently because of the increase in voice actors getting hired to do performance capture: do you need a MoCap or PCap demo? And the short answer is: unless you plan on focusing on stunts, or already have a lot of stunt/movement/martial arts/gymnastics/ MoCap experience, then probably not. The use of performance capture in games and animation is still relatively uncharted territory (see what we did there?), and we've never been asked to provide a PCap demo. Perhaps this will change, but as of the writing of this book, it hasn't.

That said, when game producers decide to hire actors who will also be doing performance capture, they often will do a little research to see what the performers look like, and to see if they have worked on television or in film, because the type of performances looked for, more and more, tend toward the naturalistic or cinematic. Don't have that kind of reel? Don't worry. But if you do, it could be another tool in your arsenal. Make sure it's easily available online in case a potential employer searches for it.

If you've already done some PCap work, pull some of your footage from the game (easily sourced from YouTube playthroughs) and put that on your reel. The animated character may not look exactly like you, but its movements and expressions provide a legitimate example of your skill as a performer, and shows you've done this before. People like working with people who know what they're doing. And knowing you worked on a particular game, the casting director may even get in touch with someone else who worked on the same game to see how you were to work with.

Or, heck, disregard everything we just said, and make your own PCap demo. Like we said, nobody who's hiring is really expecting them. Catch them off guard! Make them pay attention! Start a trend that changes the industry!

MAKING YOUR DEMO: COSTLY, BUT WORTH IT

Taking classes on demo-making and creating the demo itself can become quite costly, so make sure you understand all the hidden costs as well as the up-front costs. Do you have to pay the director and the engineer for their time as well as paying the recording studio? What about the time the engineer has to spend sweetening your demo after you're are done recording in the booth?

You may also have to make copies of your demo and possibly design (or have someone design) labels. Then there may be mailings to get your physical demos into the hands of agents, studios, and casting people. But let's be honest: who listens to CDs anymore? Maybe they did when we first wrote this book, but we haven't sent out physical copies of our demo in years. And when we've received physical demos in recent years, they've been on USB thumb drives. The custom these days is to have your demo available for streaming or download on line, or to send it directly as an MP3 attachment in an email.

From the start, research and list these costs to cut down on unwelcome surprises along the way. Make sure you have enough funding to get the job done. Start a savings account (or a glass jar) today for your demo production, and commit to putting a few dollars a week into it. How about $10-$20? By the time you're done preparing for your demo, you'll have the money to pay for it.

So how much is it gonna cost? You need to know that before you start. Depending on where you're located and who you know, you can count on spending anywhere from $500 to $2000 on a good demo. If anyone promises that they can do it for much less, be sure you check them out really thoroughly before you give them any money. Ask to listen to other demos they've produced. Go on line and see if anyone's heard of them or worked with them before. Once again, the Internet is your greatest resource, and the community you find there can be your family.

Remember, the more planning, research, and rehearsal you do before you start, the more money you'll save in the end. You don't want to show up in the studio to record and still be tweaking your scripts. The clock will be ticking the whole time, and you'll be paying for it.

By investing in a professional, high quality demo, you're showing the people who will be listening to it that you're serious about voice acting. You'll also be showing *yourself* that you're serious, and that knowledge is going to be worth at least as much as convincing the pros who do the hiring. By the same token, putting out a shoddy demo may make those listening to it think that you're neither serious nor professional. And rarely, if ever, does someone like that get hired.

Your demo is your calling card, your vanguard, your invitation to the world to come to your party. Since your demo says *this is me*, make sure it truly represents how professional, how talented, how unique and cool you truly are.

GET TO THE POINT

When I first made up my demo reel and started to send it out, I had huge expectations for it. I had put a lot of money, time, and energy into its creation and I was terribly proud of it. I knew that it had been put together professionally and really showed off my voice. It was a *two and a half minute* celebration of what I could do! I mailed it out across town to various agents and sat back, waiting for the phone to ring.

And I waited.

And waited.

Nothing. Not a peep. I made a few follow-up calls to some of my top-choice agencies in the hopes that they were just slow getting in touch, but their response was, "Oh, we'll call if we're interested," or "It sounded good, but we already have several of your type." Not responses I wanted to hear.

I was bummed. And had to come up with a solution fast. Then I remembered overhearing someone once say, "Just get to the point already." I knew what I had to do.

Knowing that I was too close emotionally to the product, I found an engineer who wouldn't have any previous knowledge of my reel, and asked him to order and re-cut the clips into a *one* minute reel. His ear homed in on the short catchy spots, and he reorganized and trimmed my material to get the listener engaged right away.

I sent this abridged version out, and within a week I had found my voice-over agent! Sometimes just giving folks what they need/want to hear gets them hooked and curious far faster than overloading them with tons of variety.

~ Tara Platt, Actress

SHORT & SWEET

A parting note on demos: keep 'em short. In this fast-paced world we live in, the folks listening to your demo will get all the info they need within a few seconds, so a good length per spot may be only six to eight or ten seconds, tops. You can *record* a longer spot or sample if you'd like, but then pull only the *very best part* of that to showcase on your reel. The length of a narration sample will be longer (perhaps a twenty second clip), but when in doubt, cut it down.

The times, they are a-changin'. It used to be that a person's demo might be much longer, but short is the new black. Try, if possible, to get the length of your entire demo down to around one minute (that's sixty seconds, in case you're counting) per category: commercial, animation, etc.

We recommend that you visit our personal websites (TaraPlatt.com and YuriLowenthal.com) and listen to our commercial demo reels so that you can hear an example of a professionally produced demo filled with a variety of tracks (yes, we wrote all those commercials ourselves, and yes, Yuri's commercial demo is longer than a minute). We also recommend logging on to VoiceBank.net to listen to other actors' demos.

One thing you may notice when you listen to our demos is that we put things that make us happy in them. You can let that be your guide, too. Let your personality shine, use your imagination, and have fun building this little ark that you're going to send out into the world.

CHAPTER 13
AGENTS/MANAGERS & PERSONAL MARKETING

"If you want to go fast, go alone.
If you want to go far, go together."

AFRICAN PROVERB

"WHO'S IN MY CORNER?"

This acting stuff is hard work. You're going to want to start building a team of people who will help you so that you don't have to go it alone. First, let's talk about these mysterious agents and managers, aka your representation. You're eventually going to want someone like this working for you for a couple of reasons:

1. You don't have time to hustle and negotiate 24/7; you want someone else to be carrying some of that weight.

2. These people have access to job information and relationships that you most likely will *not* have access to.

Having a rep who knows about opportunities you don't know about, and hustles to get them for you, should be worth the 10% an agent is going to take off the top. In the end, a small price to pay if they keep you working.

"DO I NEED REPRESENTATION?"

No. You don't necessarily need representation – certainly not when you're just starting out. The truth is, you can do much of the legwork on your own, and book plenty of work without a go-between. And having an agent or a manager doesn't mean that you won't still have to do your own hustling on top of that. But if you really want to make a living at voice work, you're eventually going to need representation of some sort.

So many jobs put out casting calls only to agencies, and some agents have long-standing relationships with specific ad agencies, clients, and casting directors. If you want a crack at those jobs, you'll need an agent. Of course, not all jobs come through agents. Many times you will end up auditioning for a job because of your personal relationship with a director or a studio, or even as a result of combing through craigslist. But you want to make yourself as available as you can to every opportunity, and being represented by a competent agent or manager can greatly increase those opportunities.

Some actors feel more professional or *safer* if they are represented by an agency, and make finding an agent a priority. Other actors try to get work on their own first and look for representation when the time seems right – or better yet, hope that representation finds *them* because of the work they've done. This is a personal decision and is different for every actor. No matter how you cut it, though, if you want to succeed, you will have to work at getting jobs on your own.

We've heard it said, "An agent gets only 10%, so expect them to do only 10% of the work." Just because you find representation with an agency does not mean that you should kick back, relax, and wait for them to bring you all of your work. Agents can be extremely helpful, but you're still the CEO of You, Inc. An agent or manager is part of your work staff.

We haven't really explained how agents and managers differ.

Managers are more a part of the on-camera acting world than the voice-over world: you hardly ever hear of voice-over managers. But, so that you understand the difference, here's the scoop.

Compared to an agent, a manager is less responsible for finding you individual jobs, and more responsible for managing your overall career, making sure you pick projects that take you in the right direction to build a successful livelihood. For this special attention, they usually require a 15% cut of any work you do.

An agent's job, on the other hand, is a little more specific: to find you work, plain and simple. This is not to say that agents don't care about your overall success, but their main concern (for which they generally require a 10% cut) is finding you jobs. They will try to find auditions that are best suited to your abilities, but they are less concerned with creating a brand for you or with other aspects of your career.

A manager technically can't legally negotiate contracts, while the agent can, but those lines can get blurry. Some actors have both an agent *and* a manager. You might not need that until you're a big shot, but some actors like to have as many people working for them as possible, and who can blame them? Sure, you'll be paying a manager's and an agent's cut, but wouldn't you rather pay 25% of *some*thing, than 0% of *no*thing? Most importantly, as much as it seems like the manager and agent have power over you, you must remember at all times that you're not working for them: *they're working for you.*

"WHERE DO I FIND THEM?"

Where will you find this elusive agent to represent you? Well, much like the VO auditions, the VO representatives tend to be located in the cities where the most work is going on. That means you could have an agent in L.A., New York, and/or Chicago, for example. You can find lists of accredited agencies through the union (SAG-AFTRA), voice-over websites, or publications like *The Call Sheet* or the *Voice-Over Resource Guide*. (More information on these publications can be found in the *Resources* section in Chapter 16, *Hints, Tips, & Parting Thoughts*.)

Some of the larger voice-over agencies may have offices in several cities, say L.A. and New York, and maybe even London. However, just because an agent is bi-coastal or multi-continental doesn't mean you are automatically represented in all of those cities if you're repped in one. Be sure you ask about things like that before signing your contract with an agency.

Here's something for you to remember: *never pay someone to represent you*. If a potential agent or manager asks for any kind of money up front, whether it's for *operating expenses* or *postage* or whatever, just politely walk away because *they are not legit*. If they say that to sign with them you are required to take classes with a specific teacher or record your demo with a specific person, just politely walk away because *they are not legit*.

Sure, legitimate reps may say it would be a *good idea* for you to take a class, and often they will have a list of people they know to be good. But anyone who insists that you study or work with *their guy* might be getting a kickback from these people. Reps should make money only when you make money.

We repeat: *never pay someone to represent you*. It may seem tempting, but we have never once heard of anything good coming of it. And besides having had some experience with it ourselves, we've heard a lot of horror stories.

From the Agent's Desk

My most successful clients are the ones who make strong choices for auditions and stick with them. They don't over-think the audition and wonder how many different ways they could've done it.

They visualize what the end product will be and then do their best to provide that. After the audition, they walk away and don't think about it again. It's this particular mind-set of being confident in one's performance and not worrying about the outcome that is the best attitude for success in this business.

~ Bradford Bricken, Agent

SELF-PROMOTION 101

Self-promotion can be hard for some people. It takes work. And how many times did your grandma say, "People don't want to hear you talk about yourself!" We're taught that *tooting our own horn* is prideful and unattractive. But in this business, you have to find as many ways as possible to let people know how great you are and why they should be hiring you. And as we said before, promoting you is not part of your agent's job. What if you don't even have an agent? What can you do on your own? Well, a lot, actually.

We'll talk about some of the things you can do to promote yourself, but there are plenty more ideas beyond what we'll go into. The more creative you get, the more effective your promotion will be. So put your fun-hat on and get cranking on some ideas.

Once you've determined what your sound is and decided where you think you might fit best in the VO market, you're done with the hard part. Use this info to promote yourself and move in the direction you want.

 MIC SAYS: Don't worry if you don't have an agent yet: you'll always be your own best promoter. So start selling yourself now.

WHAT TO DO WITH YOUR DEMO

So what do you do with your masterpiece? The demo you spent all that love, time, energy, and dough on? You get it out there and get it working for you. It's time to try to get a return on your investment.

Do a mailing to your target agents or managers, and don't stop there. Do a little research, and target production studios, ad agencies, producers, casting agents, and directors who work on the kind of projects that you'd like to be working on. Don't have a contact name or specific casting email information? Give 'em a call and ask the operator, or send an exploratory email to *any* email address you can find for the company to try and find out more. Once again, be sure to check out the *Resources* section of this book (Chapter 16, *Hints, Tips, & Parting Thoughts*) to get more direction about where you can start your search.

Post your reel on line; it's easy these days. Make it accessible via Facebook, LinkedIn, Twitter, YouTube, and any other social networking or hosting platform that may be in vogue when you read this, so that if someone wants to hear your demo, they can find it easily. Build your own personal website and host your demo there. The more online places your reel is featured and associated with your name, the easier it is for somebody to find it by using a search engine like Google.

Use whatever method you can think of to get your demo into the hands of the people who could hire you (or at least into the hands of someone who can introduce you to some of those people). There is no right or wrong way to do this, but there *is* a fine line between *catchy* and *gimmicky* – much like the line between *aggressively pursuing* and *stalking*. So do be respectful about putting yourself in people's faces.

We've found that the difference between catchy and gimmicky can be crystallized in this comparison: a personalized card with a funny note included with your demo is fine; a glitter-filled envelope that explodes all over an agent's desk when it's opened will get you remembered, but for all the wrong reasons …

A short note in case you decide to create a physical demo: you'll need some sort of packaging for it. You'll want it to look nice and professional. Feel free to use your creativity in putting your package together, but one word of warning: while it may *seem* to be a good idea to put a *picture* of you somewhere on that CD case or thumb drive, listen when we say that there are better options. Putting your face on your demo automatically typecasts you in the eyes of the person looking at it. As a voice actor you want a potential employer to think that you can be many things and many people.

If agents have a specific image of you in their heads, it'll be harder for them to consider you as anything other than what you look like. We've been telling you how important it is to use your imagination, right? Well, let the agents use their imaginations this time.

YOUR WEBSITE

Nowadays a Web presence is essential for anyone trying to market themselves in this business. It serves as your calling card and personalized news feed, letting people know what you're up to. As we've mentioned, the Web provides a way for new people to find you, and it's a fantastic place to post your demo reel for quick and easy access by potential employers.

Once you have a website set up, you can make a business card that includes your Web address (preferably an address that's your name, like *ArchibaldTuttle.com* or *TaraPlatt.com*, although sometimes, if that's not an option, you'll have to get creative: *Archibald-TuttleVO.com* or *YuriLowenthalIsAVoiceActor.com*). Then, whenever you meet people in the VO business, you can give them your card:

suddenly all your info is at their fingertips.

Even the most basic website should include a way to get in touch with you. Your name and an email contact are essential; also list your representation's contact info if you have an agent/manager. You can include your phone number, but really consider that before you do it: *anyone* could end up calling... In addition, your website might also include a list of credits and/or upcoming work, and maybe a clip or a demo reel of your voice.

Many actors choose not to include images of themselves if the site is for voice-over only, as one of the great things about voice-over is that it isn't looks-based (remember our note about packaging). Instead of displaying your photo, you can put up images that showcase either the work you've done or the qualities or essence your voice evokes.

Your website may feature several different things ranging from your professional acting experience to your personal life. If so, make sure that it's as easy to navigate to your VO info as possible, so that potential employers don't get caught up in photos of your latest class reunion when all they're trying to do is listen to your VO demo. If possible, you might want to have a separate site for your personal stuff so that professionals visiting your VO site don't see anything that might adversely affect their judgment of you: those photos may be funny to you and your friends, but a casting director might not get the joke. This is also a consideration if your shenanigans are easily viewed on Facebook. Remember, what happens online, stays online, and potential employers may not think it's as funny as you do.

You don't have to spend a lot of money, nor do you need to know how to code to set up a decent, effective website that you'll be able to update yourself. Shop around, ask around, and find a Web hosting company that works for you. Check out other actors' sites, and if you like what you see, shoot some of them an email and ask who's hosting their site and how they designed it (sometimes you'll find that information at the bottom of the Web page). There are even companies that let you design your own *free* Web page, and that can help when you're trying to get started on the cheap (although *free* often means a person visiting your site will have to contend with ads, and you don't want agents and casting directors distracted by content you don't control). In any case, creating a page is something you can do inexpensively and on your own. So full steam ahead!

POSTCARDS AND BUSINESS CARDS

In addition to having an online presence, having something a little more tangible as either an introduction or a follow-up can often be useful as well, although not as common these days. Consider it an old-school approach that may cut through a prospective agent or employer's glut of emails.

A business card is good to have when you're meeting someone in person. Having something physical like that can be even more effective sometimes than, say, an email. When the people you give your card to get home, they empty their pockets and the card sits on their desks, or counters, or bedside tables, in full view – and hopefully keeps you fresh in their minds long enough for you to get lodged there.

In addition to listing your basic contact info (name, phone number, email address, website) on your business card, you might even summarize your voice signature with a couple of key words that best describe your vocal quality. A card like that will help people identify you easily. At least at first you'll want people to associate you with a specific characteristic, so that when they're looking for, say, *spunky*, they think of you. Put that characteristic on your card, keep some cards in your wallet, and when you meet someone, you'll have just the thing to help them remember you.

You might even slip a business card into a letter or demo mailing.

Your postcard should have the same info that's on your business card, and it'll give you a little more room to be creative. For example, if you've done any work recently, you can write, "Hey, just did this job!" or "Check me out in this show/game/commercial!"

A postcard can be used as a follow-up to a demo mailing or after a meeting. You might even send your postcard as an introduction before you send your demo. The agent might get the card, go to your website (the address *is* on your postcard, right?), listen to your demo on line, and you won't have to send that agent your reel at all. (Don't assume that'll happen. Agents and casting directors are busy people. They don't always have time to type in a Web address found on a postcard; but a physical CD may be just the thing for them to pop into their CD player – if their car still has one – to while away the commute home.)

Business cards and postcards make it easy for you to keep in touch. And maybe even more important, they make it easy for people to keep in touch with you. An emailed MP3 is more likely to be listened to, and some email services will let you check to see if your email's been read by the recipient!

A note on thumb drives: With the proliferation of dangerous computer viruses and clever malware, people have become (rightfully) reluctant to accept a thumb drive from someone they don't really know and stick it into their computer, potentially endangering their sensitive personal information. So as cool as that *Millennium Falcon*-shaped drive with your demo on it may look, consider this before you hand it over to someone: you don't want there to be any excuse not to listen to it.

THE MAILING: SHIPS OUT TO SEA

Dallas Travers, an acting-career coach and good friend of ours, fondly calls mailings *sending your ships out to sea*, which we think is a wonderful analogy. You have to be prepared for some of those ships to get lost at sea, or for the cargo not to be what the port needed at that time. But some of those ships you send off just may find their way through treacherous waters and dock at the perfect spot, making your sailing – ahem, *mailing* – pay off.

Many of your postcards or demos may not make it to the agent's or casting director's office; but remember, sometimes it only takes one. You put all that work into your demo, so you might as well get it out there: that's what it's for. Thankfully, envelopes, postcards, and physical demos are cheaper than ships, and in a digital world, somewhat less common and maybe even quaint ...

NETWORK, NETWORK, NETWORK

Many people snidely call this schmooooozing, but the truth is, meeting people and developing relationships is how things get done in the entertainment business. Practicing good solid networking skills can help you move forward quickly and consciously toward the next level of your career.

Networking facilitates your being in the right place at the right time. This is part of the preparation + opportunity (*right place at the right time*) = success equation. Prepare yourself, and then put yourself in situations where you can mingle and meet people. Sometimes you can target the people you want to work with. But honestly, you never know where a job or an important friendship is going to come from. So don't limit your interactions.

How do you go about schmoozing? Well, first off, let's stop calling it that. Let's opt for *networking*. The word schmoozing has always carried a negative connotation to us because it implies that you're forcing yourself onto other people for the sole purpose of getting something from them; and that's just kind of slimy. That's probably why a lot of actors have trouble networking – because when it's called schmoozing, they feel like they're doing something gross. The less pressure you put on meeting people and wondering what they can do for you, the easier it's going to be, and the better it'll probably work out.

Where do you go to network? There are a variety of places to go and ways to make connections happen. Search for networking events and social gatherings specifically geared toward voice-over and voice acting or to entertainment in general. These events are often listed in entertainment trade papers and on certain websites, and will certainly be more plentiful in big cities like New York and Los Angeles.

Don't look just for parties (which are sometimes hard to get into). Find out where the people that you would like to work with hang out, and go there. Get yourself into the same circles they're in and see what happens. You don't have to be in a big city to make this work. You can go out with friends who are also working in the business, and meet the people they know. If you don't know anyone else who's interested in voice acting or in what you want to be doing, then *find them*.

Put an ad in a local paper or post it on line somewhere like craigslist or Facebook. Set up a gathering for people interested in the same things you're interested in. Build a support group, if you will. Things happen much faster (and it's usually more fun) if you've got a whole group working at it. Who knows, the group you assemble might end up producing a cartoon together.

If you network well, and don't put pressure on a specific outcome, it won't be perceived as *schmoozy*. Still it's not always the easiest thing for some people to do. Networking might not come naturally for you, so pay attention to people who are good at it and learn from them. In the end, being yourself is the best thing you can do when you meet and socialize with people professionally. You don't need to try to act cool so they'll like you. Remember you have as much to offer them as they have to offer you.

Networking should never be about what you can *get* from others. Treat them as you would your friends, and be friendly and personable. You just may be someone they will want to befriend and (who knows?) maybe work with one day.

And don't forget your cards! A networking event is a perfect opportunity to get your business cards into people's hands. Think of this as sowing seeds. But try to wait until later in the interaction to hand them that card. Don't lead with the seed.

You may have to plant a few seeds before anything starts growing. You never know which seed will grow and bear fruit, so sprinkle those seeds liberally. The more seeds – um, business cards – you hand out, the better your chances are. Okay, we're going to stop saying "seeds" now. If other people give you their cards, be sure to follow up and let them know that you enjoyed meeting them. Then file the cards away somewhere that you'll be able to find them again, just in case you want to get in touch. You can use your new postcards to follow up with those new contacts you made while networking.

FOLLOW UP

So how do you keep the embers glowing for those relationships you've created either through networking or actual working? By respectfully following up. After you complete a job, if you enjoyed working with that director, producer, writer, creator, stunt person, etc., ask them if it's okay for you to stay in touch and keep them posted on what you're up to, and what would be the best way to do that. They'll likely give you an email address. Put it in your digital Rolodex, and make it easy to find so you can send them the occasional update. Don't bug them often, and definitely don't reach out if you don't have something specific to report or ask. Many actors send out a fun, informational newsletter a few times a year to keep people they've met in the loop. There are many services available that make it easy to manage a database of email addresses and put together a periodic newsletter.

If you really hit it off with someone, maybe follow them on social media and keep in touch that way. If not, maybe send an email a few times a year to let them know what you're up to. People are understandably busy with their own lives and may need a reminder every now and then that you're still out there, working hard. They may get that reminder right as they're looking to hire people, or they may not; but if you stay respectful in your approach, they shouldn't ever be annoyed to hear from you. What exactly is respectful? Follow their lead and trust your gut.

REFERRALS

"Hey, can you get me into voice-over?" is a question we get a lot. Simple answer: no. We don't have that power. We don't know *anyone* who does. What we think (hope?) people who ask us this mean is, "Hey, can you hook me up with a person who can help me?" Simple answer, if we don't know you: no.

It's not that we're unwilling to help people, but you have to consider a few things. Were we to refer another person, whether it be for a job, or to an agency or a casting director, we would be putting our reputation on the line. A reputation that has taken a long time to build. And yet we have no idea if the person asking for the referral is professional, skilled, experienced, or what have you. We could just "be nice" and refer them sight unseen, but if they're not ready, then they look bad, we look bad, and it erodes our relationship with the person to whom we refer them. Maybe the person asking for a referral is talented, but we have no way of knowing if they're going to show up on a job and be less than professional. If that happens, it reflects badly on them and on us.

Remember our oft-repeated equation: success = preparation + opportunity? Well, the referral you're asking for is the *opportunity*, but you must first be sure you've done the *preparation* part. That you're already doing voice work and have established your reputation as a performer who is not only talented, but who comes to work well-prepared and on time, and who works well with the team. You can't skip the preparation and expect to be handed the opportunity – a referral from someone who isn't familiar with both your acting skills and your work ethic.

Now if we're dear friends and we're familiar with your skills, experience, work ethic, and temperament, then by all means, if you've got a specific request, ask away! But make sure you're ready when you do. Remember, there is no silver bullet to getting into this industry. It takes work first, then referrals.

SWAG

Ah, swag. The sometimes unique-and-catchy, sometimes obnoxious-and-kitschy gift that you can use to promote yourself. We'll touch on this only briefly because we've never employed this method ourselves. We do, however, know actors who have tried it, and we still remember their swag; so it must work for some people.

Often, actors will use swag in an attempt to brand themselves and become more memorable or easily recognizable. For example, an actress we know has a name that bears a resemblance to that of a popular candy bar, so she had candy bar labels (and matching business cards) printed with her name in a similar font and gave out chocolates as a fun gift. A pair of married voice actors we know also had candy bar labels made up showing them as superheroes (why didn't we think of that?). If we've learned anything here, it's that people love chocolate; and if you can get them to tie you to something they already love, well then, you're halfway there.

Other folks have created magnets, mugs, self-modeled bobblehead dolls, or even brewed their own beers to give to people they work with and *want* to work with. Studios and agencies can quickly become museums of interesting (and sometimes odd) swag created by actors. It can be a great way to stand out, but you don't want to become known just as "that actor who gives out flashlights."*

Before sending out swag, first make sure that anything you choose to give is relatively related to what you want to say about yourself. Second, be sure that you can back up your swag with real talent because that's ultimately what you want to be remembered for.

*Unless your last name is Flashlight, in which case we sincerely apologize, and applaud this tactic.

YOUR CONTACT INFO

If you're on the lam or in a witness protection program, you want to be as difficult to find as possible. Not so in this business. Just the opposite, as a matter of fact. And to help people find you as easily as possible (until you get famous, and then you can go back to making yourself difficult to find), do your best to keep your contact details constant and available. By that we mean make sure your contact information is out there and easy to find when someone's looking for you; and if possible, don't go changing it every six months or even every year.

Sometimes it takes a while for those seeds you spread to grow into trees you can swing from (okay, we promised, only a few paragraphs ago, that we'd stop saying that. We've definitely taken this analogy too far and MUST BE STOPPED.). If someone you've handed your business card to tries to call you, and all they hear is, "You have reached a number that has been disconnected or is no longer in service ..." odds are they aren't going to keep looking for you. It takes too much effort, too much time, and this is a fast-moving business. They've probably got a stack of similar business cards and they're already on to the next one.

Changing your contact info will end up costing you more than just work. It will be very expensive for you to have to change the information on your business cards, postcards, demos, website, and anything else you may have already printed with your now outdated info on it.

If you absolutely *must* change your contact info, make sure you update it on your website, and even send out an email blast letting everyone know that you've changed it. You never know when that call's going to come. Make sure it gets through.

UNION/NONUNION

Whether or not to join a union is a question that will come up eventually, and everybody's got a strong opinion on it. So rather than try to tell you how to play your cards, we'll just go over some basic information.

In the U.S., voice acting work is regulated by SAG-AFTRA, which stands for the Screen Actors Guild (*SAG*) and the American Federation of Television and Radio Artists (*AFTRA*). They used to be separate unions that divvied up the acting work, but merged in 2012. To work on a SAG-AFTRA job (a job under SAG-AFTRA jurisdiction and protected by the union's regulations), you must be a member of SAG-AFTRA. To get more details on the union and its regulations and membership requirements, please visit SAGAFTRA.org.

In other countries the jurisdiction may fall to unions such as the Alliance of Canadian Cinema Television and Radio Artists (ACTRA), and the British Academy of Film and Television Arts (BAFTA). Check to see what union might apply in your country.

Some employers may choose to go *non*union, meaning that only people *not* belonging to a union may apply for voice acting jobs with them. If you are just starting out in the U.S., odds are you will not belong to the union and your only option will be to work nonunion jobs. There's nothing wrong with this, despite the fact that union work will seem like the Holy Grail to you because of the benefits and the often higher pay scale.

Don't obsess over joining the union. That time will come when it's right. If you force your way there before you're ready, you may find yourself in a different pinch: now you're limited to union work only, but you have no agent, haven't built a name for yourself, nor have you amassed many contacts. So how are you going to get this union work? You're better off working the jobs you can until the opportunity to join a union presents itself naturally. The nonunion work is out there. And some of it pays as well as union work.

Once again, if you *are* in the union, you cannot work on non-union jobs that would be covered by that union.

All union jobs are paid the same basic scale rate for the same type of job, so you will always be assured that Job X = $Y. No one else will be getting paid a different amount for doing the same type of job. A common exception, of course, is a well-known or celebrity talent who may be able to negotiate a higher (*above scale*) rate. The union is also responsible for making sure working conditions are safe and that the needs of its membership are taken care of.

Similarly, if you are nonunion, you cannot work on union jobs and usually can't even *audition* for union jobs. There are, however, exceptions to this rule. For example, if you are nonunion, but have a specific skill or talent that is hard to find, an employer may be willing to pay a fee and *buy* your way into the union if they exhaust their union options without finding someone suitable for the job. This is achieved through a Taft-Hartley agreement, and you can research that if you'd like to learn more.

Say producers of a video game are looking for an actor who speaks fluent Tupi from South America – but specifically Guarani dialect, not Nheengatu. They hold auditions for union actors who speak Guarani, and don't find any. But the video game *requires* it. Now they've got to look further afield, and if you're a nonunion actor who speaks Guarani, you may be in luck. This may be your golden ticket. Book this union job and they'll Taft-Hartley you and you can start the process of becoming a union member.

And that's another reason to be a well-rounded actor with many interests and skills. Not only will it make you more interesting as a person (and hence, actor), but your odd hobby might pay off in ways you could never imagine.

A common misconception about nonunion jobs is that they pay less than union jobs. This is often the case, but not always. They will sometimes pay more than union jobs since they aren't regulated; but a nonunion job without regulations might mean you are working longer hours or under conditions that aren't up to the standard of union requirements. Many studios will have both types of work depending on the producers and the clients they work with.

We can't say that there is a limit to the success you can attain by staying nonunion, but we have noticed that most of the working actors we know have had to join the union at some point in order to keep their careers moving along. The choicest jobs are most often the union ones. Don't let this be a hindrance. Let it be a goal. One you will reach when the time is right.

SCRATCH TRACKS — WITH TARA & YURI

HEY, TARA, WILL YOU BE MY VOICE-OVER AGENT? I'LL GIVE YOU 10%!

NOPE.

WHY NOT?

BECAUSE 10% OF NOTHING IS STILL NOTHING...

CHAPTER 14

PRACTICE MAKES PERMANENT

"What you practice every day is what you will become."

AUTHOR UNKNOWN

Time to take the stuff we've talked about and practice on some real live scripts, since the best way to be comfortable and confident when you get in the booth is to have practiced beforehand. But before we throw you into the fire, let's give you a little lesson on hieroglyphics. Okay, well, maybe not hieroglyphics *exactly*, but the first time you see certain kinds of script notations it might feel like you're dealing with a new language. These cryptic markings on your script are there to make things easier on you. Let's take a look at them now so you're ready to translate them when the time comes.

SCRIPT NOTATIONS

Script notations are used to give you, the actor, a heads-up about such things as where you should pause when reading a line of dialogue, and how long the pauses should take. There are some notations to let you know if your character has an intake of breath or some sort of reaction, and still others to indicate what the character's mouth looks like on screen so you can best match the lip flap.

The notations themselves can differ slightly from original animation to dub work, from video game to commercial, from writer to writer, and even studio to studio. We're going to introduce you to some script notations that we see most frequently, especially working in ADR/dubbing. Let this list be a general guide, but as always, never hesitate to ask the director what a notation means if you're unfamiliar with it.

TIME CODE

In the corner at the top or bottom of the screen might be a black box with numbers in it showing the *time code*. The time code indicates how far the program/movie has progressed, and enables everyone to stay on the same page. The numbers break down into *Hour:Minute:Second:Frame* so that if, for example, you have a line for which the time code is *01:02:03:04*, that means the line would begin at one hour, two minutes, three seconds, and four frames into the movie/program. Hours, minutes, and seconds, you're probably pretty familiar with; but *frames*? Allow us to *framesplain*.

When dealing with a recorded moving image (film/video/ animation), the illusion of movement is essentially created by flashing still images in rapid succession (hence the term *moving pictures*). This process fools the human eye – in much the same way an old-fashioned flip book did. Only these days we're talking much more high tech, with the individual images, or *frames*, generally going by at a rate of twenty-four or thirty per second. Because these frames go by so fast, you need not concern yourself too much with the frame number in the time code. That number will be much more important to the engineer, who may have to make very specific adjustments to lines that you'll record.

The engineer will always cue you up to the correct time code so that The Three Beeps bring you in at the exact moment you need to speak. Sometimes a script will show both an *in* and an *out* code so that you know when to begin speaking and also when to be done. The notation *01:03:12:19 – 01:03:25:20* indicates that the line begins at one hour, three minutes, twelve seconds and nineteen frames, and ends at one hour, three minutes, twenty-five seconds and twenty frames, giving you about thirteen seconds to speak.

LINE OR LOOP NUMBERS

A *loop number* or *line number* is just another number (usually found to the left of each line in the script) that makes it easier for the director/engineer/actor to refer to a specific line. Lines are numbered in consecutive order. Sometimes, when a line has been added after the original script was written, the new line number might be followed by a letter to avoid confusion (e.g. 1, 2, 3, *3A*, *3B*, 4, 5 …). In motion capture scripts and video game scripts, because of the enormous amount of content, a line number may be a really big number (98765) or a file name (*Kirby_OpenWorld-001*), depending on the internal organization the team is using for their scripts. Sometimes a line in a script may have multiple names: one for you, one for the engineer, and one for the audio/animation team. In that case, your director should let you know which line numbers/names you should be paying attention to. And if it's confusing, just ask.

MOUTH MOVEMENT

When recording *to picture* (recording dialogue to what has already been animated or filmed), you might encounter notations specifically dealing with a character's mouth movement, or lip flap. Below we list some of the most common notations.

MNS is short for *mouth not seen*, and indicates that the character's *mouth* is not visible, even though he/she/they/it might be on screen at the time. Perhaps the character's face is turned away

VOICE-OVER VOICE ACTOR

from the camera, or there's something blocking it from view – like a fan or a giant sword, for example. The *MNS* loop can be a boon to actors because you won't need to pay attention to mouth flap; you need be concerned only with timing. Similar to this notation is *MBS*, or *mouth barely seen*. This refers to a loop during which the character's mouth is so far away you can barely see it move even if it is flapping.

Similar to *MNS* are the straightforward notations *OFF* and *ON* which mean exactly what each word indicates: the line is spoken either *off*screen or *on*-screen. (The notation *OS* is also used for *offscreen*, or sometimes *OC is used* for *off camera*.) Sometimes both of these notations are used in the same loop. An example: a character wanders offscreen and then back on again, or an on-screen character turns away from the camera for a portion of the line.

Sometimes an even shorter shorthand is used to indicate an *off* line: *underlining*. Underlining comes in handy particularly in the abovementioned case, where some of the line is *on* and some of it is *off*. An example of an *on-off-on* line might look like this on the script:

"*You know <u>you'll never be able to get away with</u> that, Toshi, you're gonna get caught.*"

This gives you a heads-up that you'll have to pay particular attention to the mouth flaps at the beginning and at the end, but that you won't see several mouth flaps in the middle at all. This notation can become confusing if a writer is also using underlining to indicate to the actor that a certain word should be stressed, but this is only rarely a problem.

CM indicates a *closed mouth*. "How would that apply to someone speaking, you ask?" Well, remember, not all lines involve speaking. Many of them involve things like laughing, grunting,

228

or humming. So if you see a notation that says, *CM grunt* or *CM chuckle*, you know that the mouth won't be flapping, and that you should grunt or chuckle with your mouth closed to get the right sound. Similarly, you might see *OM, open mouth,* to denote the opposite.

CT is similar to closed mouth, but means *closed/clenched teeth.* Pull your lips back like you're growling or snarling: that's pretty much what CT is going to look like. Some people can speak through clenched teeth. Some can laugh. Some can only growl. Give it a shot; see what you can do with your teeth clenched. *Okay, killer. Back to reading.*

Other notations you'll come across in your script might include *sigh, inhale/exhale, reax* – shorthand for *reaction* (e.g. *fight reax, fear reax*), or *thought filter* (i.e. because the dialogue is going on inside the character's head, the mouth won't be flapping).

HITCHES

Standard punctuation can't always be trusted to ensure that a phrase times out (synchronizes) with action that's happening on the screen. To help you match specific timing, notations called *hitches* are included in the script. Hitches warn you of breaks in the line (pauses within a line of dialogue). You'll have to pay attention to these breaks/pauses when you're trying to match specific timing. Some of these notations might appear as one of the following marks: - ' ^ / ... and they all indicate varying lengths of pauses. Different writers will sometimes notate hitches differently, so you'll have to stay on your toes.

When considering the length of a pause, the idea of a *beat* (about a second) is a pretty good starting point. Often, if directors just want a *slight* hitch, they actually want less than a second. A shorter hitch is usually indicated by one of these marks ^ *or* ' while either / *or* ... may be used for longer pauses.

SOMETIMES IT ALL JUST WORKS ANYWAY

We dubbed the original *Voltron* series without seeing it. In those days, anime was new and there were no set systems for doing it. So the writers would watch the show and use the time code to time each line by frames, then convert it to seconds. In the script, next to each line of dialogue, they would place a number such as 5.46 or 1.23 indicating seconds, tenths and hundredths of seconds.

When the actors went in to record, they would *not* see a video of the show. There were no monitors at all. Instead, the director, Franklin Cofod, would have a stopwatch, and each time the actors said one of their lines, Franklin would time it and check the stopwatch. If it matched the number on the script, he'd move on. If it didn't match, he'd redo the line until it matched. Pauses were not indicated, so the actors would talk right thru pauses. As new characters came in or out of the series, there were no visuals or audio for the actors to go on, so they had to guess at what the character would sound like. Often they'd use a little weasely voice for a big burly character or a childish voice for an old man.

The result of all this should have been disastrous. Instead *Voltron* was a mega-hit show – once again proving Henslowe's theory in *Shakespeare in Love*, "Strangely enough, it all turns out well ... It's a mystery."

~ MARC HANDLER, DIRECTOR

PRACTICE SCRIPT & COPY SECTION

You will want to get your hands on as much copy and as many scripts as you can to familiarize yourself with the work you'll be doing. Although each project is unique and each session will have its own specialized copy, reading through a variety of scripts before you start working will get your brain going as well as your mouth, and you will find that you'll be more comfortable when you actually need to read a script for work.

As you know by now, *copy* is the material you will be working on in an audition or recording session. Below you will find some examples of various types of copy with which to put your VO skills to the test. You might want to use a similar variety for the clips on your demo reel.

You should notice that each example below has a different feel to it. The feel of a scene or phrase can indicate the types of vocal qualities you might want to employ when reading it.

MIC SAYS: Specs are a good starting point, but ad execs don't always know what they want; so don't be afraid to bring your own magic to the material.

COMMERCIAL COPY

Following is a series of different types of commercial spots you might come across, from hard sell to soft sell. The most important thing to remember is that with all commercial copy, personalizing the identity of the individual you're giving the information to can make the copy come to life. In our examples, we give you a spec to use as a jumping off point; but after you've tried it our way, feel free to bring your own ideas to the copy to give yourself more of a workout.

Hamburking Burgers Copy

Spec: Cool, laid back, talking to your buddy

The cheapest place to get a burger is also the healthiest place to get a burger. At Hamburking Burgers. We only sell burgers. And for just 99 cents. All natural, all fresh, all fast. A burger for a buck. Yeah!

Alive Insurance

Spec: Honest, folksy, wise

Your family is more important than anything, and luckily, now you have someone who thinks you're just as important as they are. At Alive Insurance, it's our goal to make sure you and your entire family are protected through life's many adventures. Call your Alive Insurance Representative today at 800-555-1234 to find out how you can make the most of tomorrow – today.

HipKool Back-to-School Clothes

Spec: High energy, fast-paced, hip and fun, but not cartoony

Right now at HipKool all the coolest clothes are 30-50% off. That's right, just 30-50% off. And if you come in this Saturday you'll find clothes for him at an additional 10% off. Girls get an additional 20% off all accessories and jewelry. So come on down and get all the best back-to-school gear this weekend just in time to show off your new jeans. And with all his-and-her denim for less than 30 bucks, there'll be plenty to show off. The HipKool Back-to-School shop-off, now thru August 30th, and with additional 10-20% discounts this Saturday. Get back-to-school savings at HipKool.

Awesome Action Toys

Spec: High energy, aggro, X-games-type read, but not shouting

You can jump 'em! You can rock 'em! You can roll 'em! Cool Wheel Carz! For the lightning-fast action of a real race, use them on dirt, water, or grass! See if you can win the race! Cars and racetrack sold separately. Cool Wheel Carz: a division of Awesome Action Toys.

Diabetes PSA

Spec: Personal, confessional, genuine

I still remember the smell of smoke on a crisp, cool, autumn evening, the sounds of laughter coming from the house, my sister and me eating fudge and marshmallows 'til our tummies hurt. I lost my sister to her fight against diabetes almost 2 years ago, and it could have been prevented. With almost 8% of the U.S. population currently diagnosed with diabetes, there's no time like the present to deal with this growing disease. Now more than ever, we need your support to fund vital diabetes research and save the future of our children.

Equator Flyy Travel Site

Spec: Wry, simple, not too charactery

Let Equator Flyy take you around the world for less than $2000. With round-trip fares from tons of major U.S. cities to destinations in Mexico, Australia, and Europe, getting away has never been so easy. Just visit us at EquatorFlyyTravel.com and click on "Around the World" to see our latest deals and destinations.

Bank 'R Us Tag

Spec: Fast-paced, intelligent, factual

Bank 'R Us Banking is a Member FDIC, Equal Opportunity Lender. Products and services are offered by Bank 'R Us Banking and its affiliates. Programs, fees, rates, and features are subject to change without notice.

ANIMATION SCRIPTS

Remember when we told you there are original animation (pre-lay) jobs and dubbed animation jobs, and that there are differences between recording them? Well, now's our chance to show you how the *copy* for each of these jobs differs as well. The content may be similar, but the scripts look very different, and the way you read them won't always be the same.

Original

We've dusted off an old script from an animated show called *Yuratari the Goat* – okay, so we just made it up. But humor us and just imagine for a moment that it's an excerpt from a pre-lay animation script.

---

pg 37

<u>EXT. DEEP DARK WOODS NEAR THE
FORTRESS OF EVIL – DUSK</u>

Sam and Yuratari the Goat look at the fortress, black smoke rising from behind its walls.

245   SAM
We're not gonna be able to make it!

246   YURATARI
Baaaah! We can do it. You go down that
side and I'll come at them from the front.

247   SAM
Aren't you worried they'll see you?

248   YURATARI
I'm more worried about what might happen if
we don't get the Crystal of Light back soon –
Baaaaaah.

Sam reluctantly turns and starts to run to the gorge.

249   SAM
                                  (turning back)
                    Be careful you crazy goat. I don't wanna have
                    to tell Princess Mona you didn't make it back!

                                                      FADE TO BLACK.

Dubbed animation

We can't very well include *actual* copy from a series we're working on, so let's pretend we just licensed a new Japanese animated
show that's being dubbed into English. Below is some of this
exciting copy from *Best Dub Show Happy Time, Go!* Enjoy...

Loop Number	Time Code	Character	Line	Notes
4.	01:12:27:21 01:12:29:24	Kira	Stop right there!	*Very frightened*
5.	01:12:30:07 01:12:34:09	Suki	What? ^ No, it can't be.	
6.	01:12:35:18 01:12:38:10	Suki	Is it ... ^ (OM SURPRISE REAX)	*mouth moves a lot on reax*
7.	01:12:39:05 01:12:43:07	Kira	Why do you look at me like that?	
8.	01:12:45:09 01:12:49:18	Kira	(thought filter) What a strange girl this is.	
9.	01:12:50:03 01:12:53:05	Suki	It's you. / The Chicken ^ of Destiny.	
10.	01:12:55:15 01:12:57:10	Kira	(CT DISGUST REAX) How dare you!	*dialogue a little fast*
11.	01:12:59:01 01:13:02:20	Suki	I am dishonored!	

VIDEO GAME SCRIPT

Each video game session is different, but many of the scripts we've worked with actually have each character's lines separated from the rest of the script to make it easier to record them all at a run. That said, for the video game dialogue below, let's say you've been asked to do an ABC (series) take of each of the efforts as small, medium, and large.

To explore a variety of sounds, imagine different types of movements your character might be making. Are you blocking a hit with your arm or your leg? Do you take the hit to your gut, your chest, or your head? This distinction will affect the reaction sound you create and help differentiate your efforts. Variety will get you rehired.

When you come across lines in the script that describe only the *type* of effort or sound they want you to make (e.g. *attack, throwing effort, fall, jump, death*), you should not only remember to really go for it, but imagine a variety of different vocalizations for each effort. Consider different consonant and vowel combinations. Getting hit in the stomach could sound like *ooof!* but it could also be *aargh!* or *kugh!* Perhaps an attack might sound like *hyyyah!* or *raah!chuh!*

Line #	Character	Dialogue	
15	MELCHIOR	Never! We will take this ship ...	
16	MELCHIOR	(Shoving Effort)	3x
17	MELCHIOR	(Attack)	3x
18	MELCHIOR	Yield, or perish!	
19	MELCHIOR	(Take damage)	3x
20	MELCHIOR	See you on the other side of hell!	
21	MELCHIOR	(War cry)	3x
22	MELCHIOR	I never ... thought ... I'd hear you say –	
23	MELCHIOR	(Death)	3x

PROMO/TRAILER COPY

Similar to commercial copy, but specifically promoting a particular network or TV show, the promos below give you just a taste of this type of copy.

The YT Network

Spec: Real, Hip, Girl/Guy-next-door, ex. Jennifer Lawrence, Ryan Reynolds

Why tea? Just because. Check it out. Only on YT.
Check it. The funny. Why? Tea. Only on YT.
Coming up next, on YT. Check it.

The Toppies Award Show

Ladies and Gentlemen, please take your seats, sit back, and enjoy the most riveting, most exhilarating, most action-packed awards show this season. The Toppies, the top awards given to the best, the brightest, and the most promising actors, writers, directors, and engineers in the field of voice-over. First up for Best Female Performance in an animated series …

Tumbling After *Trailer*

In a world where darkness meets light, one man is forced to choose between the two. A dark secret will threaten to tear these two lovers apart. Will Jack and Jill make it up the hill? Or will it all come … *Tumbling After?*

NARRATION SCRIPTS

Narration might be for anything from a story to an instructional manual. Below is just a little sample of this burgeoning area of voice work. Try your hand at reading an audiobook or reading more cut-and-dried medical or legal text for further practice.

Children's Book/Story

The Little Girl Who Grew Up To Be A Snowman, by Yuri Lowenthal

"Oh, honey," he blurted. "I can't let myself get sidetracked by that business. My brain's overheating on this project as is."

And with that, he pulled a chain that tripped a switch that activated a mechanism that fired a spark that started a pump that compressed some air that sprayed his head with liquid nitrogen with a terrifying hissing sound.

"Ahh, that's much better. I'm close! I'm close!"

Classic Literature

Hone your skills on a classic; try something out of Dickens or Homer's *The Odyssey* for a little classical language practice. You can even use a play by Shakespeare or perhaps Molière. Pick whatever sounds like it might be fun. There's plenty to choose from. If you try something and don't like it, grab something else. Take advantage of free books at the library! For now, try reading the Aesop's fable below.

The Prophet, an Aesop's fable, translated by George Fyler Townsend

A Wizard, sitting in the marketplace, was telling the fortunes of the passers-by when a person ran up in great haste, and announced to him that the doors of his house had been broken open and that all his goods were being stolen.

He sighed heavily and hastened away as fast as he could run. A neighbor saw him running and said, "Oh! You fellow there! You say you can foretell the fortunes of others; how is it you did not foresee your own?"

Instructional Copy

How to build a tasty PB 'n' J

First gather your ingredients. Lay out two fresh slices of bread (toasted if you prefer). Using a butter knife, apply one thick, even coat of peanut butter to one of the slices. Wipe the knife clean, and use it to apply an evenly matched coat of your favorite jelly to the other slice of bread. Carefully pick up the peanut buttered slice and place it on the jellied side of the other slice, so that the peanut butter is directly against the jelly. Press gently together. Voila! An American classic!

Legal/Medical Text

There are thirty-one pairs of peripheral spinal nerves which emerge from the spinal cord through spaces between the vertebrae. Each of these nerves divides and then subdivides into smaller branches. There are dorsal and ventral branches. The dorsal branches service the rear area of the body, while the ventral branches service the sides and front.

All rights reserved. Without limit to the rights copyright reserved above, no part of the publication may be reproduced without prior written permission of both the copyright owner and the publisher. Published in the United States, © 2009

GET ON YOUR FEET: PCAP SCRIPTS

You may do performance capture for a character in a film or a video game, and the style and genre can vary wildly. For this sample section, practice learning the script, getting off book, and performing the scene while on your feet going through the physical motions indicated in the script.

Better still, get a friend (or a tripod) to film you. Extra credit points if you wear spandex and a helmet, tape a brick to your chest, and paint dots on your face with eyeliner. *Just kidding. But you do get bonus points for sticking with us through this paragraph.* Once you've performed one character in the scene, try the scene again, but as the other character!

Script for Act3_DarkPowerHQ

Line Count: 6

Cinematic

Act3_DarkPowerHQ

28939

EXT. DARK POWER HEADQUARTERS – DAY

36789

Quill and Styles have just broken into the Dark Power HQ. They stand on a second-story catwalk and survey the room below. It is dark and quiet. TOO QUIET. We CUT TO:

Heavily armed Dark Power forces spill out of doorways on the floor below and from the darkened recesses of the warehouse. Quill looks at Styles. Styles grabs a gun. Quill reaches out.

03245   QUILL_CINE_DARKHQ_001
I got this.

12452   STYLES_CINE_DARKHQ_005
Are you kidding? I helped you get in here didn't I?

12453   QUILL_CINE_DARKHQ_002

Against my better judgment. I don't need a partner. Stay here.

22487   STYLES_CINE_DARKHQ_006

I've taken on more than this without your help. I'm fine.

36871

Suddenly two of the Dark Power mercenaries press guns into their backs. But before they can even utter a word, Styles drops to the floor, kicking one of the mercenary's legs out from under him! The mercenary's rifle FIRES LOUDLY into the air!

12949   QUILL_CINE_DARKHQ_003

So much for the element of surprise…

36890

Quill FIRES a grappling gun across to the far railing, using another DP mercenary as anchor, and pulls himself across. Styles does some grappling of her own, YANKING one of the mercenaries off the catwalk.

36892

Quill dispatches the mercenaries on the far catwalk with flair that our stunt team will make look great, while Styles brutally takes down the last mercenary on the catwalk with her. Machine gun fire pings off the catwalk they're standing on.

02453   QUILL_CINE_DARKHQ_004

Shall we… partner?

36892

END CINEMATIC CAMERA:

As Quill and Styles leap over the catwalk, we transition to gameplay.

End Cinematic

PODCASTING TEMPLATE

Podcasts are tricky to write out scripts for because they are usually unscripted and each one has a personality of its own. You could, for example, do a very structured show which is broken down into the same specific segments for each program, or your episodes could vary drastically from recording to recording. Your show could even be scripted like a radio play. For the purposes of this section, record yourself hosting an interview show for a few minutes. Don't worry, you'll never have to play it for anyone else, but you never know what may happen…

Start first by deciding what your show is about: we recommend something that you're passionate about. Then come up with a name for your program and see if you can loop a friend or family member into being your first victim – uh, guest. Not all podcasts interview guests, but doing so can definitely help you not feel like you have to generate the whole show yourself.

Decide whether or not you want to have prepared questions or just let the wind take you where it may. Having a cheat sheet could help you out in the case of awkward pauses or a reticent guest. If you want to be extra prepared, listen to a few podcasts to get a feel for how it all works (or doesn't).

How will you record your show? Well, it can be as simple as using whatever voice memo recording app came with your phone, or you can set up something that's a little more elaborate. Will you each have a mic (recommended), or will you share? Remember, the same rules for setting up a space that sounds good for recording an audition apply here, too. Test your setup before you invite your co-conspirator over. Once they've arrived, agree that you will keep recording the "show" for at least five to ten minutes. Then, start recording, and introduce your show ("Hello my name is Tara Platt and you are listening to the *Talking with Tara Today Show*"), your guest ("We are here today with Johnny John

Johnson talking about [insert your brilliant topic here]"), and then start chatting (this is the meat of the podcast sandwich). When you want to wrap it up, thank your guest and listeners and sign off ("Thanks so much Johnny John for enlightening us about [insert topic here] today. This is Tara, and you've been listening to the *Talking with Tara Today Show*. Talk to YOU next week!"). You may be surprised at how the time flies when you're interviewing!

Now listen to the playback and note aspects of the show you liked, things you'd choose to improve, and pitfalls to avoid in the future. Worst case scenario, you got to hang out with a pal and chat for a bit. Best case scenario, you just recorded the pilot for a soon-to-be award-winning podcast!

Has all this copy inspired you to do some more digging of your own? Great. Anything you read can be turned into practice copy. Take a look around and see what you might use as inspiration. The materials you compile will help you write commercial, narration, or even promo copy for your own demo!

WRITING: NOT SO SOLITARY AN ENDEAVOR AFTER ALL

I have had to sit in a studio watching some irritating former child-star ruin one of my best-ever scripts.

"My character wouldn't say that," she said.

"It's not *your* character," I replied. "It's mine. Now read the line the way I wrote it!"

Shortly afterwards, I was asked to leave. The writer is king in his little head, for as long as he is typing alone. Once the script reaches the studio, it belongs to the actors. Get used to it. Over the years I have learned to write scripts that are more open to interpretation, that allow the actors freer rein. I suppose it's because I trust them more now. I understand that on the day they have my script, it is theirs, and that I should credit them with the talent to do it justice.

The joys outweigh the miseries. I have listened as an actress took something I had written and utterly transformed it, adding nuances of her own, reading every line just as I had intended, but then adding tiny moments of unexpected comedy, pathos, and character. She took it to new heights, and she made it indubitably her own. Her name was Sheridan Smith, and she made me sound a lot smarter than I really was.

Those memorable little snickers from Mark Gatiss when he plays the Master in my *Doctor Who Unbound: Sympathy for the Devil*? They weren't scripted; he put them in himself. That filthy Scottish slang from Middenface McNulty in *Strontium Dog: Down to Earth*, largely invented by Mark McDonnell, who is a filthy Scot. That comedy snort from Johnny Alpha when he wakes up in *Strontium Dog: Fire from Heaven*, put in there by Simon Pegg, who is a comedy snorter. The decision to play the bad guy with the voice of Sean Connery in my translation of *Kekko Kamen* – all down to Rupert Degas. But don't tell anyone; I am happy to take the credit for their decisions, as long as I look good.

~ Jonathan Clements, Writer

A FUN EXERCISE: THE PHRASINATOR!

Scientists and technicians have been working around the clock at TaraYuri Industries and have finally devised a little something that we hope you'll enjoy: *The Phrasinator* (see below). Choose a phrase from the list on the left, and say it using each of the qualities (feelings) listed on the right. Be sure to try each phrase with each quality to discover how a different intention can change your reading of a line.

The Phrasinator can be a particularly helpful exercise for working on video game copy. If the director asks for two different takes of the same line, try giving a different intention, or quality, to each. Trust us; it'll be much more exciting than reading the copy twice exactly the same way. For the director *and* for you!

The Phrasinator

PHRASE	QUALITY
Watch out	Angry
Help me	Happy
I'm here	Frustrated
Not that way	Annoyed
What do you mean	Scared
I like green ones	Sleepy
I don't want any	In awe
Were you serious	Frightened
Get down	Excited
Yes and	Overjoyed
Hooray	Uncomfortable
That's what I'm talking about	Secretive

SCRATCH TRACKS　　　　**WITH TARA & YURI**

CHAPTER 15
SUCCESS STORIES

*"Success is stumbling from failure to failure
with no loss of enthusiasm."*

SIR WINSTON CHURCHILL, BRITISH
STATESMAN, WRITER

NOT JUST US

Each and every person's path to success is unique and exciting – with ups and downs, setbacks and detours, stalemates and leaps forward. But no matter what the person's story, we can learn from it.

That's why we decided that, for this updated and revised edition, we would reach out to readers of the book to see what has or hasn't worked for them over the years. Perhaps, as you read their stories, you will find similarities to your own experience, or you'll find encouragement in knowing that it wasn't that long ago that they were where you are and reading this book (*errr… the slightly shorter, slightly earlier version of this book*)!

READER STORIES

The first story comes from reader David Errigo, Jr. who is now living in Los Angeles and represented by a great agency. He worked hard to make his career something that he wanted. His story shows that there are things you can do to take bold action towards your dream. And we aren't just saying that because he liked our book (*thanks, David, for the kind words*).

CONFIDENCE MAKES A DIFFERENCE

I found voice-over by accident. I always loved cartoons. Always loved Disney. Always loved creating character voices. I was a born ham. I started acting in 7th grade in Florida. After high school and college in Montana, and a couple of years as a graphic designer/photographer at a regional theatre in Arizona, I moved to New York. After a couple of adventures, I found a manager, and he set me up with a meeting at Paradigm for on-camera commercials. The agent and I chatted for nearly an hour before he stood up from his desk and said, "Come with me." He walked me through the office to the voice-over department: that day I started freelancing with them.

I knew nothing. Well, nothing useful. I could create a character, create a funny voice, speak clearly (and quite loudly – thanks, theatre!), and I had many other skills gained through theatrical training and experience. But I didn't know what to do in the booth. Bless Matt (my agent), he kept letting me audition for a while, and I even booked a small ad pitch job for Sony. Still, I needed more knowledge. I kept pursuing theatre and creating relationships in the city and across the country as I traveled for shows.

At some point I was reminded of something a personal trainer had said to me at the gym during one of those free get-people-to-buy-sessions deals. He asked me, "Are you likely to buy any sessions?"

"No. I don't think I can afford it," I replied.

"Okay," he said. "Then buy books. Buy Magazines. Do it yourself. You'll get results. *And* you'll save money."

Boom. Books. Self reliance. There it was staring me in the face. If it worked for fitness, it could surely work for voice training. I started picking up books. I started listening to podcasts. I started taking workshops when I could find them. I watched *I Know That Voice* on repeat. I started working. A lot of what was available to me was dubbing for foreign properties, and I started working a few times a month in that realm. As I went down the rabbit hole, a through line popped up for animation: if you want to do this for real, you have to go to L.A. This is where *VOVA* came in.

I was sitting in Barnes and Noble at Union Square browsing through the book when I stumbled on the dubbing section. It stopped me in my tracks. I knew I had to buy the book. By then I had gotten fairly comfortable with the techniques and skill associated with dubbing, and one passage in the book stood out to me: *If you can master the skills required for dubbing, you'll look really good in a pickup or ADR session for a pre-lay animation project. The engineer will love you, and you'll save everyone time and money.* This became a weird source of confidence for me as I geared up to make the move to L.A. I would think, "Well, if I'm not good at any of the other stuff, at least people will like me for this."

Then I went deeper. *Get comfortable with your boundaries as well as your strengths… A common misconception among actors is that to make a bold choice is to do something crazy or intentionally weird… Don't ever fear that your voice sounds too* natural *to be interesting.* And so on, and so on. There are similar gems to be found all throughout this book. Those are just a few of the highlighted passages in my copy (which I keep at my desk for occasional reminders). Armed with new knowledge, a couple of trials overcome, and many auditions completed (and with an awesome pal's referral), I found actual full representation with Stewart Talent in NYC. Shortly thereafter in 2016, serendipity and tragedy combined to spur me to make the move to Los Angeles where I found representation with SBV and can happily say I make my living as a voice actor.

To say that *VOVA* was what got me here would be to ignore the many contributions and support of friends, family, and colleagues. However, to say that this book had a lot to do with my confidence level when deciding to make the change would be absolutely appropriate. I got the gift of feeling like I had something of value to contribute in a world I so desperately wanted to join. Not only that: I had seeds to plant for other skills that I didn't know I needed. And the cover looks cool. (*Sorry, couldn't resist something light.*)

> Thank you for an outstanding resource, and if you'll excuse me, I think I'll go have a refresher read. After all, who doesn't like more work?
>
> ~ DAVID ERRIGO, JR., ACTOR

Now let's look at someone who started taking action when they were still in high school. Matt Shipman is here to share his journey, from garbage pails to studio tales. In his own words…

WORKING HARD AND FINDING ANSWERS

When I was in middle school, my class took a career aptitude test. It was dozens of pages long, with many questions like "Do you enjoy being outside?" I remember answering "no" to a lot of questions because I just couldn't imagine myself doing anything that they were suggesting. At the end of the test, the program excitedly told me I'd make a great janitor. I'm not making that up. When I think back to that seemingly insignificant moment, it helps me understand why I chose the path I did. I eventually chose voice-over because there really wasn't anything else that I could see myself doing for (potentially) the rest of my life.

A year or two after that test, I started to notice that some cartoon characters' voices sounded the same. I didn't quite understand what that meant at the time, but that curiosity led me to do some research. It didn't take long before I realized that there were real people behind these characters that I loved, giving them life. And that was their job! The more I learned, the more fascinated I became with the concept. (Maybe I didn't have to be a janitor after all!) So, I started recording myself on my terrible computer microphone. I'd listen to what I'd recorded, compare it to professional performances that I respected, and try to understand what made it feel so...amateur.

I learned more and more, and practiced on my own after school. When I was fifteen, I decided that voice-over was what I wanted to do with my life. At the time of this writing, I'm ten days shy of twenty-five, and I'm just scratching the surface. This can take a LONG time.

I knew I needed to get better. So I joined my theatre club at school and performed in their productions. I graduated, went to college, and started auditioning for ten times more shows than I was cast in (because that's just how it works). I invested in better home recording equipment and started booking small voice-over gigs on line: low budget commercials, indie video games, anything that I could find. I took acting and public speaking classes to help get over my nerves when I'm performing in front of someone. I took voice-over classes and workshops, and met people. I worked other jobs like food service and retail to start saving money so I could put myself where the voice-over work was. *Voice-Over Voice Actor* came out and I snagged a copy right away. It answered so many questions I had! (*They didn't pay me to say that.*)

As time went by, I auditioned for every character that I could feasibly voice: main characters, their rivals, their wacky friends, the sassy kid, the over-the-top dad.

Months went by, and I didn't hear anything. Eventually I got the email saying I booked the part. It was a pretty major recurring character, and I'm still playing him to this day. That's the closest thing to my "big break" that there ever was.

I started working with a couple of other studios regularly, thanks to the people I had met. A lot of voice-over doesn't pay that much, so I decided to expand. I inquired about script adaptation, I started booking bigger parts, and I started meeting more people. I learned how to engineer an ADR session and filled in directing on a few projects. With all of the knowledge we gained, people we met, and resources we slowly built up, Brittany Lauda (who has a different success story) and I started our own studio, Kocha Sound, where we record VO for games and shows. I still record *Yu-Gi-Oh!* but now from our own studio. I used my previous script adaptation experience to get a job writing with Funimation. I've got a voice-over session in 3 hours, and I'm celebrating my birthday as a guest at an anime con back in NYC soon.

It's probably easy to read all that and think, "Okay, well things fell into place for this guy. How does this help me?" But keep in mind that you just read a ten-year journey in a few paragraphs. There were so many times I doubted myself. So many people who told me I'd never do this. So much rejection and SO much learning: how to take direction; how not to be starry-eyed when you meet an actor you admire; how to effectively criticize your own performances so you can grow. And then there's the technical side: how to read and understand contracts; when to go slightly off-mic to avoid a plosive; what in the world does "[OM REVVING UP >> 01:12:03:16]" mean?! Point is, you want to learn all you can, and it will take a lot of time. This isn't easy.

And at the end of the day, I've still got a long road ahead of me. But I'm in a place where my voice-over and writing can pay the bills. And that's pretty cool. What's less cool is remembering that I *did* end up working as a janitor one summer during college (it paid well, and I was saving up!), so that career-aptitude test wasn't so far off after all...

P.S. Every day I warm up using a routine that evolved from the one in *Voice-Over Voice Actor*. "Puh-tuh-kuh-tuh, buh-duh-guh-duh, puh-tuh-kuh-tuh, buh-duh-guh-duh!"

~ Matt Shipman, Actor

Our next success story comes from someone who recognizes that success is a journey, and he is still very much on the journey, learning as he goes. We hope that your wake-up call won't take the form of a medical emergency like it did for Cyrus Nemati, but however it appears, we hope you are ready to take action!

Finding the Pathway to Possible

I always wanted to be a voice actor, deep down. My favorite toy as a kid was my tape recorder. I would make shows and audiobooks – audiobooks I'd actually listen to, which I'm aware now is extremely bizarre. But a career like voice acting wasn't a thing that was done in my cultural upbringing, so I put acting away, aside from doing the occasional theatre or independent film role.

At 31 (already "knowing" I was too old to get into voice acting), I had a bad experience with an ENT doctor that left my hearing significantly impaired. It was only for a little while, but it definitely gave me a scare. I remember being terrified that I would lose my relationship with my voice. Luckily, my hearing got back to normal, but I took the experience as a wake-up call to do what I always wanted to do with my voice.

I was working in Washington, D.C., at the time, doing Web development and communications work for a tech advocacy non-profit (not a great career track for someone who wants to get into voice-over). I dug through every resource I could on line. I looked into those classes that you pay a ton of money for and get a demo for your efforts. But in the end, I just grabbed as many scripts as I could from the Internet and cobbled together a demo. An agency in Washington, D.C., took me in after an open call, but never really got me any work.

That's when I found *Voice-Over Voice Actor*. I'd already stumbled upon some of the guidance that Yuri and Tara wrote about, and that gave me the confidence to know that I was at least on the right track. But there was a wealth of information I did not know yet. I didn't know how to do things *right*. All I had was a sleepy agency and a pretty unprofessional demo. What *Voice-Over Voice Actor* really gave me was the realization that this voice acting thing wasn't an impossible endeavor.

I pushed myself hard, flying around the country to put myself in front of casting directors, auditioning every night, making friends, and building my skills. I put away my natural introversion and made sure to take advantage of every opportunity that came my way. It started to pay off, with commercials and video games making up the bulk of my work.

I'm using the same strategies today, and I imagine I always will. I realize I've got a lot to learn, and once I learn those things, there will be more to learn after that. But I know that being a voice actor isn't impossible. I see my peers succeeding by thinking the same way, yet still encountering the same stumbling blocks I do. It doesn't seem like hard work, but it is; but it's definitely not impossible. The pathway is right there in *Voice-Over Voice Actor*, and in the attitudes of anyone who actually becomes a voice actor.

~ CYRUS NEMATI, ACTOR

The specifics of each person's path to success will be different, but are you starting to see certain recurring themes emerge? Our next story comes from Jay Preston, an actor we met early in his career, and to whom we actually gave a copy of the book ourselves...

MIC SAYS: Whatever your story is, it is YOURS. Own it. Be proud of it. It got you exactly where you are now and will take you to your own greatest heights!

KNOW YOUR GOAL AND FOLLOW THE SIGNS

In an interesting turn of fate, in my very first month telling people I was "getting into voice-over," I met Yuri and Tara, they handed me their book, and the journey literally began. Every 2 months, I would make some progress and then I would read the book again, make some progress and read the book again: each time picking up on something I didn't fully understand the first time. So now, knowing you are reading my words in a book I've so frequently read myself is kind of surreal.

What follows (along with starting to act when I was 16 and being involved in theatre ever since) are the reasons, I believe, for my success so far. Steps that you, too, can take.

1) Find the path you were born to be on, trust it, and follow every sign. I'll be the first to throw skepticism at the "put it out there and the world will provide" mentality. Until I fully understood how it worked, there was no combination of words in a book or from a friend's mouth that helped it make sense to me; there was no real guide for how to do it. But if you are truly on your right path, doing what you think you should be doing, you will eventually create the world in which you are successful. The craziest thing is, it's that simple a concept. And still you think to yourself, "Great. I've heard

that before: what does that mean?" I'll tell you how it worked for me. I fell into voice-over by accident, and realized it's exactly what I was born to do. So I asked how to do it better. Mary Ellen Lord at SBV told me, "Go to this class, then that class, and then let me know when you want the next step." Those classes were far more expensive than any class I'd attended in L.A. before... and I was broke.... and I *hate* "classes in L.A." But I took them anyway. I met a sound engineer, Morgan Gerhard, who introduced me to Yuri, who told me that I should meet Bill Holmes and go to his networking event. I didn't know who that was or why, but I trusted Yuri. Fate had already brought us together as friends, so I did it. Bill "The VO Doctor" Holmes was the start of another year and a half of training. Then someone told me about Talk Shop, so I went there for workshops and trained more. I trained at every VO booth I could squeeze into. Through Bill, I met the incredible director Jamie Mortellaro and one of the best friendships in my life was formed: with his guidance, I've grown even more. *Something* told me I should create a network of like-minded voice actors, friends, and co-workers. So I did, and the VO Collective has become a haven for knowledge, work, and friendships. *I must note that I trained for 3 years before creating my first professional demo. Why? Because everyone who's successful tells you not to make a demo until you are ready. So don't.

2) Believe in yourself, and take that leap of faith. You will never have "enough" money. You will never feel like "now's a good time." The more you put it off, the more things will get in your way, the more reasons you will give yourself to wait. Don't be afraid of success. Quit that job you hate, and go all in. But remember to put *all* of the time you were spending on that other job *plus* the time you were already putting into VO *into* your voice-over career: learning, classes, auditioning, marketing. When you quit that job you hate, you immediately start your new job. And that job has 12- to 16-hour days. "But Jay! That's just too much work!" you say. Well I say to you, then you don't love it enough. Because my 12+ hours a day still feels like I'm on a magical vacation in which money keeps showing up. Take a moment and *think* about it. When you were working that other job, you were trying to do all the things you needed to do *to*

get into voice-over, right? So all you are really doing is turning that temp job into a VO job.

3) Keep up with new technology and new innovations. All I heard when I was getting into VO was how different the business is now. Well I wasn't around then: I showed up in the *now* and in the *different*, and I found ways to make it work for me. Stay current, and adapt with things as they change. Change is inevitable.

4) Don't stop having fun outside of VO. Make new friendships, fall in love, go on little and big adventures, have game nights, visit family, find new restaurants, go to concerts, do anything that can be perceived as *living*, and do it often. As an actor, you only have so much you can pull from in your bag of life experience. And every time you pull from that bag, it gets lighter. The only way to fill it up is to live life and interact with the world around you. You can't be a *wise storyteller* without stories, and you can't be *conversational* without having conversations.

Now, if you've been paying attention, you'll understand that you couldn't possibly take my *exact* path to success. It's the one I'm on. I was just being me, trying to pay my bills in L.A. So just be you. Be kind, keep your eyes open, and when you ask for advice, be ready to take it and run with it.

~ JAY PRESTON, ACTOR

And last, but not least, we'll leave you with a story from Darin De Paul, an actor who embarked on this specific journey much later in life than most. But it just goes to show you not to let anything hold you back from pursuing your dream. Even if you haven't heard *of* Darin, you've probably *heard* him…

LEARN ACTING *AND* THE BUSINESS

Barnes & Noble. Union Square. New York City. That is where I picked up *Voice-Over Voice Actor*. I was doing theatre and commercial voice-overs in New York, but I wanted to learn more about every facet of the industry. I was an avid listener to Rob Paulsen's amazing podcast "Talkin' Toons," and an episode featured Tara and Yuri. They spoke of their careers, their lives … and their new book. I remember just where I was sitting when I heard it. The café called Cosi in Union Square which sadly no longer exists. But I remember the exact place I was sitting as I listened to Rob interview Tara and Yuri. I loved their passion for the business of voice-over and I ran out and bought a copy of their book. I think I pretty much devoured it. So much practical and insightful information told with humor, heart, and wisdom.

I loved the advice on how to set up a home studio because in New York, you always went in to your agent or to a casting director's office to audition, whereas in Los Angeles, for the most part, you could record an audition at home. And it better sound good. I discovered proper mic placement and other tools that I needed to know. Each facet of the business is different. And if you want to break into a business that is tough to break into – you have to be talented, and you have to know how to properly present yourself as a professional. That is something I also got from Tara and Yuri. I needed to learn more about the nuts and bolts of every aspect of voice acting. Because, yes, you do have to have the proper acting training to make it in show business. That is essential. But what is also important is knowing the business side as well. Yuri and Tara brilliantly share their knowledge of the business side of show business.

In 2013, when I took the crazy chance to try and see if I could break into the Los Angeles voice-over world, I reread *Voice-Over Voice Actor*. I wanted to be ready. Because it is always a gamble, but the more prepared you are, the better your odds. And then when I met Tara and Yuri … I pretty much stammered and fanboyed. But I told them what the book meant to me. How they had been the guides on my journey. Yuri and Tara were, in a way, the Lewis and Clark in my VO trip westward. (I didn't really say the part about Lewis and Clark to them. But I thought it really hard.)

Success is indeed preparation meets opportunity. I have gotten to work on voice-over projects, and play roles I always dreamed of. Whether it be animation, video games, commercials, or looping … I have been lucky. But my crazy way of preparing is to learn everything about the world I want to be a part of. To learn about my fellow performers, writers, directors, game developers. As an actor you never stop learning.

That copy of *Voice-Over Voice Actor* is still on my shelf in my New York apartment. It seems like I first read it a lifetime ago. And now ... Yuri and Tara asked me to write this. I was overwhelmed by their kindness. They were part of the start of my journey. If you are reading this, they are part of the start of yours. Each career in the performing arts will be different. Being a working actor is hard. It is hard. It is HARD. Never stop learning. Never stop challenging yourself. Always be joyful. Always be professional. That is what I got from reading *Voice-Over Voice Actor*. That is what I got that day in Barnes & Noble. Union Square. New York City. And so, here we are. All the best on YOUR journey.

~ DARIN DE PAUL, ACTOR

[YOUR STORY GOES HERE]

Hopefully, at this point, you recognize there is no reason that, with your own passion, drive, determination, and focus, you couldn't someday share a story on par with or better than the ones above. But remember, success will always look different to different people.

For some, having a steady job doing a weekly promo gig is perfection, while others may see success as nothing less than working on five or more AAA game titles a year. And be aware that success will never be exactly as you foresaw it. Let your dreams be flexible, and embrace success in *all* forms. As we've mentioned, we didn't come out here to get into voice acting, but we're very happy it turned out that way!

Remember, try not to compare yourself to others. This business appears to be a competition, but it's not. For another person to win, you don't have to lose. There's enough to go around. Compare yourself instead to your own past. Look how far you've come already! We look forward someday soon to reading your story...

SCRATCH TRACKS

WITH TARA & YURI

CHAPTER 16
HINTS, TIPS, AND PARTING THOUGHTS

"I've got a tip for you: Longnose in the fourth."

BARRY PLATT, DOCTOR, ROCKET SCIENTIST

We don't like to give *advice* per se because everyone's experience is different, and advice implies that you think you know other people's lives better than they do. But we wanted to share the lowdown on things that *we've* done, since they've worked for us. And not just for us, but for a lot of people we work with. So as we've said about the rest of the suggestions in this book, try one on, see how it works. If, after a while, it isn't quite right for you, change it, or move on to the next idea. There are plenty of tips to go 'round.

ACTOR, DIRECTOR, *CHEATER?*

I'll admit it. Being both an animation voice actor and voice director kinda feels like cheating. Cheating, because I get to peer behind the curtain in ways my fellow actors and directors do not.

Sitting in my voice director's chair is a daily thrill. It's a permanent front row seat to fantastic performances by masters of animation acting: Tom Kenny, Tara Strong, Grey Griffin, John DiMaggio... I sit back while they try to make me laugh. Directing cartoon sessions is hilarious, and exciting, and weird. But most of all, it improves my own acting immeasurably.

Yes, I help these actors land their jokes and finesse their dialogue, coaching them through the beats of a scene. But I'm also studying them. Learning their tricks. Seeing what kills and what bombs. Every day is like a master class acting workshop with the best of the best – except I actually get paid to be there! And it has no doubt made me a finer voice actor in the process.

Then there's the flip side. When I'm on an acting gig, I also stay keenly aware of what my director is up to. Picking up the language they use to convey an adjustment. Learning how they break down the rhythm of a sequence. Yes, I always focus on giving a good performance, but who's to say I can't also pick up some directing tips at the same time?

So, once and for all, I confess. Acting has made me a better director. And directing has certainly made me a better actor. Now if I could just get into writing…

~ SAM RIEGEL, ACTOR, DIRECTOR

HOW TO STOCK YOUR PANTRY

All the actors we know have their own tricks and tips for keeping their voices healthy – because if you lose your voice, there's no real way around it.

Some of our favorite tools for soothing a sore throat or tired voice, or for getting your voice prepped for an upcoming session, include all natural *black licorice, non-caffeinated hot tea, honey* (especially *Manuka honey*, an anti-bacterial, medicinal honey from New Zealand which you'll have to go to a health store to find), *primrose* or *fish oil* capsules, *lots of water, fresh pineapple* or *pineapple juice*.

Also, we eat a lot of *ginger* and *garlic* which are said to have natural antibiotic properties; and while that might not directly affect our voices, it seems to keep us healthy. Staying healthy is important because we've found that when we get sick, our voices are the first things to go. We've also found that *zinc* helps nip a cold in the bud, or at least loosen its grip on us. You may want to keep these things around so you'll have them when you need them.

New favorite thing: downing a massive dose of Vitamin D (50,000 IU at once) when you're feeling sickly. It's apparently an old commercial airline pilot trick, but it has worked wonders for getting us back on top again. They call it "the Vitamin D Hammer" for a reason. We're not doctors (although we've both played them), so please do a little research on your own before trying this tip.

You may find other things that are good for you. Great: add them to the list. Pay attention to what makes your voice feel good and what makes it feel bad.

Many people will tell you that, before recording, you should avoid *milk products* at all costs because it makes your voice thick and phlegmy, and in most instances they're right. But sometimes we actually like to have a little dairy if our voices are particularly scratchy or raw because it tends to coat our vocal cords a bit. Another colleague of ours travels with a little bag of potato chips because he says the oil from the chips helps coat his throat when he's scratchy. Hey, whatever works! Obviously (because we've said it so many times), drink as much water as you can without starting to feel sloshy. Not just before a session, but as often as possible. Staying hydrated will help a lot more than just your vocal health.

Black licorice (natural, not candy) is said to have anti-inflammatory properties which can soothe and slightly numb the vocal area, so it can be nice after a grueling session. But many people don't like the sharp taste. Yuri used to hate it, but after realizing how positively it affects his voice when it's scratchy, he's come not only to tolerate it, but maybe even like it. *Maybe.* Just a *little*.

Many types of *cough drops* can also be soothing. And while *lemon* and *menthol* (not necessarily together) are appreciated by some as a remedy, see how they affect you. Some people actually find that the harsh properties of both lemon and menthol can aggravate a throat irritation.

Hot, *non-caffeinated tea* is nice for multiple reasons: it is warm, which keeps your voice loose and relaxed; and it keeps your throat moist. Honey, which can be mixed into tea or taken separately by the spoonful, has soothing and anti-bacterial properties. *Throat Coat* herbal tea, by Traditional Medicinals, is a classic, and a staple in our pantry. *Primrose* or *fish oil* capsules, when ingested, are said to help strengthen your vocal cords and keep them lubricated. However, be sure to check the dosage: eating too many at a time could have … runny results. As with many types of natural *cures*, there is no scientific evidence proving that these oils will do something for the voice specifically, but the folks we know who use them seem pretty happy with their results.

Using fresh *pineapple* and pineapple juice as a natural anti-inflammatory is a tip that was given to us by a friend who has starred in many a Broadway musical. Singers often drink pineapple juice or munch on pineapple before, during, or after a show to keep the swelling in their vocal cords down when their voices are tired from overuse. Hey, good enough for Broadway is good enough for us; and besides, pineapple tastes good.

Some folks will tell you that besides *green apples* for combating smackiness, green apple-flavored hard candies or even a sip of soda will help. We prefer the apple since it's easier on the teeth and healthier in general. But once again, before you make your final selection, check with your body: it usually knows best. *Another new favorite thing:* We're not affiliated with, nor do we receive any kind of money from Tazo teas, but Yuri's been mixing their *Passion* and *Sweet Orange* teas for a tart and delicious non-caffeinated cocktail that seems to work as well as any green apple.

Things that we're pretty confident you should avoid to keep your voice as healthy as it can be are *smoke* and *caffeine*. Hey, like we said before, we're not your mom, your teacher, or the boss of you; but smoking and being around smoke seems like an obvious no-no, as smoke dries out your vocal cords and can change your voice, over time. Not to mention the effects of smoking on your lungs, mouth, etc. (we're sure you know this already). Once again, it is very much a personal choice. We know both highly successful voice actors who are regular smokers and highly successful voice actors who never smoke.

Caffeine has a very similar side-effect to smoke: drying out your voice and often creating more strain on it when you use it. So think twice before swigging that morning cuppa joe on the way to your VO session, tasty though it may be. Or at least consider decaf. Again, that said, we know some voice actors who can't start their session *without* a cup of coffee. So it all goes back to being aware of how things affect your body and voice, and knowing what works best for you, personally.

 There are many great voice-savers, but always staying well-hydrated goes a long way toward heading off problems at the pass.

TARA & YURI'S SHORT LIST

Below is a short list of some of the things we think are most important. Hopefully, as you read through them, each will be a reminder of what you've read throughout this book and an inspiration for your journey. With everything you'll have going on all at once, it's always nice to have a little cheat sheet.

- **Agents**: Find a person (or more than one) that really *gets* you so you feel comfortable and confident with them as your go-between for job opportunities and clients. Don't just settle for whatever agent will take you.

- **Auditioning**: Remember the Ws when looking at a script. It'll put you ahead of the game and help you stand out from the rest of the pack. Come up with a short ritual that will focus, relax, and ground you. Improv can help set you apart, but mind the script. Make strong choices, but be flexible enough to take direction. And never forget that YOU ARE ENOUGH.

- **Confidence**: If you can't hear what's going on in the control room, assume all's well. Make bold choices about the material and people will take notice. Don't feel you need to apologize if you're given direction to go another way; simply take it and move on. Don't ask the directors if they need another take, or if your last take was good: they'll let you know.

- **Creating Characters**: Playing with pitch, speed, and volume can be an easy way to find and develop a variety of different characters. But never underestimate the beauty of your own natural voice. And, remember, the script will give you a lot to go on if you pay attention!

- **Demo**: Start with the voice closest to your natural speaking voice. That way, listeners will get *you* right away, even if they listen to only the first bit of your demo. When looking for commercial copy, feel free to flip through your favorite magazine and pull ads for real products. Then rewrite the material or tweak it to create your very own copy.

- **Efforts:** When it comes to efforts, just do it. But make sure you're breathing and supporting your voice.

- **Home Booth**: Home is where the heart is, but with a little effort and few bucks, it can also be a great place to record. The clothes hanging in your closet are a good substitute for expensive foam.

- **Hydrate**: Choose non-caffeinated beverages over drinks that have caffeine in them. Caffeine can dry out your mouth and voice and may not do you any favors in the booth. Water is best. Begin hydrating the night before a session to make sure you're well-lubricated come morning.

- **Imagination**: This is your most powerful weapon. Cultivate it and never underestimate it.

- **Location**: Go to where the work is. Your chances will always be better if potential employers can see your face.

- **Networking**: Use every opportunity to meet 'n greet as a way to build a network of people you can work with. You never know where your next job is going to come from, and most things are easier when you have other people to help you do them.

- **Popping**: Use your finger (or a pen or pencil) pressed into the *shhh* groove between your nose and your upper lip to help eliminate a plosive *pop* sound. Another great trick is to turn your head slightly off-axis (to the right or left) of the mic.

- **Professionalism**: Be on time. Be prepared. Be respectful. And just be a fun person to work with.

- **Read**: Read everything you can get your hands on. Read aloud. Read to yourself. Sir Ian McKellen once said that reading aloud is how he learned to act. Become better at reading and use this skill to your advantage.

- **Self-Promotion**: There are plenty of things you can do on your own to put yourself out there. Create a website, design postcards, carry business cards in your wallet, do a mailing. And that's just a start.

- **Warm Up**: Warm up your face and tongue as well as your voice. This will help your voice resonate and create a warmer richer sound, as well as help prevent injury. So massage your face a little with your hands, loosen your jaw, and move your tongue around. You'll be surprised how much it helps. And how nice it feels.

IN A NUTSHELL

Few understand that voice acting is *acting*, first and foremost. At the mic, there is nowhere to hide. Voice acting allows you to be ubiquitous and anonymous at the same time. Voice actors are like studio musicians – most are hired for their versatility, dependability, and because they bring a good energy to the studio. No one hires a resume. They hire you because they want one less thing to worry about. My job is a service. My job is to provide producers something better than they thought they wanted.

Starting out in the big city, dig in, get a sustainable existence, and connect. Expect it to take years, not weeks or months. Every gig is ultimately an audition. Wanting to *break in* to voice-overs is like wanting to *break in* to being a professional athlete or the mayor of a city. Most who say they want it prove ultimately unwilling to earn it. Never take the meeting or hand in that demo *before* you are ready. You probably won't get a second chance. You must surround yourself with people going where you want to go, some hopefully a few steps ahead of you.

~ DEE BRADLEY BAKER, ACTOR

RESOURCES

One resource we've found invaluable, especially for people just starting out in voice-over, is the *Voice-Over Resource Guide*. This is available as a super-helpful and handy-dandy periodical guide as well as a website (*www.VoiceOverResourceGuide.com*) with tons of great information. Here, you'll find info regarding classes, teachers, voice-over talent agencies, recording studios, union rates, demo reel producers, casting directors, and more. And the site is constantly being updated and expanded, so check back often.

We have no affiliation with the *Voice-Over Resource Guide* website, nor are we endorsing any of the services advertised on it, but we recommend it because we've never found a better repository for this kind of knowledge. It can be a great jumping-off point to find a class, make a demo, or if you're already set in those areas, to research talent and casting agencies and do a mailing. We give this site *two mics up.*

Backstage Magazine (*www.Backstage.com*) is a popular trade publication that also offers information on classes, agents, auditions, and voice-over related services. *Backstage* offers regional editions with more specific information related to local auditions. And we always love to recommend our friend Dee's blog *iwanttobeavoiceactor.com* (his original anecdote's above, and another one is in Chapter 5, *The Audition Itself*). He created his blog for the very same reason we wrote this book, and it's a terrific place to start. And by no means stop with these resources. A simple Internet search will turn up many more websites that provide information and resources related to voice-over.

For even more information, you might want to contact the unions that have jurisdiction over voice-over. As we mentioned before, in the U.S. that would be *SAG-AFTRA* (*www.SAGAFTRA.org*). You can find the closest chapter of SAG-AFTRA as well as info on joining, dues, and much more on their website. If you're outside of the U.S., find what union(s) regulate voice-over work in your location and ask them for more information.

You are, of course, always welcome to visit our personal websites (*www.YuriLowenthal.com* and *www.TaraPlatt.com*) and go to our *voice-over* pages. Here you can click on our different demo reels and listen to what we're using. Hopefully our demos will give you an idea of different types of spots, sounds, and qualities that might be helpful as you put together your own materials.

Also, our trusted friend and resource for all things audio and VO, Juan C. Bagnell, (who kindly contributed an anecdote to this book *and updated it for this edition*), has a helpful and entertaining blog (*someaudioguy.blogspot.com*). While he's been too busy lately to update his blog regularly, it's still a great archive of information for people wanting to set up their own recording space. Visit it at your own risk ... of *learning* something!

And your final resource: the website for this book (*www.Voice OverVoiceActor.com*), which is filled with additional information.

As always, a wonderful resource is someone who is already doing what you want to do. Every voice actor that you know or have met will have their own story on how they got where they are today. Which brings us to our next section ...

STANDING ON THE SHOULDERS OF GIANTS ...

A lot of our friends and people we work with on a regular basis are in the voice acting business. Some are actors, some directors, writers, engineers, agents, and more. We consider ourselves fortunate to work in a business with such talented, generous, amazing people who, by their sheer awesomeness, push us to step up to the next level and constantly improve our game.

Several of them had words to offer us, anecdotes or observations, that we thought might be helpful to include as we wrote our book. You probably noticed them sprinkled liberally throughout the chapters. We figured it'd be more interesting if occasionally you heard about the magical world of VO from people other than the two of us.

Here's what we want you to know about these people and why

they're important to us: they're our family. You want to remember that you're going to build a family if you decide that you want voice acting (or any acting, for that matter) to be your life. The stronger your group is, the more you'll be able to accomplish, and the more fun it'll be. Be conscious of your growing family as you push towards your goal. As much as it'll sometimes seem as if you're all alone on your voyage, remember it's a team effort. So build a team you like, and they'll help you reach heights you never imagined possible.

MORE THAN JUST ENTERTAINMENT

I was a guest at Anime Next in NYC a few years back with a few other voice actors from *Fullmetal Alchemist*. In that series my character, Edward Elric, is a young boy with a metal arm and leg who seeks a mystical stone to restore his body and that of his younger brother. While signing autographs that Saturday afternoon, a young woman approached the table.

"I cannot tell you how much Edward has meant to me. He has gotten me through such a difficult time in my life and I feel like I identify with him so much."

As I listened to her, I wondered how she identified with Ed. She was probably in her twenties, seemingly healthy, and a girl. She started crying and said, "I don't care what my mom thinks, I want you to sign this." She stepped around the table to reveal that she had a prosthetic leg. She'd recently lost her leg in an accident and made such a connection with *FMA* that helped her through that difficult tragedy. We all proceeded to sign her artificial leg, not a dry eye around.

From that point on, I realized that even though we are simply voicing animated characters, there are many people out there who draw great strength, encouragement, and support from our work. I came to learn that what we do has the potential to do much more than I ever thought before.

~ VIC MIGNOGNA, ACTOR

AND *THAT'S A WRAP!*

Much like at the end of a recording session or on a film set, we're *wrapping* this book.

Or as a favorite director of ours (*we're looking at you, Mary Elizabeth*) likes to say in a thick Austrian accent, "Get out of the booth!"

We hope you've learned a bunch of interesting, exciting, and thought-provoking things during your read. And that you feel more prepared and more confident with the knowledge you now carry.

We wish you extra happiness and a second helping of fun in your many adventures. To move you toward your goals, take *daily* action – whether that's reading aloud, mimicking the radio, or training your body.

Here's to passing you in a recording studio one day. Be sure to say hi!

SCRATCH TRACKS   **WITH TARA & YURI**

TARA! I FORGOT I HAD A SESSION TODAY AND JUST DRANK A MILKSHAKE!

AND A POT OF COFFEE! WHAT DO I DO?!

MAYBE THEY'LL ASK YOU TO PLAY "UNINTELLIGIBLE ALIEN #3".

OH, BOY.

DON'T WORRY ABOUT IT.

APPENDIX
THE WORKBOOK

"Success isn't always about greatness. It's about consistency. Consistent hard work leads to success. Greatness will come."

DWAYNE JOHNSON, ACTOR

VOICE-OVER VOICE ACTOR ACTION GUIDE

Funformational auxiliary action guide, complete with extended exercises and extra info, as well as some just plain fun stuff.

So, you've read the book and you want more, you say? Or you're in the process of reading it but already want to get to work? Great! We know how exciting and fun this can be, and there is so much time and so little to do. Wait a minute. Strike that. Reverse it. Let's go!

We have devised a series of exercises and tasks that will simultaneously help you create a solid self-marketing plan and build your skills using a variety of copy and practice material as well as warm-ups and physical exercises.

STEP ONE: YOUR VOICE

First, let's work on the *vocal quality list* to help you identify your sound and understand your *signature* (vocal style), so you can better market yourself. As we brought up in the book, a simple list might help you to begin narrowing things down; so let's use the list below as a starting point for several exercises. Begin by reading the adjectives and adverbs below and brainstorming what each particular word means (and how it may or may not apply) to you. Going through the list this way will help you focus on the particular ways that you use your voice. You might find that there are adjectives or adverbs that you feel are missing, so add them as you go.

Exercise 1: Adjective/Adverb List

wry	calm	perky
honest	open	cut-to-the-chase
sarcastic	happy	clipped
giddy	haughty	innocent
secretive	emotional	bored
inquisitive	playful	cool
sexy	witty	crazed
earnest	angry	grounded
trustworthy	confident	relaxed
_____	_____	_____

Start with the first word on our list: *wry*. What does that mean to you? Who is someone you think is *wry* and what are the qualities associated with that? What pictures or images come to mind when you think of the word *wry*? As your thoughts on each specific adjective or adverb start to solidify, jot them down.

For example, someone who is *wry* may be someone who cuts

to the chase in a very tongue-in-cheek kind of way. Someone who is *wry* almost seems to be smirking as they tell you the facts. Maybe picture a weary mom telling you about trying to keep her kids clean in a *wry*, "What are you gonna do? I love them, but they just get so darn dirty," sort of way.

A good example may be Allison Janney. When you hear a Kaiser Permanente commercial that she has voiced, you can almost feel the truth and the humor mixed together in her delivery. Whereas, unlike the *wry* read, a *clipped* delivery might not have any humor in it, or the humor might come from being overly earnest or innocent as the actor gets to the point as quickly as possible.

See how much work and time we've invested in examining that one little word? It takes time to start sorting out your vocal signature; but once you have a starting point, then you can grow from there. It's kind of like building a house: sort out your foundation first, and then you can put up the walls. After that, you can start decorating and painting. In other words, know what you naturally bring to the table, then start playing with it.

Your next assignment is to go through the following list and write the description you came up with for each of the words. (As well as any words you chose to add).

Exercise 2: Detailed Adjective/Adverb List

wry _____

calm _____

perky _____

honest _____

open _____

cut-to-the-chase _____

sarcastic _____

happy _____

clipped _____

giddy _____

haughty _____

innocent _____

secretive _____

emotional _____

bored _____

inquisitive _____

playful _____

cool _____

sexy _____

witty _____

crazed _____

earnest _____

angry _____

grounded _____

trustworthy _____

confident _____

relaxed _____

_____ _____

_____ _____

Once you've filled in the list and have a good idea of what the various adjectives and adverbs mean to you, you can begin to see where your voice falls. Circle the qualities that you feel are reflected in your natural, everyday speaking voice.

It can be difficult to look at ourselves objectively, so if you're having a hard time applying the list to yourself, try it on another person first. Pick a friend or relative (or even someone famous) as a reference, and use the list to evaluate their voice. Sometimes stepping outside of yourself for a few minutes can give you a new perspective on you. Now try you again!

Another idea is to try it with a friend or two. Use the list to figure out what their vocal qualities are, and have them, in turn, identify yours. Then you each will have discovered your unique sound while helping a friend.

If you choose a well-known voice to begin the comparison, think about the ways you would describe that voice to someone who couldn't hear them. Who are celebrity spokespeople who have unique or interesting sounds? Describe the qualities that make their words or thoughts stand out. What do you notice when you listen to television or radio commercials that makes you tune in to certain spots? How do they make you feel about the product?

Use the next exercise to examine particular qualities that a few famous folks have, as well as qualities of some people you may come in contact with daily.

Exercise 3. Other People's Qualities

George Clooney _____

Robert Downey, Jr. _____

Morgan Freeman _____

Peri Gilpin _____

Jeff Goldblum _____

Samuel L. Jackson _____

Angelina Jolie _____

Lucy Liu _____

Johnny Lee Miller _____

Kumail Nanjiani _____

Barack Obama _____

Chris Pratt _____

Julia Roberts _____

Seth Rogen _____

Oprah Winfrey _____

Steven Yeun _____

Your favorite radio DJ or newscaster _____

A family member _____

A friend _____

_____ _____

Spending a few minutes assessing another person's vocal qualities may make it a little easier to finally turn that lens on yourself. Now, using the descriptions you've created for the people listed, go down the list and eliminate any qualities that really don't sound like you naturally. This is the honesty part, so don't cheat and say, "Well, I can do anything. I'm an AC-tor…" We all have natural tendencies that make us who we are, and the sooner we own them, the sooner we can really lean into our strengths. And once you do that, you can start expanding.

Once you've narrowed down the list to your particular qualities, cross out the ones below that don't fit you. The words that are left should start to give you a better "picture" of your voice.

Exercise 4. Elimination Adjective/Adverb List

wry	calm	perky
honest	open	cut-to-the-chase
sarcastic	happy	clipped
giddy	haughty	innocent
secretive	emotional	bored
inquisitive	playful	cool
sexy	witty	crazed
earnest	angry	grounded
trustworthy	confident	relaxed

Now, use the remaining descriptors from this list to help you create a sentence that describes your natural vocal quality. The sentence might read something like:

"I have a perky, honest, intelligent, playful, friendly, warm voice."

Or

"I have a confident, clipped, sarcastic, inquisitive, smart sound."

Now fill it in for yourself. Use around five descriptive words to write your vocal signature sentence.

Exercise 5. My Vocal Signature Sentence

I have a _____, _____, _____,

_____, _____, _____ voice."

This sentence will become part of your voice-actor toolbox since it will help you to focus on the types of products/projects you might naturally be right for.

Knowing your signature will put you ahead of the game since being clear on your natural strengths gives you confidence and can even make it easier for a potential employer to slot you somewhere specific. Tell them you can "play anything," and they don't know what to do with you. Those Greeks really knew what they were talking about when they said, "Know thyself."

> Tara had postcards printed with her contact info, voice actor details, and vocal quality list. She sent the cards out and attracted work from various studios and production companies. Using marketing tools like the "quality list" as part of your mailings and demos can be extremely helpful, not only in getting you representation, but also in securing work.

STEP TWO: EXPANDING YOUR RANGE

Stepping outside of your natural voice can be a lot of fun. And once you've got a good feel for where your voice falls naturally, you can start to color outside the lines, expanding your range as they say. When you push those boundaries by experimenting with different vocal qualities, you increase both the number of characters you can play and your chances of getting hired!

This next exercise is designed to help you play with a range of emotions as you read the following phrases. We have removed all punctuation so as not to influence your interpretation of the dialogue. First, see what your natural inclination is when you read the phrase. In the blank provided, write down the adjective you feel most fits the phrase/sentence. For example, a single-word sentence such as "Stop" might be angry, it might be afraid, or it might be agitated.

Exercise 6. Phrases

over here _____

I need that _____

let go _____

what are you talking about _____

don't do that _____

I don't think that's a good idea _____

give me the new one _____

no _____

try it again _____

listen to me _____

alright _____

stop right there _____

wow that's huge _____

Now, review the list you just filled in, and see how you naturally "heard" the specific phrases. Perhaps your "No," was inclined to be frustrated.

Okay, let's move outside of your first instincts. Try the following exercise, keeping each phrase the same, but using the assigned quality (shown on the right) as you say it. Are you beginning to feel old patterns melting away as you expand your vocal toolbox?

Exercise 7. The Phrase/Quality Combo

over here	excited
I need that	overjoyed
let go	secretive
what are you talking about	frustrated
don't do that	uncomfortable
I don't think that's a good idea	annoyed
give me the new one	angry
no	scared
try it again	sleepy
listen to me	happy
alright	in awe
stop right there	lovingly
wow that's huge	frightened

SCRATCH TRACKS   **WITH TARA & YURI**

Let's go one step further. Use the following exercise – which we like to call *The Phrasinator* – to shake up your own rhythms by trying out multiple ways of saying the specific phrases on the left. This time say every phrase in the style of every one of the qualities listed on the right (ex. "over here" *uncomfortable*, "over here" *scared*, "over here" *frightened*…), and notice how your reading changes as your intention changes.

Exercise 8. Phrasinator: Mix'Em'Up

over here	uncomfortable
I need that	scared
let go	frightened
what are you talking about	in awe
don't do that	sleepy
I don't think that's a good idea	happy
give me the new one	overjoyed
no	annoyed
try it again	lovingly
listen to me	angry
alright	secretive
stop right there	frustrated
wow that's huge	excited

How'd it go? Did you discover some fun things simply by shaking things up?

> You don't always have a lot of time to think when working on a video game. The nature of games involves a number of branching possibilities in gameplay and story, and game designers have to cover their butts in recording. Because of this, the director will often have you move through your lines in the script by saying each line 2 or 3 different ways, without a lot of context. Using The Phrasinator technique will help to train you to think quickly on your feet, and that'll make you look professional, prepared, and talented (because you will be). It'll also contribute to the session running more smoothly and quickly, almost ensuring the director and producer will want to work with you again.

Now let's add punctuation to mix it up a little more...

Continue playing with the phrases by trying each of the different quality descriptions above with each phrase, as you did with The Phrasinator. But this time add punctuation (. ? ! ...) to see how that might change the way you say the lines.

Exercise 9. Punctuation Trials

	.	?	!	...
Over here	.	?	!	...
I need that	.	?	!	...
Let go	.	?	!	...
What are you talking about	.	?	!	...
Don't do that	.	?	!	...
I don't think that's a good idea	.	?	!	...
Give me the new one	.	?	!	...
No	.	?	!	...
Try it again	.	?	!	...
Listen to me	.	?	!	...
Alright	.	?	!	...
Stop right there	.	?	!	...
Wow that's huge	.	?	!	...

As you're doing your detective work on a script, punctuation will always be an important clue to the intention, motivation, or emotional life behind a line. Ideally you'll be doing all your Who, What, Where, When, Why, and hoW work. But when you don't have much time to dissect a script, punctuation'll be an important element to help send you in the right direction quickly.

Now, let's head into pitch, speed, and volume, and examine how you can tweak each of these to expand your range and create a variety of characters. The natural pitch (highness or lowness) of your voice is pretty set, but everyone can usually pitch up (higher) or down (lower) a bit if you push it a little. The natural speed (fastness or slowness) of your voice is also probably pretty constant for you, but can be easily manipulated. And volume? Well, from a whisper to a scream… Let's go back to the cube and try some exercises.

Exercise 10. Pitch, Speed, Volume

Find a piece of copy from pretty much anywhere (you could even use this very paragraph). Then, using the "Rubik's Cube of Choices" for pitch, speed, and volume, practice pushing yourself into uncharted territory. Start on one side of the cube and move yourself toward the other. See below for some examples.

1. a fast, low-pitched, soft voice

2. a slow, mid-range, loud voice

3. a medium-speed, high-pitched, conversational voice

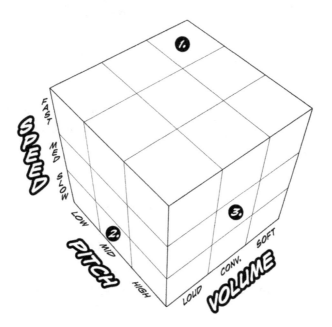

Don't just stop with the suggestions above. Try as many different combinations as you can stand. Even just looking at ways to
vary the first option above: what about a fast, high-pitched, soft
voice? Or a fast, low-pitched, loud voice? What about slow, low,
and loud? Keep going!

Now try some of these voices on a variety of copy: technical,
animation, commercial. Make notes of your favorite combos for
future auditions!

We've had you use your brain a little bit to start examining
where your voice sits naturally, and how you can begin to push
it into different directions, but let's get back into your body for
a minute to really make sure your voice (and the rest of you) is
prepared to start working. Let's warm it up!

Exercise 11. Sirens with Lip Trill

1. Press your lips lightly together like you would to make
   imaginary car noises, "broom, broooom." Now allow
   your lips to trill a siren (police, fire, or ambulance –
   your choice), beginning at the bottom of your range
   and moving up to the top.

2. Reverse direction: start at the top of your range and
   move downward through your natural pitch to your
   lowest note.

3. Repeat the sirens 3-5 times until you feel like your
   voice is beginning to get warmed up.

Lip trills are a wonderful way to not only warm up your face,
but to help prevent your vocal folds and neck muscles from
tensing up while you are stretching your voice. Don't worry if
your voice cracks during the sirens. That's just a natural part of

expanding your range. We all have a different range from head to chest, and in order to move through them continuously, you have to move over your natural "break," which is the sound that people often associate with a teen boy hitting puberty. Here's another sirens drill to help stretch your range.

Exercise 12. Sirens without Lip Trill

1. Make sounds similar to those for the last exercise, but allow your mouth to remain open, and let your tongue pull back a little. Begin a "yee" sound at the bottom of your range, and gently increase your pitch until you hit your high note.

2. Now reverse direction: start at the top of your range and move downward through your natural pitch to your lowest note.

3. Be conscious of your face and jaw, and make sure they are relaxed comfortably open while making the siren sound. Don't force it.

4. Repeat the sirens 3-5 times until you feel like your voice is warming up.

Practicing these siren trills can begin to stretch your range gently as your own specific musculature begins to get used to where the sound resonates in your head, face, and body.

Whether you have a high- or low-pitched voice, begin to think about the placement of the sound as separate from the pitch. Pitch is your range from low to high, and placement relates to where in your body your voice resonates. For example, if you had a head cold, you might sound very frontal, or nasal, since your sinuses would be clogged and thus blocking the sound from escaping completely. If you dropped the sound way back to the back of your throat, then you would almost sound like you were swallowing the sounds, creating a very different quality altogether.

Begin to play around with an extremely frontal, a mid-range, and a back-placed sound. This awareness will help in creating a variety of characters.

Exercise 13. Chewing Your Voice

1. Keeping your mouth and lips closed, begin to hum.

2. Start chewing an imaginary item as you continue to hum.

3. Lightly place your hands on your cheeks and feel your voice resonate in your face, your nose, your cheeks; and gently allow your hands to move to your neck and throat, and perhaps even down onto your diaphragm.

4. Feel the different vibrations in the different areas.

Use the *chewing hum* to warm up the areas where you really want your voice to resonate.

To continue to explore *where* different sounds resonate in your body, let's examine some specific sounds that tend to resonate in specific areas. If you can control where you want the sounds to resonate, you can engage more of the power of your own unique voice.

Exercise 14. Front-Mid-Back Sounds

1. Using a "ne, neee, nee, nee" sound, try squinting to create a more nasal resonance as you produce some of the sounds.

2. Now switch to humming normally to feel a very mid-mouth placement

3. Move the sound to the back of the mouth and throat by changing what you're saying to a "guh, guh, guh, guh."

4. Switch between the separate utterances ("nee," "hum," "guh") to move the sound from your frontal resonators to your more glottal, rear resonators.

Now that you're warmed up a little, try speaking in your natural voice, and then move the sound forward and back, as in the exercise. What do you notice about where your voice sits naturally, and what happens when you push it around? Again. Make notes of things you like and store them for later!

STEP THREE: BETTER BREATHING & MOVING YOUR MOUTH

Breath control is extremely important when it comes to voice acting. With better breath control you can speak longer and louder, and more effectively protect your voice from injury. We all have to breathe, so it seems like a no-brainer, but the breath is what creates the sound of your voice by vibrating your vocal folds. So the more control you have over this process, the stronger an actor you can become.

One way of gaining control is by expanding the length of time you can hold, and can exhale, your breath. And you do that by strengthening your diaphragm. The diaphragm is the muscular sheet that separates your heart and lungs from your intestines, stomach, and other organs, and it is responsible for inflating your lungs so you can breathe. In order for you to inhale, the diaphragm must contract and pull down, which expands your lungs, allowing them to fill with air. When your diaphragm relaxes, it allows your lungs to contract, and then you exhale through your mouth and/or nose. And luckily, the diaphragm mostly does this without us even having to think about it.

Exercise 15. Your Breath

1. Begin by lying comfortably flat on the ground and placing your hand on your abdomen, right over your diaphragm at about the level of your solar plexus.

2. Feel the rise and fall of your breath as your abdomen rises and falls.

3. Notice the natural "pause" between inhale and exhale.

Without trying to control it, feel how you breathe naturally. As you breathe, there should be four parts to every breath: 1. an inhale, 2. a pause, 3. an exhale, 4. a pause. We usually don't notice the pauses when we're breathing normally. Pay attention to them here.

Tara once had a voice teacher who could breathe in and out on a thirty-count, but that comes with a lot of practice. Being able to control your breath allows you to play with your instrument more, increasing your range, and helping to maintain a strong voice even through the most grueling audiobook recording sessions.

This next exercise focuses on lengthening your natural breath. Begin inhaling for a slow three-count, hold for a three-count, then exhale for a similar three-count, and hold again for a final three-count. Now work your way comfortably up to a four-count, a five-count, and so on. How high can you go? Remember, it's very important that you stop immediately if you start to feel light-headed or woozy. That's *too* high a count.

Exercise 16. The Count

inhale-2-3 ....hold-2-3............. exhale-2-3 .... hold-2-3

inhale-2-3-4 ....hold-2-3-4 .... exhale-2-3-4 .... hold-2-3-4

inhale-2-3-4-5 .....hold-2-3-4-5..... exhale-2-3-4-5 .... hold-2-3-4-5

Having a strong diaphragm not only helps you support your breath for longer periods of time, it can also help you yell, scream, shout, or make fighting and reaction noises, which you're probably going to be doing more often than you thought in this job. Continue exercising and strengthening your diaphragm so that you have this important tool in your acting toolbox.

Certain sounds can naturally help you slow your breath when you're practicing, and you'll use this technique in the following exercise.

Using an "s" or "z" sound, (rather like a snake hissing, or a *French* snake hissing, respectively) try to push the air out as slowly as you can. As before, start at a low number – let's say four – and inhale for a four-count, then exhale on the hiss for a four-count (don't forget your four-count pauses in between your in and out breaths). Once you're comfortable, up the number by one and try again. Another helpful exercise is to rapidly pant, much like a dog when it is hot, which forces your diaphragm to repeatedly contract and relax, which strengthens it. If you pant through your nose, then it's yoga (see "Breath of Fire" in another book: one about yoga)!

Exercise 17. Snake Hiss

1. Inhale deeply and then, holding your hand an inch from your mouth so you can feel the air, let out a hiss.

2. Hiss for as long as you are comfortable, and then take another deep breath.

3. Repeat this 5 times alternating between an "s" hiss and a "z" hiss.

4. Begin increasing the length of your breath and your hiss.

Hissing can strengthen the muscles around your diaphragm because the muscles must work to maintain one strong, steady, continuous flow of air.

The panting technique works to strengthen the muscles of the stomach and diaphragm for creating short bursts of air rapidly, which will help with shouting or yelling. It's a harder workout than you may think. Do it enough, and you may even get that six-pack you've always wanted.

Exercise 18. Dog Pants (everybody's wearing them these days!)

1. Place your hand on your diaphragm.

2. Open your mouth and allow your tongue to relax and hang out of your mouth.

3. As quickly as possible, inhale and exhale (panting), getting the diaphragm to work, moving in and out as quickly as you are comfortable with. (Again, if you

feel dizzy or lightheaded, stop immediately and
take a break.)

Let's move on to articulation. Besides a strong diaphragm, it's
also important to have a limber mouth, tongue, and mind. Articulation, or being able to speak words clearly, is a crucial element
to a voice actor's repertoire. Not every character will need good
articulation (see "Benicio del Toro"), but it's better to have such a
skill up your sleeve, just in case, so that if you're going to mumble
or slur, it's a *choice*.

Exercise 19. Articulation

1. P-T-K-T (puh-tuh-kuh-tuh)
   Repeat the sounds P-T-K-T over and over
   (p-t-k-t-p-t-k-t...).

2. B-D-G-D (buh-duh-guh-duh)
   Repeat the sounds B-D-G-D over and over
   (b-d-g-d-b-d-g-d...).

3. P-T-K-T-B-D-G-D
   (puh-tuh-kuh-tuh-buh-duh-guh-duh).
   Repeat the sounds P-T-K-T-B-D-G-D over and
   over (p-t-k-t-b-d-g-d-p-t-k-t-p-t-g-d...).

4. Vary which consonant sounds you go between (*P* or *B*)
   to make it harder for yourself. Try also going up and
   down the scale while doing this articulation exercise.

5. This would also be a wonderful time to practice any of
   your favorite tongue twisters.

This next exercise will help your mouth warm up while working
on plosive sounds. Also be aware of your breathing throughout

the articulation exercises, as this will be a good gauge of whether the previous exercises are working.

Exercise 20. A Trill of a Different Color

1. Roll your tongue on the roof of your mouth (in an *R* sound) while going up and down the scale.

This is a different kind of trill than the sirens we did before. This is more of a classic Spanish or Italian roll of the *R*. If you're not familiar with the rolled *R* (many of us who speak English as a first language are not), you can get an idea of what it feels like in your mouth by saying the word "butter." When your tongue hits the "tt," that vibration is the trill. **This doesn't work for everyone. You can also try another technique:** place the tip of your tongue just behind the top front teeth and relax your tongue, letting it vibrate against the back of your front teeth as you breathe out through your mouth for a sound like a cat purring. You may need clearer examples, and if so, head on over to YouTube and search "rolling your Rs."

Once you've got a feel for this kind of *R*, give these trills a try. They'll warm up your vocal folds and wake up your tongue, which should do wonders for your articulation.

> Great articulation, and rapid tongue movement is what a ventriloquist uses when speaking through a dummy.

STEP FOUR: PUTTING IT ALL TOGETHER

Below is a step-by-step sequence of exercises to help you get ready to work. It incorporates many of the above exercises into a total body warm-up. Don't like the order they're in? Mix 'em up until it works for you! And as always, stay safe. If anything hurts, stop. It ain't worth it.

Exercise 21. Complete Body Warm-up

1. Lie down on your back.

2. Hum/sigh in and out.

3. Practice panting.

4. Roll over to one side and move into a squatting position as you get your feet back under you. Now stand slowly with your head hung low, slowly rolling up your spine, vertebra by vertebra, with your head coming up last. Don't forget to breathe throughout.

5. Very gently, drop your chin to your chest and roll your head slowly side-to-side and then in circles, both clockwise and counterclockwise, warming up your neck and throat

6. Gently hunch your shoulders and roll them first forward a few times, then back. This should loosen up your back and neck a little more. Make sure when you're done with this that your shoulders are relaxed so that they are down, away from your ears.

7. Get your circulation going by lightly shaking out your hands and feet for a few seconds each.

8. Take 10 small jumps.

9. Vigorously rub your hands together to warm them, then use your hands to gently massage and relax the bones and muscles in your face.

10. Lion/Mouse (also known as Lion-face/Lemon-face) is a fun exercise to do in front of the mirror (but can be done anywhere). Basically you go back and forth between two expressions, one for which you make the biggest face you can, eyes wide, mouth wide open, like a scary lion; and then, right away, make your face as small as you can, like you've just sucked on an entire lemon. Do it a few times and your face'll definitely feel more awake. Feel free to add a sound or vocalization to your expression.

11. Stick your tongue out of your mouth as far as it'll stretch, then pull it back in, several times. Now try to touch your nose with the tip of your tongue. Next, try to touch your chin. Now lick around the clock – with your nose at 12 and your chin at 6. Now counterclockwise. Full disclosure: this exercise can be messy, but it's really good for getting your tongue warmed up.

12. Sirens!

13. Trills!

14. PTKT, BDGD

15. Finish up with a couple of tongue twisters of your own choosing. Don't know any? That's what the Internet's for! Actors all have their favorite tongue twisters, but among the most popular are *Red Leather, Yellow Leather; Peter Piper; and Unique New York.*

Hopefully, at this point, you feel awake, alive, and ready to play. And the above sequence is merely a suggestion, not a bible. Feel free to modify the routine and make it your own depending on where you are and how much time you have.

Warming up becomes even more crucial if you're going to be doing a job that requires fight sounds or efforts, both of which are common in video games and animation and can lead to vocal injury if not approached correctly. Let's practice some below.

Exercise 22. Fight Sounds

1. punch	small	medium	large
2. kick	small	medium	large
3. attack	small	medium	large
4. injury	small	medium	large
5. death	small	medium	large

When performing efforts, you will often be asked to give a variety of sounds for, say, being hit or for hitting someone else. Be sure to vary your approach, so that all your efforts don't sound exactly alike. Open mouth, closed mouth, different lengths, different vowels, and different consonants are ways to create variety: *hy-ah, ki, shah, rah, gar, huh, hnng, ngh*. Often in a video game session they will ask for an A-B-C of a small, medium, and large effort per fight sound. Another way to mix it up is by really imagining what makes the effort. Get specific. Are you poking someone with a dagger or swinging a two-handed battle-axe? Did you get socked in the jaw or punched in the gut? Or did someone just take a pair of shears to your Achilles tendon?

These kinds of efforts can be intense, so be sure you are generating the sound with good diaphragmatic support and not tensing up your throat to create the sound. All that tension in your throat will put pressure on your vocal cords and could damage your voice, so be sure you're warmed up and relaxed before you, y'know, charge that pillbox or attack that orc.

Another great (and free!) voice-over exercise is to mimic things you hear. Listen to your favorite radio station and simply mimic the DJs, the commercials, even the news stories. Not only will this clue you into the types of voices that are working out there, but you may end up accidentally creating characters you can add to your repertoire.

Exercise 23. Radio Follow Along

1. Turn on the radio or TV and mimic what you hear. You in no way have to do a perfect match of what you're hearing. Just trying is enough.

Now find a station or a program that you wouldn't normally watch or listen to. This can shake up your mind and be a little more challenging. And through the mimicry of *other* people's voices, you'll learn a lot about your *own* voice.

SCRATCH TRACKS   **WITH TARA & YURI**

I JUST AUDITIONED FOR THE COOLEST PROJECT!

YOU SHOULD TOTALLY GO IN FOR IT!

GREAT! THANKS! WHAT WAS IT?

I CAN'T TELL YOU. I SIGNED AN NDA.

STEP FIVE: PRACTICE WITH SCRIPTS & COPY

So, your body is warmed up, your mind is awake, and you're ready to get down and dirty with some actual voice-over work. There can be a lot to take in when you're looking at a script, so here are a few hints to guide you.

You'll likely find the most notations on the script if it's for ADR/dubbing: terms such as *time code* to indicate where the dialogue is in the program, symbols to let you know where pauses (or, hitches) fall, abbreviations that signify when the dialogue is on or off camera, etc. If it's original animation, you'll likely have fewer things to look out for: maybe only line numbers to refer to as you're recording. Let's see what you remember from the notation section of the book as you look at the scripts below. And always remember, different studios and different writers can have their own notations. If you don't recognize something, ask!

∧ or … or / or _	hitch (pause)
MNS	mouth not seen
OM, CM, CT	open mouth, closed mouth, clenched teeth
OS, OC	off screen, off camera
01:02:03:04	time code

Below are some new practice scripts, original animation, and an ADR script. There's also commercial copy to practice with as well. Add a little realism to your practice work session by recording on your phone or computer. Listen to your recordings afterwards, and just assume we would've cast you!

Exercise 24. Practice Scripts

1. As you read, try circling all the notations you notice and be aware of the information you can gather from everything on the page.

2. Ask yourself the Who-What-Where-When-Why-hoW questions and let your answers guide what choices you make. Underline this information as you find it.

ORIGINAL ANIMATION Script:

You've been cast on the *Sloopy School Haus Show* as a main character. Congrats! What will you do with your script to make your performance shine?

<u>INT. SCHOOL HOUSE – DAY</u>

Inside the Little Red School House, Sloopy sleeps at his desk. Wrex and Chazzy are finishing their classwork as the bell rings.

1.   WREX
             And....done! See ya, losers!

He grabs his backpack and races for the teacher's desk. Chazzy nudges the snoring Sloopy.

2.   CHAZZY
             Wake up, Sloopy. We're gonna miss next period.
             Hey, check it out, my third gold star this week!

Sloopy groans and then perks up.

3   SLOOPY
             I want one! I want a star! I want ALL the stars!

3A   CHAZZY
             You? I love you, man, but not a chance.

4   SLOOPY.
             What do you mean?

5   CHAZZY
             You gotta do work to get stars, Sloop.

6   SLOOPY
             I do? Oh, well then forget it...

He puts his head back down on the desk and goes back to sleep. Wrex sticks his tongue out at his friends before running out the door.

ADR Script:

You recorded the previous script several months ago, and the dialogue track was sent to a group of animators and has been animated to your performance. But now that the finished animation has come back, the writers, directors, and producers realize that there are some sections that need more efforts/reactions to fill in the story; or sometimes, with the animation completed, new lines or rewrites become necessary. The following script is the ADR script for the same *Sloopy School Haus Show* scene.

4A   SLOOPY
01:00:21:14   <louder>
What do you mean?

6   SLOOPY
01:00:33:17   <missing>
I do? Oh, well then. Sloopy, OUT.

6A   WREX
01:00:34:00
(gives a raspberry)

16   WREX
01:01:04:19 – 01:01:05:22
(impact HIT & LAND)

18   CHAZZY
01:01:07:00   <multiple takes>
What? What?

21   WREX
01:01:12:09
Woah! <surprised>

```
21A              WREX
01:01:13:00
(impact grunt

26               CHAZZY
01:01:17:00      <softer>
I'm gonna get Wrex, just you wait…
```

DUB Script:

You are working on the *Greatest Dub Show Ya Ya Boom!* Unfortunately, Pro Tools crashed, so while the engineer reboots, you have a minute to look over your script ….

1. Amanda	01:01:03:12 01:01:05:20	Wait for me guys…please?	
2. George	01:01:06:00 01:01:10:00	<u>Well, then hurry up</u>.	MNS
3. Amanda	01:01:10:20 01:01:15:12	I am ^ sheesh, I. Am.	
4. George	01:01:16:00 01:01:19:05	I mean <u>we can't wait all day</u> you know.	ON/OFF/ON
5. Amanda	01:01:22:00 01:01:25:07	(effort) Ahhhh! Ouch. Help me up!	CM/OM
6. George	01:01:25:20 01:01:27:12	(laugh) Sorry ^ I hope. you're alright	
7. George	01:01:30:00 01:01:34:05	See…I told you we can't wait <u>all day.</u>	
8. Amanda	01:01:35:20 01:01:37:12	(laugh) Right. I ^ I knew that.	
9. George	01:01:40:00 01:01:44:05	(effort) Ugh. Well, I told you we… can't wait <u>all day</u>.	

VIDEO GAME Script:

The client listened to your audition for Hitarr, The Conqueror, in the new *Universe of Demon Dragon Blood II,* and everyone agreed that you're the Hitarriest. Congrats! You've been cast for both the performance capture and the voice recordings. You head into the studio to record a session for the character, and will be going to the soundstage next week for your first of several PCap sessions over the next few months.

Today though, the director lets you know that Dwayne "The Rock" Johnson, who's also in the game, has to come in earlier than expected, and you've got to record everything in about half the time they had budgeted. They've just been doing A-B-C takes for each of the lines. No need to slate each new line. Just give them three different takes and move on unless the director chimes in to give you direction. And … you're rolling:

Line #	Character	Dialogue
68	HITARR	(Pain groan) Aaarg!
69	HITARR	Stop, or I will shoot.
70	HITARR	(Effort/being blasted) Unghh.
71	HITARR	You've got two on your six!
72	HITARR	There are two more, twelve o'clock!
73	HITARR	(Hit) Rah.
74	HITARR	(Taking damage) Euhh.
75	HITARR	(Attack yell) Yaaarrgh!
76	HITARR	(Death) …uugh…unn.

Your agency calls to say you have a full day of motion capture in two days ("performance capture," you correct them politely) and they want to send you the script to work on right away. Don't put it off; get started now. Read and do your work. Sleep on it. Then work it again tomorrow. Get on your feet and practice it as if you were in the audition. Get off book. Then revisit this scene later.

Script for Act2_Forest Demons
Line Count: 7

Cinematics

Act2_Forest Demons

08971
<u>EXT. MAGICAL FOREST – DUSK</u>

23546
Our rough band of travelers is holed up in the Magical Forest trying to keep a low profile while getting ever closer to the Mothmar's Castle.

Meiliandra sits by the fire while Kluxx scopes out the horizon from a tree. Hitarr paces angrily below, tensions running high. An arrow sails through the air and hits the tree near Meiliandra, narrowly missing Hitarr.

Three Forest Demons POUNCE! While Meiliandra steals behind a tree and nocks an arrow, Hitarr goes hand-to-hand with the closest of the Demons.

> 01980   MEILIANDRA_CINE_FOREST DEMONS_001
> Kluxx! A little warning next time?

23547
Kluxx drops from his perch, using a Demon to break his fall.

> 01981   KLUXX_CINE_FOREST DEMONS_002
> On it. Literally.

> 01982   MEILIANDRA_CINE_FOREST DEMONS_001
> That's more like it. What about you, Hitarr?

23589
Meanwhile, Hitarr has cleaved one of the Demons in two, and has

---

just chopped off another Demon's clawed hand just in time. Hitarr holds up the severed limb.

| 22248 | HITARR_CINE_ FOREST DEMONS_001 |

I can give you a hand.

23691
Meiliandra laughs and launches a volley of arrows, blanketing the seemingly endless horde of incoming Demons. The Demons scurry for cover but a persistent bunch regroups immediately to attack Hitarr.

| 23098 | HITARR_CINE_ FOREST DEMONS_002 |

Come, hellspawn!

| 01981 | KLUXX_CINE_FOREST DEMONS_003 |

Looks like you could use a hand of your own, Hitarr!

29807
Hitarr ignites the Sword of Rathnoth to vanquish the assailants, but more continue to dogpile. Our heroes are being swarmed. Meiliandra's arrows are running low, and Kluxx, unsurprisingly, uses his camouflage ability to blend into a tree.

| 12949 | HITARR_CINE_ FOREST DEMONS_003 |

(roaring)
Rahhh! I will defeat you all! Come, and be ripped asunder!

29911
END CINEMATIC CAMERA:

Begin gameplay.

End Cinematics

COMMERCIAL Copy:

Your new VO agent would like you to come in and read some of the spots they just got in today so they can start to see what your strengths are. So go ahead and show 'em what you've got.

Luxury:

The Jewelry Outlet at KnollCrest is having a pre-Valentine's Day engagement ring sale. Come down today and surprise your loved one with the proposal of a lifetime. 24 karat gold and platinum rings on sale for up to 30% off, this weekend only.

High Energy:

It's Faaaaaaantastic! Super Fruit Bowl O'Sugars gets you ready for a day of fun in the sun. Filled with vitamins, minerals, and naturally sweetened real fruit pieces, Bowl O'Sugars is part of a complete breakfast. Start your morning right. Be fan-tastic.

Promo

This October, *The Best Show* on TV is moving to a new time...five days a week. Catch your favorite characters Mindy, Bobbi, and Karl, now at 7p.m. on KOOLTV.

Partner read:

A: Honey did you forget to pay the phone bill?
B: What do you mean? I thought it was automatic?
A: Oh, right! Sorry. It's just so easy, I keep forgetting.
B: Yeah, now we can spend time thinking about more fun things.
A: Yeah, like if you paid the cable bill...
Announcer: Don't let bills get you down. Use Earth Bank's auto bill-pay feature to pay for all your monthly charges. Earth Bank: the bank of the Earth. Not available on intergalactic space station Giltex.

SCRATCH TRACKS **WITH TARA & YURI**

Soft sell:

Soft CleoPattra Egyptian sheets are specially designed to become softer with use…and every time you wash them, the natural bamboo fibers relax just a little bit more…which makes your bed even more comfortable to get into… Who wouldn't want to sleep in…Soft CleoPattra Sheets. Easy to sleep on, easy to sleep in.

High Energy:

I love hitting the BergerJerk on the way to the game. I can fill up on all my favorites: a real ice-cream shake, a 100% beef patty, and a large Idahome fries for under 5 bucks. And I can even grab something for the coach so if I'm a little late to practice sometimes, no harm, no foul.

Legal Tag:

Prices based on participation and subject to change without notice, offer good only in the continental United States, all entries must be postmarked by July 4, or will not be considered.

Need more? Remember, you can always tune in to the TV, radio, or Internet (which will all probably be the same thing by the time you read this) for more examples!

Exercise 25. Audition Time

1. This exercise is meant to simulate an audition experience. Remember to mine the page for all its valuable information so you can make the most informed choices and knock it out of the park.

2. Do a trial run with each of the specs, and record yourself. Play it back and listen to hear if what you planned in your head came through in your recording. Not sure? Play it back for a friend whose opinion you trust.

Try out the following commercial and animation audition copy. See how changing up the spec changes the choices you make.

Commercial

Specs:

1. young, cheerful, spunky
2. wants to be everyone's friend
3. eternally optimistic
4. intelligent, honest, down-to-earth

1. In the summer heat, 2 bucks can go a long way. Now, at Boone's Burger Joint, grab a large drink, large fries and your choice of hamburger or cheeseburger for only $1.99. Come in and fill up for less than 2 bucks.

2. Why choose one of those other companies that might lose your package or handle it with less-than-optimal care? Let *BoxYouUp* come by your office or home and package, mail, and deliver your important items at your convenience. Visit BoxYouUp.com for pricing.

Animation

Specs:

1. energetic, sporty, hot shot
2. is always having a good time
3. goofy, crazy, wild
4. nervous and easily excited

1. Hey little monkey, I have no idea what you're doing in there, but you need to come out right now. You hear me? I don't wanna have to yell. C'mon now. Get out. Get. OUT. Monkeeeeeeeee! OUT. Now see, that wasn't s bad, now was it. Ha! Silly monkey.

2. You mean there is more out there than this? Robots even? Wicked!

Because I've been waiting my whole life for this. I just know I can take them on.

Let's go.
What are you waiting for? Let's do this thing.

Woah. Did you see that? I'm pretty awesome.

So, how'd it go? If you were anything less than impressed by your auditions, be sure to cut yourself some slack. You never know what they're looking for. And remember, all you can do is prepare yourself and bring *you* to the table. Oh! Speaking of which, did you forget? You have a MoCap booking. Remember that Hitarr scene you prepared? The big day is here. Are you PCap ready? Get a move on. Get there early enough, and I hear they're catering a hot breakfast...

Of course, these exercises can't exactly duplicate an audition experience, but the more prepared you feel before you go into an actual audition situation, the more confident and relaxed you will be, and the higher your chances of doing your best work, and occasionally even booking the job!

You will want to begin putting together some of your own copy so that you can practice reading it aloud, making choices, and having copy to choose from when you get to the point of putting your demo reel together. Of course, we still recommend taking a voice-over class before the step of putting the demo together, but early preparation can never hurt you.

Exercise 26. Getting Your Own Practice Copy Together

This is a short final exercise to help you begin to create your own practice copy which you can either work on or use to create your commercial or animation demo reel. Again, this is only a guide to help you if you don't feel you know where to start. If you've got better ideas (and you probably do), start writing!

1. For commercial copy, grab a couple of magazines, see which ads really pop for you, and write down whatever words are on the page (or if the magazine belongs to you, pull that page right out). Remember that print copy often reads very differently from commercial audio copy (because there's a visual right there to go with it), so use this copy as a starting point, and then tweak it 'til you like it.

2. To build animation copy, find an inanimate object in your house, then write a short monologue or conversation that this object/character might have with you about its needs, hopes, or dreams. Another way to spark your creativity is to jot down a few of your favorite characters from books, movies, or even from existing animated shows. Now rename them for good

measure, and start writing conversations with them that you imagine, or wish, they'd have (if you've ever written fan fiction, you're already good at this.).

3. For performance capture copy, try searching on line for movie or TV scripts for your favorite action, horror, fantasy, or sci-fi scenes. If it's a scene you already know well, you'll have a feel for what it would look like acted out. Compare what you know of the scene to what the script says (often it's very different), and put it on its feet!

4. Listen to a bunch of ads (either radio or TV) and note which style of delivery goes with which type of product (hard sell, soft sell, partner read, tag, etc.). Also review your animation copy and start to determine where your strengths are. Hint: They're usually the ones you have the most fun with.

5. Put all your found (and tweaked) copy into a binder, and practice randomly flipping to different pieces and reading and performing them as you would if you were in the booth or on the soundstage.

Outstanding work! You've honed your unique vocal qualities and probably learned a thing or two about your body and voice that you didn't know before. You've found warm-ups that work for you, and learned what makes you feel the most prepared and confident before heading in to an audition or a work session. You've studied and dissected copy, and made choices; and maybe you've even begun the process of building your own stack of practice copy that you can use as you move toward making your demo reel.

Voice-over isn't what it used to be. There really aren't "voice-over" voices. There's a need for voices of all shapes and sizes, so don't feel limited by what you sound like. Concentrate on the things you *can* affect: work on your acting, make sure you're professional and considerate, and get familiar with working in a studio with the people and equipment that live there. Is that all you need? Possibly. Is there more you can do? Of course! Make your demo; send it to agents and production companies. Hunt for auditions. Take classes, and take care of yourself. Make the investment in *you*.

What's the payoff? Creating amazing characters. Entertaining, maybe even teaching, or at least touching, the people who are lucky enough to bear witness to your performances. A richer imagination. Adventure. Maybe even financial remuneration. But above all, hopefully, fun and fulfillment. The path is a twisty one, and we can assure you that things will NOT go as planned. This life of voice acting has its ups and downs, but if this is what you really want, we hope you'll learn to appreciate both (if not entirely equally). It's a hell of a ride. So gather all the tools in your toolbox, muster the passion that made you pick up this book, fire up your imagination, and get to fun! Uh, we mean work, get to work – no, wait, we mean fun… Hopefully, they'll be indistinguishable! Now get out there and *Raise Your Voice*!

SCRATCH TRACKS   **WITH TARA & YURI**

GLOSSARY OF TERMS

ABC take (series) – multiple *takes* of the same line in succession, usually to give the director variety

ADR (additional dialogue recording or *automated dialogue replacement)* – dialogue recorded to picture after something has been animated or filmed

agent – a representative whose job it is to find and broker jobs for a client (the actor), and for which they typically receive a 10% commission

articulate/articulation – using the various moving parts of the mouth to create the vowels and consonants used in speech

bed – a continuous layer of background dialogue (*walla*) created by a *loop group* in post production to help create the illusion of a group of people; final audioscape may be composed of many beds layered together

beep(s) – a specifically timed sequence of audio cues (almost always three beeps) that, like a metronome, establish a rhythm and help the actor come in (start speaking) at the right time

booth – the room that you record in; a soundproofed space where the microphone and you create the magic of voice recording *callouts* – shouts that you might record to break up a *bed* of background dialogue; created when you work in a *loop group*

cans – headphones

clicking (smacking) – the mouth noises the *mic* picks up when your mouth becomes too dry; often makes a *take* unusable

copy – the *dialogue* you'll be recording; i.e. the stuff you need to say

demo – a brief recorded demonstration of your vocal talents; used as a calling card or introduction to a potential agent, manager, director, or producer

dialogue – spoken words between two or more characters

diaphragm – the muscular partition between the thorax (chest) and abdomen; facilitates breathing

diaphragmatic support – using your *diaphragm* to support and protect your voice when vocalizing

direction – the information which someone (usually the director) gives you to guide your performance

donut – group movement that involves the actors circling in front of the *mic* while conversing with others in the *loop group* to create a specific *bed* of background *dialogue*

dub/dubbed – to rerecord *dialogue* translated from the original language or from temporary *scratch* tracks; also called *ADR*

efforts – the non-dialogue vocalizations you create to add life or action to a scene; sometimes called *reax* (*reactions*) or *onos* (onomatopoeias); usually grunts, groans, moans, or KI-yahs!

enunciate/enunciation – to create each sound clearly; to speak clearly *facial capture* – using markers and often makeup to mark the face of an actor during *motion capture* performance, so the technology can render an in-game or in-film computer generated character with the facial reactions of the actor's performance

flap(s) (mouth/lip flap[s]) – the opening and closing motion of a character's mouth on screen

frames – the shortest increment into which a time code is broken down; each frame representing a still image of action which, when flashed rapidly in succession with other frames, creates the illusion of movement

free and clear – a direction used in group recording sessions indicating that the actors should not let their *dialogue* overlap

hitch – a slight pause that breaks up a line of *dialogue*

level – the volume at which you are speaking (engineers often ask for a level so they can accurately calibrate the recording equipment)

loop – a single line of *dialogue* (this term is a holdover from when recordings were done reel-to-reel and there was actually a loop of magnetic tape on to which audio was recorded)

loop group – a group of people (usually five to eight, but we've been in groups for films that were upwards of twenty!) hired to *loop* or record all the extra or background *dialogue* necessary in film, TV, or games; sometimes called a *walla group*

manager – a personal representative hired to *manage* your career (for a 15% commission on all of your work), and help you make decisions that will advance you to the next level

mic – microphone; that thing you talk into

Mike – a common abbreviation of the name Michael (not to be confused with the aforementioned *mic*)

MoCap – short for *motion capture*

motion capture (MoCap) – a process by which the movements of an actor are recorded simultaneously by multiple cameras. This captured data is then mapped to a 3D character model which is used to animate a character in a video game, film, show, etc.

networking – broadening your circle of work contacts by going out to meet people in the hopes of creating new *mutually beneficial* relationships

node (vocal node) – a swelling on the vocal chords, often resulting from vocal strain; can affect the quality of your voice; an untreated node can become a *nodule*

nodule (vocal nodule) – a callus-like bump on the vocal chords; similar to a *node*; heals more slowly than a node and sometimes requires removal via surgery

nonunion – not belonging to a professional labor association that looks out for the welfare of its members (e.g. *SAG-AFTRA*)

notations (script notations) – specific details noted in the script that give you extra information regarding timing or visual cues; used especially with *ADR/dubbing* scripts

off book – able to perform scripted material from memory, without need to refer to the text

off-mic (off-axis) – turning your head slightly away from the *mic* so you don't *blow out* the *levels* when you have to scream, yell, whistle, blow …

OJ – original Japanese; the original Japanese animation voice recording from which an English *dub* is made *on tape* – sometimes said by the director or engineer to indicate that your next *take* will be recorded (a dated term that comes from a time when all recordings were made to magnetic tape rather than digital files)

original animation (pre-lay) – a recording of a character(s) that will be drawn and animated later specifically to match an actor's voice

pass-bys – movement that involves multiple people in conversation walking across the *pickup* area of the *mic* to give the illusion of movement during a *loop group* session

pay-to-play – arrangement by which actors are charged a fee in exchange for access to auditions and other services

PCap – short for *performance capture*

performance capture (PCap) – a term that has come to prominence with the improvement of *motion capture* technology, and is often used interchangeably. As capture technology has improved, the ability to record and use an actor's full performance, including facial expressions and micro movements, has gotten much more precise, leading to this change in terminology. Many actors prefer this term, as they feel "motion capture" ignores the nuances of their performance

phone patch – a telephone connection that allows the actor, the director, the producer, and/or the client to communicate during a recording session, even while physically in two or more locations (often with at least one participant in another city)

pickup – the rerecording of a line because of a flub, rewrite, or a technical error, either during the original session or at a later date *pitch* – the tonal placement of the voice as in high, medium, or low

plosive – the burst of air that comes with certain types of sounds, most notably the *P* and *B* sounds

podcast – a new form of audio programming made available for download from the Internet (often by subscription), usually for free; easy and cheap to produce, this format is rightfully popular among those wanting to start their own talk show or radio-type program – usually a themed series

Popper Stopper (specific brand name) – a metal or fabric mesh barrier that sits a few inches in front of the *mic*; used to cut down on *p pops* or other bursts of air that may distort the recording of sound; also sometimes called a *pop screen* or *pop filter*

popping (p pop) – the sound made when a violent burst of air rushes into the *mic*, distorting the sound; often created by a *plosive*

pre-lay – another way of referring to original animation recordings; laying down a recording before creating the animation

pre-viz – a roughly animated pre-visualization of a scene to help guide the production of the actual scene in a show, film, or game.

preview – viewing the moving image that you will be syncing to, before you record a *take*

promo – a voice-over recording commonly used to promote a network, show, film, or other special event

reactions (reax) – sounds that are used to color lines and give them a more realistic quality; similar to *efforts* but usually smaller *reel (demo)* – a compilation of examples of your work, or demonstrations of your different characters or qualities

register – the range of an actor's voice, relating to pitch and placement (a high register tends to resonate in the head, while a lower register resonates in the chest and belly)

remote recording – process of recording outside of a recording studio

rolling (on tape, recording) – expression that indicates that the engineer is recording and that you're free to begin speaking

ROM – range of motion

safety – refers to an *additional take*, recorded as a different option, or to be used if the original take is unusable due to a technical issue

SAG-AFTRA (Screen Actors Guild and American Federation of Television and Radio Artists) – a performers' labor union typically known for its jurisdiction over motion pictures, but also governing voice-over contracts

scratch tracks – temporary recorded tracks that act as a placeholder for dialogue to be recorded later; also, a side-splittingly funny series of 3-panel comic strips found in this book

script – sometimes the lines you will be saying; sometimes the complete written story, including scene descriptions and every character's *dialogue*; usually seen as printed pages, but sometimes projected on a screen in the VO studio

script stand (stand) – a rack or other device on which you rest your *script* while you record

session – a scheduled period of time during which you record *series (ABC take)* – multiple *takes* of the same line in succession, usually to give the director variety

sides – the partial script or copy that is made available to an actor for an audition; in the case of longer scripts, usually not the entire script

slate – an audio marker such as "Take 12" or "Tara Platt reading for Cinderella"; allows the engineer to identify a specific section of recording

smacking (clicking) – the mouth noises (clicking of the lips, cheeks, and tongue) picked up by the *mic*; caused by your mouth being too dry

sound check (level check) – a request from the engineering team at the beginning of the session for you to read a few lines so that they can accurately gauge your volume

soundstage – the part of a performance capture studio (or film/TV studio) in which a production is filmed

spec – directions included on your *script* to let you know what the client is looking for in your delivery of a character's lines

speed –how fast or slowly you speak your lines

splashy – a condition that occurs when your mouth is too wet and which causes unwanted mouth noise

spot – another word referring to a commercial

studio – the location where voice-over is recorded as well as sometimes mixed; includes a recording booth and a control room

swag – promotional goodies that you give out (or receive!)

GLOSSARY OF TERMS

sweetening – adding additional sound (music, sound effects, additional *dialogue* tracks) to a VO performance to enhance it

sync – matching (synchronizing) recorded *dialogue* with mouth movements of on-screen characters

tag – a short bit of VO at the end of a commercial *spot*; identifies a certain product, or presents legal or other information regarding the product

take – one specific recorded performance of a line or series of lines, from the time the engineers begin recording to the time they stop recording; identified by a *slate* ("Take 1," or "Take 35B," etc.)

talkback – system for the actor to communicate with director/engineer while in the booth; usually means you (the actor) are hearing the others via a speaker in the booth; sometimes refers to communication over headphones

travel rig – a compact, portable recording setup designed or assembled for ease of transport and use when a dedicated studio is unavailable

union – a professional labor association that looks out for the welfare of its members (e.g. *SAG-AFTRA*)

vocal attributes – your specific vocal qualities that create your unique sound

vocal cords (vocal folds) – the tiny flaps inside your voice box that press against each other to help create sounds as you push air out of your lungs

vocal creators – the moving and non-moving parts of your face and mouth (lips, teeth, tongue, roof of the mouth) that help you *articulate* words *vocal node* – a swelling on the vocal cords, often occurring as a result of vocal strain; can affect the quality of your voice; untreated, can become a *nodule*

vocal nodule – a callus-like bump on the vocal cords; similar to a *node*; more difficult to heal than a node, sometimes requiring removal via surgery

vocal signature (style) – your own unique collection of vocal attributes; like a vocal fingerprint, identifies you and sets you apart from others

voice match – the near perfect replication of one actor's voice by another

volume – basically, how loud you're speaking; sometimes how loud someone is speaking to you via your headphones or a speaker

walla – the background vocal sounds that fill in a scene, sometimes made up of several layers of recordings to give the impression of multiple speakers

wild – to record without stopping to *slate* the *take* or otherwise give a marker identifying it; often occurs at the end of a session when trying to record options or anything that might be needed but hasn't been scripted

REFERENCES

"audio engineering." (2009). In *Some audio guy*. Retrieved July 13, 2009, from http://someaudioguy.blogspot.com/

Baker, Dee Bradley. https://iwanttobeavoiceactor.com/

Blum, Steve. http://www.steveblumvoices.com/ how-to-be-a-voice-actor/

Fitzgerald. Erin. http://www.erinfitzvo.com/erins-ebook

Johnstone, K. (1992). *Impro: Improvisation and the Theatre*. New York: Random House.

"luck." (2009). In *Merriam-Webster Online Dictionary*. Retrieved July 8, 2009, from http://www.merriam-webster.com/ dictionary/luck

Mamet, D. (1997). *True and False*. New York: Pantheon Books.

Meisner, S. & Longwell, D. (1987). *Sanford Meisner on acting*. New York: Random House.

"off book." In *Wiktionary* (off-book: adj.). Retrieved January 25, 2018, from https://en.wiktionary.org/wiki/off-book#English

Parker, S. (2007). *Human body book, The.* (1ˢᵗ American ed.). New York: DK Publishing.

Parkin, K. (1994). *Ken Parkin's anthology of British tongue twisters.* London, UK: Samuel French.

Paulsen, Rob. http://robpaulsenlive.com/hear-rob/

"plosive." (2009). In *Webster's online dictionary.* Retrieved July 12, 2009, from

http://www.websters-online-dictionary.org/definition/plosive

"radio." (2009). In *Wikipedia: Radio: history and commercialization of radio.* Retrieved July 8, 2009, from http://en.wikipedia.org/wiki/Radio

Raferty, B. (2017, October 24). Watch Andy Serkis give you a history of performance-capture technology. *Wired Magazine RSS.* Retrieved from https://www.wired.com/story/video-andy-serkis-history-of-performance-capture/

Rainford, N. (2002). *How to agent your agent.* Hollywood, CA: Lone Eagle Publishing Co.

"Simpsons, The." (2009). In *Wikipedia: The Simpsons.* Retrieved July 17, 2009, from http://en.wikipedia.org/wiki/The_simpsons

Skinner, E. (1990). *Speak with Distinction.* New York: Applause.

Stanislavski, C. (1989). *An Actor Prepares.* New York: Routledge.

Taylor, James Arnold. http://www.jamesarnoldtaylor.com/jat365/

Townsend, G. F. (2009). In *The Internet classics archive: Aesop's fables: the prophet.* Retrieved July 8, 2009, from http://classics.mit.edu/Aesop/fab.3.3.html

"voice-over." (2009). In *Merriam-Webster online dictionary*. Retrieved July 8, 2009, from http://www.merriam-webster.com/dictionary/voice-over

"voice-over." (2009). In *Wikipedia*: *voice-over*. Retrieved July 8, 2009, from http://en.wikipedia.org/wiki/voice-over

"War of the worlds, The." (2009). In *Wikipedia*: *The war of the worlds (radio)*. Retrieved July 17, 2009, from http://en.wikipedia.org/wiki/The_War_of_the_Worlds_(radio)

Yukelson, D. Ph.D. (2007). In Penn State University: *Teaching athletes visualization and mental imagery skills.* Retrieved March 30, 2018, from http://sites.psu.edu/mascsatest2/wp-content/uploads/sites/17619/2014/11/Visualization-Handout.pdf

INDEX

AUTHOR BIOS

Yuri Lowenthal, in addition to being an unrepentant nerd, is an award-winning actor of stage, screen, and voice. He has worked on hundreds of video game titles, but may be best known for playing the titular roles in the popular *Prince of Persia* video game series and Insomniac's new *Spider-Man* game for the PS4. He's voiced multiple Supermen (mans?) and a host of other heroes for DC and Marvel animation, and is also particularly proud of his work on the Emmy-nominated *Afro Samurai, Ben 10* for Cartoon Network, and *Camp Camp* for Rooster Teeth. Anime fans may also know him from such series as *RWBY, Naruto, Gurren Lagann, Bleach, Code Geass, Persona, Durarara!!* and the film *Robotech: The Shadow Chronicles.* You may also recognize him as the voice of ABC Comedy.

For additional credits, fun facts, and information, please visit his website: www.YuriLowenthal.com or follow him on Twitter @YuriLowenthal.

Tara Platt is not a nerd but is proudly married to one. She has performed internationally from London to New York to Los Angeles in film, TV, animation, and theatre. In the VO world, she is best known for her work on the *Naruto* series and video games as Temari, *DC vs. MK* as Wonder Woman, *Legion of Superheroes,* and *Ben 10.* Anime fans may also recognize her from animated series and features such as *RWBY, Sailor Moon Crystal, Aggretsuko, Buso Renkin, and Persona;* and from video games including *League of Legends, Drakengard 3, Skylanders, Mafia III, World of Warcraft, Saints Row III,* and *Sunset Overdrive.* Tara and Yuri's production company, Monkey Kingdom Productions, has two feature films, *Tumbling After* and *Con Artists,* in addition to comedy series *Shelf Life* (4 seasons) and *Whatta Lark,* and travel show *Up, Up and Away* (3 seasons and counting). Tara has also authored children's book *Relax Your Toes* and interactive journal *Zartana.*

For more information on Tara, please visit her website: www.TaraPlatt.com or follow @TaraPlatt on Twitter.

CPSIA information can be obtained
at www.ICGtesting.com
Printed in the USA
LVHW041118251019
635331LV00006B/112

9 780984 074051